Thirty years ago, women across America began to recognize a shared experience.

Suddenly, they began to talk with each other about frustrations, obstacles, joys and sorrows they had never before dared to articulate.

Today, women have moved on to a new experience—and discovered that while some things have changed, others stay the same. They've learned that—especially in male-dominated fields—it can be lonely at the top...and in the middle and at the bottom.

In *Working With Men*, women talk—with each other, about themselves, about other women, about men, about work. It's a lively, personal, enlightening collection of observances that paint a portrait of the working world for women today...

Working with Men

Women in the Workplace Talk About Sexuality, Success, and Their Male Coworkers

Beth Milwid, Ph.D.

BERKLEY BOOKS, NEW YORK

Originally published as *What You Get When You Go For It,*
Dodd, Mead & Company, 1987.

The case studies in this book are real; however,
the names, circumstances, and locations have been
substantially changed to protect the anonymity
and confidentiality of all cases.

This Berkley book contains the complete
text of the original hardcover edition.

WORKING WITH MEN

A Berkley Book / published by arrangement with
Beyond Words Publishing

PRINTING HISTORY
Previously published by Beyond Words Publishing
Berkley edition / September 1992

ISBN: 0-425-13482-2

A BERKLEY BOOK ® TM 757,375
Berkley Books are published by The Berkley Publishing Group,
200 Madison Avenue, New York, New York 10016.
The name "BERKLEY" and the "B" logo
are trademarks belonging to Berkley Publishing Corporation.

PRINTED IN THE UNITED STATES OF AMERICA

10 9 8 7 6 5 4 3 2 1

*To the parents of
tomorrow's working women*

Contents

Introduction 1

The School-to-Work Transition 7

Establishing Credibility 39

Learning the Informal System 65

Understanding Sexual Dynamics 91

Scrutinizing the Power Game 127

Hitting the Cement Ceiling 179

Striking a Balance 213

Epilogue 267

Acknowledgments

First I wish to thank the 125 professional women whose insights and observations appear in this book. I am grateful to each woman for her unique contribution and for her courage in speaking out candidly about life on the job.

I am also indebted to a set of talented colleagues who have helped immeasurably in the preparation of this book. Here my thanks go to Robin Bartlett, Julie Bennett, Jim Dennis, Mike Edelhart, Dave Fleenor, Jerry Garchik, John Greenleigh, Sally Hertz, Susan Kazan, Betsy Lathrop, Richard Newcombe, Lisa Orta, Kay Radtke, Kathleen Sindorf, and Cynthia Vartan.

To my friends and colleagues at Apple Computer, I owe a special note of thanks. I am grateful to Stephen Sieler for his clarity of thought and superb sense of design; to Diane Dyson, my editor, for her magnificent command of language, subtlety, and wit; and to Beth Anne Moore for her tireless ability to make the Macintosh sing.

My original publishers, Cindy Black and Richard Cohn, have supported this project from beginning to end. I salute their dedication to high-quality small press publishing.

Finally to the friends and family members who have contributed their time, ideas, and encouragement, I offer my appreciation.

Beth Milwid
San Francisco, California
June 1, 1990

Where, after all, do universal human rights begin? In small places, close to home—so close and so small that they cannot be seen on any map of the world. Yet they are the world of the individual person—the neighborhood he lives in; the school or college he attends; the factory, farm, or office where he works. Such are the places where every man, woman, and child seeks equal justice, equal opportunity, equal dignity without discrimination.

Unless these rights have meaning there, they have little meaning anywhere.

— Eleanor Roosevelt

Working with Men

Introduction

The statistics are impressive and the trend seems clear: Women in the 1990s are making it in a man's world.

Or are we?

In discussions over coffee, professional women empathize secretly with one another's frustrations. In therapists' offices, female executives ask, "Am I crazy? Am I the only one?" In the privacy of their homes, couples try to figure out why a lifestyle that looks so easy in the cereal commercials is in reality so incredibly hard.

Everyone is affected, but few talk publicly. We know that statistically there are more and more women in business today, but we don't know how it's affecting them personally.

To learn more about the texture of today and to predict what will happen tomorrow, we need to supplement statistics with stories. We need to find out from the women themselves how it feels to be making history.

I got the idea for this book when I worked in an office with ten professional men. On the surface, I was doing fine. I was several years out of school, had a master's degree, and had been hired in the San Francisco mayor's office to help coordinate housing plans. I was the only woman professional in that branch. Day after day, I sat in meetings, trying to laugh at the jokes, trying to keep up with the latest names in football, tennis, and golf—in other words, trying to learn a new job and a new male culture all at the same time. I knew I didn't fit in and wasn't taken seriously, but I was determined to give it my best.

A turning point came one February night. After a tense, all-day meeting, my boss suddenly asked me to make copies of a forty-page report and distribute it to twenty city agencies before nine that night. He explained that the support staff had left for the day, and I seemed to him the next obvious choice.

As I stood over the copying machine hour after hour, I found myself wondering if professional life was all it was cracked up to be.

On my way home that night, I picked up a copy of Studs Terkel's *Working* and read it nonstop, searching for the words of someone like me.

Terkel's book was filled with lively portraits of Americans talking informally about life on the job. I read excerpts from interviews with bricklayers and executives, day-care workers and plumbers, paperboys and secretaries—but none with professional women breaking into the all-male management ranks. That phenomenon—of which I was a part—had only just begun. Flipping through those pages, I decided then and there that someone should give professional women a chance to tell their stories. Someone should afford career women a candid opportunity to speak from the heart.

Years later I embarked on that project. As a psychologist, I wanted to find out if, after more than a decade, professional women across the country were still facing the emotional challenges I had faced back then. I wanted to learn whether time and increased numbers of women in management had made a difference, and if so, what kind. Finally, I wanted to know whether working women encounter new challenges midway through their careers.

My own work with organizations had convinced me that the professional world is a psychologically loaded environment for men and women alike. My goal was to document the dynamics in a way that would capture the changing cultural landscape. I decided to search not for numbers and statistics, but for a sampling of images and anecdotes. I sought to create a composite picture of a unique historical time.

To write this book, I traveled to all parts of the United States and interviewed 125 women in a variety of industries and professions. I spoke with stockbrokers on Wall Street, computer programmers in Silicon Valley, and women up and down the management ladder in manufacturing companies across America's heartland. Some interviews took place at television stations and industrial plants, others in law offices, design firms, living rooms, restaurants, and hotels. A total of twelve professional fields were represented in a sample drawn from fifteen cities.

The women ranged in age from twenty-six to seventy-two, but most were in their thirties and forties and had worked in their fields for more than ten years. Each had spent the majority of her career in settings where she had been one of few professional women. I found the women of this cross section through a nationwide network of colleagues and friends—men and women curious about the project and eager to help out.

I was surprised at how quickly the women accepted my invitation to be interviewed. When we met, however, I sensed that their enthusiasm was tempered with hesitancy. Some were puzzled about why they had been selected. Accustomed to reading articles about superstars, they found it hard to believe that there would be a book about "ordinary" women like themselves. Many worried that if they disclosed too much, their jobs and professional reputations would be threatened. Despite my assurance of confidentiality—that I would reveal neither individuals' names nor employers' names, and that I would disguise the identity of participants—some remained wary and quizzed me extensively before they would talk.

On the one hand, the women seemed dying to tell their stories; on the other hand, they had understandable fears. I could tell from their ambivalence that the interviews would prove controversial. It wasn't until much later that I discovered how powerful and moving they would be, as well.

3

Each interview had a decided momentum. When a stock-broker first recounted a deal, or a lawyer described a hard day in court, I probed for details, asking what had happened, who was involved, and how the woman herself had felt at the time. With the advantage of hindsight and perspective, the women could reflect on their experiences and sift through what they had learned. Long-buried memories were quickly resurrected. The women were surprised by how much they had to say.

How to Use This Book

This book reveals a collective story showing that despite unique personalities and positions, professional women are facing a remarkably similar set of challenges as they break into all-male fields. These challenges emerge in a clear, regular sequence, regardless of what industry the women work in, or in what part of the country. Whether I spoke with a graphic designer in New York City or a personnel manager in Detroit, I heard the same recounting of unfamiliar situations, on-the-spot decision-making, and valuable lessons learned. In short, American working women were—and are—jumping through the same sets of hoops in an almost identical order.

The organization of this book reflects that order, with each chapter portraying a set of issues that women must confront and deal with in order to move on in their careers. The book opens with an exploration of how young women handle the transition from school to office. In later chapters, working women describe their struggles for credibility, for acceptance in the informal aspects of their working world, and for equity in promotions. They scrutinize power games and ethical standards; they critique the eighty-hour work week; and over and over they wonder aloud about the dominating role of work within their lives. Finally, the last chapter of the book presents a compelling reexamination of the meaning of success.

Each chapter in this book is made up of two parts. The first is a collection of interview excerpts in which women explain what breaking into a man's world has really been like. All the stories within a chapter address the same theme—the same psychological challenge confronted by a diverse group of women.

The second part of each chapter is reserved for Tips From the Trenches. Here the women describe how they handled tough situations and what they learned. Whether the challenge took the form of a sexual come-on or an ethical dilemma, each woman had had to create a solution tailored to her needs, and the variety of stories found in each chapter provides a sampling of approaches from which to choose. This collage format also illustrates clearly that there is no "right way" to handle male-female dynamics in the office. Solutions that work do so because they are specific; they reflect a woman's personality and values, and the corporate culture in which she operates. The stories here are brought to you by veterans, and the tips they offer come straight from the trenches.

This is a book designed for browsing. It is filled with anecdotes, drama, and wit—occasionally satiric. Open to any page and find stories of determination. Skim through any chapter and find courage, laughter, and soul.

Unlike a novel, this book need not be read from start to finish. You might think of it as an owner's manual. For different readers at different times, certain chapter titles will jump out immediately, depending on the need of the day. Each chapter functions both individually and as one piece of a large and profound story.

Voices of Hope

As an outsider privy to confidential information, I had the rare opportunity to hear from a generation of women in the throes of social change. I learned that despite their progress, many still feel fundamentally excluded from the male-run business world. Though indebted to individual men who have provided encouragement and support, these women remain psychologically separate from the dominant cultures of their organizations.

Further, I learned that women are intellectually aware of the complexity of their situation and are able to view it in a broad historical context. They recognize now that early promises of equal opportunity did not take into account the tremendous adjustments male coworkers would have to make. They realize, too, that the presence of thousands of new females competing in the job market does, in reality, threaten the financial future and self-esteem of many aspiring men. The women I interviewed are bright; they understand that the causes of discrimination are intertwined and complex.

The women in this book are primarily survivors. They are persevering amid emotional pressures none had imagined, and are continuing to make remarkable gains. As I traveled across America, meeting working women in Boston, San Diego, Atlanta, Denver, Houston, Cincinnati, New York—all across the country—I was struck by their energy and enthusiasm, their hope and optimism.

This book presents an intimate look at one diverse sampling of women. It does not claim to draw conclusions about all professional women, nor does it pretend to offer solutions that would apply to all groups. Instead, it exposes multiple dimensions of a drama that had not previously been revealed in this compelling way: through a chorus of women's voices. Women reading this book may recognize their own experience in the voices of others, and may appreciate in a new way that they are not alone.

For men, these candid accounts may provide new insight into the daily work experiences of wives, sisters, colleagues, and friends.

For fathers of all ages, these stories will illustrate the discrimination their daughters will encounter in the future, unless changes in attitude and behavior finally take place.

For all of us to benefit from the potential power of a strong, integrated, and healthy workforce, we need to face directly the issues these women raise.

1

The
School-to-Work
Transition

The Fall from Innocence

In an all-glass conference room high on the forty-third floor, Cathy, a marketing manager, smiles as she contrasts her earlier dreams with the present realities of daily life.

> I always figured I'd be in a "female" profession—I never thought about going into business. I didn't think I'd work in a male-dominated profession. It was all a total surprise to me. Actually, I didn't think I'd work much at all. I thought maybe I'd work until I was thirty, then that would be it. I was a product of the fifties and sixties. I thought I'd work my way up and become pretty famous pretty fast—maybe as a newspaper editor. Then I'd quit and get married and move to Westchester, have two children, write novels, and live happily ever after.

From Atlanta to Dayton to Los Angeles, other women described similar transformations, and a clear pattern emerged from their experiences of the past twenty years.

When young professional women entered the work world in the mid-1970s, few knew what to expect. Most were from families in which fathers had discussed business only with their sons. Their mothers, who worked only inside the home, could not be the role models their daughters suddenly needed. With no direct access to professionals, schoolgirls and female college students turned to television for images of success. As they studied Lois Lane and Mary Tyler Moore, they created fantasies of offices like the Daily Planet and colleagues like Clark Kent.

For institutional models, they relied on school—the only organization they knew. Young working women expected that the rules of behavior in the office would be clearly spelled out, as they had been in the university. They anticipated "grades" in the form of raises and promotions, and recognition that would come regularly and be based on objective criteria. Few could predict that gender would influence their work experience. Just as they had competed successfully with men in the classroom, most women expected to compete easily and effectively with men on the job.

Since these expectations were rarely grounded in the work world, it's not surprising that the realities and pressures of corporate life caused considerable shock.

When I heard women contrast their expectations with their actual experience, I realized that at the outset most were totally unprepared for the psychological challenges they met. Given this, the women's accomplishments seem all the more impressive, their disappointments that much easier to understand.

The words of Brenda, a thirty-five-year-old black woman, capture both the naiveté and the determination of many women I interviewed.

When I go to see her, it is snowing in Detroit, and rush-hour traffic is intolerable. I have never been inside an automotive plant before. Its size and the after-hours silence are awesome. I sit across from Brenda at a gray steel table. Her office is impersonally furnished with metal bookcases, green file cabinets, and company manuals. Only a glass dish of Hershey kisses bespeaks a personal touch.

Brenda has worked here for ten years, most of that time in management. She is one of very few women in the plant, and most of the time has been the only black female. In thinking back on her career, Brenda draws a sharp contrast between her initial hopes and her current beliefs. Though her speech remains calm and matter-of-fact, her eyes blaze.

> When I signed on with this company, I didn't have any preconceived ideas. I just knew the Big Three were in Detroit.
>
> Come to think of it, I did have some expectations. I expected a sophisticated environment. I expected very businesslike, professional personnel. I also expected a predominantly male organization, which I found—that expectation was true. And all I was hoping for—actually this wasn't an expectation, I think it was more of a hope— was that I was really going to have an equal opportunity to maximize my potential as an employee.
>
> I'll tell you one thing: I surely thought that most of my problems would be because of my race and not because of my sex. What I wasn't expecting was the sexism I experienced after starting to work in this industry. It was worse ten years ago than it is now.
>
> I wasn't ready for these experiences. I think I was somewhat naive because when I was young, I was elected president of a major high school, one of the top in the United States. That was perfectly acceptable. I went to college and earned undergraduate and graduate degrees in schools where there were males and females, and that too was acceptable. So I really think I was blind to the fact that a woman joining the team was going to be unacceptable here. Nevertheless, I was determined to be a team member.

Many women Brenda's age—those now in their thirties and forties—recalled how little they had known about the work world prior to signing on. And back then few had really believed that "getting a job" would lead to a long-term career commitment. Even in the mid-1970s, many of these women secretly hoped to marry and retire from the labor force. For them, the goal was love, not work.

Marilyn supervises the regional offices of a major telecommunications corporation. She sighs as she reviews her twenty-year career. When I ask how she chose telecommunications, she laughs. She explains that initially she had viewed her job as "just a tide-me-over" until something better—notably the Prince—swept her off to suburbia. Like Marilyn, many women told of meandering into their jobs, of never really expecting to stay long, and of discovering that they had somehow embarked on a de facto career. Marilyn's story is a classic.

In undergraduate school, I prepared to be a teacher, but when I did my student teaching, I didn't like it at all. Then one of my sorority sisters went to work for the telephone company. She suggested that I come in and take a job there until I found something better. So I applied and was hired in a nonmanagement capacity—in a job classification that was for women college graduates. This was in 1965. In those days, the company hired male college graduates into first-level management and brought women in two levels below that. No one, including myself, openly challenged that.

It's hard for me to go back to 1965 and talk about my goals and aspirations, because I was brought up and schooled to become something different from what I am today. The world is very different now from the world I was prepared for. I totally expected to marry—hopefully, someone wealthy—and to have a family, to entertain, to have a beautiful home, to take cruises, to go on nice vacations, and to entertain my husband's business associates.

My expectations were so dramatically different from what they are now. In college, I believed that women should work only if they had to. That's how I was brought up. Actually, I don't think I thought very much about it at all. When I did think about work, I thought I would work until I got married. I looked to somebody else to be the breadwinner. I would be the wife and mother at home.

Quickly the women realized that they had to come to grips with the unknown, both on the job and in their personal lives. For many, the first challenge came in confronting the fears of their parents.

During the 1970s, most of the women's parents still expected their daughters to become wives and mothers. When this didn't occur on schedule, many of those parents grew anxious and concerned. Though proud of their daughters' achievements, they worried about financial security, physical safety, and the possible sacrifice of a family in favor of a job.

The women recognized their parents' mixed messages immediately. Many commented that starting a career had made their psychological separation from Mom and Dad a very complex task.

Jill, a twenty-nine-year-old corporate attorney, sits behind her desk and takes off a pair of tortoise-shell glasses. She leans back, gestures at file folders on the floor, and wonders aloud if her parents have any idea of what her life is really like. Softly, Jill acknowledges that her mother and father may never fully appreciate her accomplishments. To them, Jill is failing as a woman because she is not a wife.

> My father is threatened both because professional women threaten him in general, and specifically because he's afraid he won't "marry me off"—I think he still sees it as that. My mother's confused. I think she's probably a little jealous. Also, she's concerned that I'm going to be lonely and miss out on experiences that she feels are essential. I don't think that either of my parents has ever connected the words "gentle," "soft," and "professional" in the same sentence.

Jennifer's family believes that the purpose of a young girl's education is to train her to be the cultured, articulate wife of a successful professional man. Sitting in her fashionably funky design office, Jennifer tells me that when she chose to become a "lady architect," she was consciously rebelling against that family rule.

> I think my parents thought that my becoming an architect was just kind of a cute idea. They encouraged good education and hard work. But it turned out that, although it was nice to go to these good schools and do well, once you met a man and got married, that was supposed to be it. I don't think, even to this day, that they think it's so great that I have a career.

Even women whose families openly encouraged them noted that their parents usually thought of a career as "something to fall back on in case your husband dies or leaves." In addition, the professions these parents pushed were limited in number and in scope. As Sandy, a corporate loan officer, looks out over a sea of blue suits and red ties, she contrasts her current world with the world her parents had originally prescribed.

> What did my parents think of banking? Not much. I was raised for marriage. It was a big surprise to them that I would become a businesswoman. On the other hand, they thought I should support myself. My father advised that I should be a teacher or a nurse, because then I would always be able to find a job. But neither of those things appealed to me. My brother was an engineer, and in our family that was very important. What I did in terms of a career was "nice," but it wasn't at all important.

As women explored new career options, their family relationships changed dramatically. When a young woman's professional goals clashed with those of her parents, the resulting tension sometimes lasted for years. Understandably, this additional burden increased the woman's own doubts about entering an all-male field. Usually she felt torn between loyalty to her parents' traditional values and loyalty to her own values, which were now gradually taking shape.

But not all the women I interviewed rebelled against parental expectations initially. Some had begun work in roles traditionally assigned to females. Later they moved up.

Natalie, an executive with a large midwest land development company, started as a secretary. She shakes her head in disbelief as she remembers her "career aspirations" circa 1970.

> I honestly think I didn't have any expectations other than if I could just make $10K, I would never want to make another dollar. I would have succeeded. Having come from a family where my mother worked as a secretary for so long, I really never thought about women being any more than secretaries. I really thought my goal in life was to be the best secretary I could ever be. I don't think I ever, ever thought about doing anything other than that.

Another group of women began their careers immediately competing with men for nontraditional jobs. But before 1970, few expected to break in successfully. Back then, most women felt resigned to the status quo.

When Janet was in college, she decided to apply for a management trainee position with a nationally renowned consumer products company. After researching the opportunity extensively, Janet was delighted to learn that the company was interviewing at her school. As she recalls her bout with the campus recruiters, she smiles triumphantly. Today, twenty years later, she works as a senior executive for that company's major competitor.

> I had some very bitter experiences in the interviewing process, because interviewers came to campus and said that they were only interviewing men. That was pretty awful. I was very angry. One company in particular posted a notice on our board saying, "No women need apply." I was flabbergasted, because I was sure that this was the era of equality, even though it was only 1971. I wrote a letter and expressed my concern. They actually called me from

13

their headquarters and apologized. They said that the reason they weren't considering women was that the job required lifting forty- to fifty-pound boxes to stock the shelves of the stores. My rejoinder to that was, "Women have been lifting forty- to fifty-pound children for centuries." I couldn't understand the difference between the two. I was very aggravated.

I said to them that it was fine with me that they didn't want to interview me, but I would never purchase another one of their products in my life. The fact that my company now competes head-to-head with that company is gratifying. I still appreciate having a chance to zap them in the marketplace. It's wonderful.

Ellen is divorced and the sole supporter of three sons in college. She is tall, soft-spoken, and shy. A whiz with numbers, she majored in accounting in the 1960s and looked forward to a business career. But when she saw other female students being rebuffed by corporate recruiters, Ellen changed her plans. Her voice shakes as she explains how she waited fifteen years for the job she should have landed then.

In my junior year, there was another girl in the sorority, a senior whose name was Dale. She was also an accounting major. Companies came to campus to interview, and Dale was set up for a lot of interviews. But when she went in, they took one look at her—now this is in 1960—and realized that this "Dale" was a woman and not a man, and said, "We can't hire you. You'll get married and have a baby. We're not going to train you." So Dale dropped out of school during her senior year to look for an accounting job on her own. I saw that happen my junior year and decided I wasn't going to go through that. I switched into business education then and became a teacher.

Even having an MBA didn't necessarily open doors for women in the early 1970s. Courtney, one of the nation's top-ranking retail sales executives, describes her experience one year out of business school. At a very early age, Courtney learned that what some people consider strengths, others consider liabilities.

When my husband and I were calling around the country to decide where to work, we chose Seattle because his parents were there. I called all the banks in town, and they said, "Well, I'm sorry, the salary's this," which was only half what I had been making in my first job out of business school. "And besides," the personnel people would add, "we don't hire women." It just went on and on and on and on. That town was so out of it. But back then even the banks in New York City said things like that to me.

Someone at one of the places where I really wanted to work said, "I'm sorry, but there are five things wrong with you: You're a woman, you have an MBA, you were an officer at another bank, you were highly paid, and you're intelligent." I said, "But I thought that was all the good stuff I had."

Yet in another way, none of that really surprised me. I had grown up thinking that of course women didn't have a shot at things. Even when I had some interviews on campus before I left college, it was obvious that women had clear roles in business. You know, even with an MBA from Berkeley, my greatest aspiration back then was to be an entry-level professional making $15,000 a year. I thought, "That's the most I can do, and that's fine." I wasn't depressed because I just knew that was the way it was. Women didn't have a chance. That was fine with me then. It was a reality I accepted.

Blind Faith

The more I questioned the women about their initial expectations, the more I realized that powerful internal myths prevailed. These myths served both to set women up for later disappointment and to keep them from preparing themselves realistically for the challenges all professionals face.

The most popular myth defined "working" as something exclusively glamorous and exciting. Since few women I interviewed had heard adults discussing their jobs, they had turned to the media to learn about office life. From television images and magazine articles, many developed exaggerated fantasies of glitter, power, and political intrigue.

Marion, a litigator for the Justice Department, chuckles as she tells me how she chose to become a lawyer.

> When I was twelve, we had to do a project on what we wanted to be when we grew up. I interviewed the only woman attorney I knew at that time. I don't remember it much now. I just know I always watched Perry Mason. I always wanted to be a lawyer, but I never really thought I could. I'd have settled for being either Mary Martin or Perry Mason—both were fine with me.

Jane works as a loan processor and does freelance writing in her spare time. Her articles are published regularly in a small neighborhood newspaper. When she talks about her earliest career dreams, she remembers with a grin her favorite childhood friends.

> I always thought I'd work on a newspaper, like Lois Lane. Of course, growing up, I didn't realize that the newspaper world is one of the most sexist. I figured that there were always female reporters out there. Brenda Starr and people like that—they were my role models.

It's understandable how media images initially served as role models for these women. More surprising to me was the tenacity with which the women seemed to hold on to their idealized expectations. Often, even after they had begun their careers and had become familiar with the daily grind, many clung to naive dreams.

Ruth, an immigration attorney, now likes her job. Several years ago, though, she worked in an area of law ill-suited to her skills and temperament. Ruth had chosen the wrong subspecialty initially and had remained in it too long. She had been trying to remold herself, hoping to become one of the lawyers she'd met in a magazine.

In law school, I didn't have any idea of what it was going to be like to be a lawyer, even though I was working around a lot of lawyers by that time. Somewhere along the way, I read an article in *Time* magazine about insider trading, and so—just like that, without any idea of what I was talking about—I decided I wanted to go into insider trading. I wanted to be in *Time* magazine. If someone asked me what I wanted, I said "insider trading"—with a great deal of assurance. You'd have thought for all the world that I knew exactly what I was talking about.

Part of my problem was that I had no idea of what being an attorney would be like. It never occurred to me that lawyers worked particularly hard. Not that I hadn't seen lawyers working hard, because I had, but I didn't realize what tremendous pressures are put on a successful lawyer in terms of continual performance, and the incredible responsibility a lawyer has for what people's lives are going to be like.

I thought it would be like *Time* magazine. I thought it would be dramatic. I thought that every case would involve some interesting issues, something vibrant, something constitutional, something important—you know, things that make *Time* magazine. I thought that one day soon I'd see myself in "Milestones."

The women's career goals were strikingly abstract. Some wanted money, though not a specific amount. Others wanted power, security, sophistication. Many sought status. A few wanted to emulate friends or relatives. Most women described how they had hoped to feel, not what they had wished to do.

17

I sit in Mandy's New York City apartment admiring her mounted posters, paintings, and photographs. Shyly, she explains that she used to be the "arty" type. Today she works in the public relations department of an import-export firm. Mandy went into business for reasons she still doesn't understand.

> I think I always wanted to be in the corporate world because I imagined that it was this wonderful thing. I have an older sister who used to work for an important law firm and now is an attorney with a big corporation. Her life always seemed really glamorous, so I thought working for a corporation must be a marvelous thing to do. Somehow, because my background was more in the arts, it seemed as if a corporate job would legitimize me in some way in the eyes of the world.
>
> In a certain respect, it has. Now I feel as though people take me seriously, because I have this job. But it doesn't feel like it's all it's cracked up to be. My having this job changed people's responses to me, but it doesn't make me perceive myself any differently.

Lynn's career history follows a pattern common among the women I interviewed. With a bachelor's degree and little work experience, Lynn headed for California in search of sun and opportunity. Today she's an investment banker. Ten years ago, she worked as a secretary, carefully observing the flow of money and power inside a large manufacturing company. When Lynn chose to go into finance, she had no idea of what she really wanted to do. All she knew was that a professional credential meant a better salary and more prestige.

> After graduation, I moved out to San Francisco with a very loosely defined idea. I thought, "I've got a college degree and a year's experience." It didn't take me long to realize that there were thousands of people in San Francisco just like me. So I ended up becoming a secretary to

an executive. I smiled every day, got him coffee, and didn't work very hard at all.

I did that for almost four years, and in that process I realized it was time for me to do something else. I was just beginning to realize that maybe I would be supporting myself all my life. I saw clearly that, where I was, the opportunities were very limited. I also was aware that some of the managers in that company weren't particularly bright, and that it was really the secretary that ran the whole show. Why should one guy be getting a lot of money and the secretary not getting much money at all? I decided to get training in providing financial services.

Those who believed that professional training would ensure credibility were often those most disappointed. Many women I talked to had worked in low-level positions and had observed that people with advanced training seemed to command more authority. What the women neglected to observe was that those in authority were older, more experienced, and usually male.

For women whose main professional goal was to be taken seriously, early difficulties on the job proved the most disheartening. Several told me that in choosing professional careers, they had cared more about how they would be treated than about which job they would ultimately hold. For them, dashed expectations were particularly painful.

I went to law school because I wanted to be taken seriously as a person. I figured that the best way to do that in this system is to have money and power. Being a lawyer would give me both.

I made a very pragmatic decision that what I really wanted was a career, and it probably didn't make any difference whether it was in law or business. I wanted the credentials so I wouldn't have to fight my way up through an organization. I wanted to enter at a professional level and be taken seriously from the start. So I just decided,

"Why not go to business school?" Mine was a very backwards way of making a career choice.

Those who went to graduate school explained that the focus of their academic programs had been on gathering information and developing skills, but not on applying those skills in real-life situations. In retrospect, given this academic bias, it's predictable that the transition from campus to workplace would be difficult for many young adults. But for women who had been raised to remain in the home, leaving school and entering the corporate world presented an added psychological challenge.

Carla, a television writer, sums up her transition from school to the newsroom.

I really didn't have any preconception about what it would be like. I didn't know what I was getting into—basically because they don't teach you that at school.

One of the Guys

The most intriguing part about discussing expectations with these women was that very few had carefully considered what it would be like to work mostly with men. At first, I was puzzled to find such apparent naiveté in so sophisticated a group. I wondered aloud why they had chosen to overlook the male-female issue. Gradually I learned that some women equated thinking about the issue with "going looking for trouble." Others had decided not to consider it because they didn't want to bring a set of preconceptions to the office. But for the majority, the reason was quite simple: Women chose not to think about male-female issues because they didn't want to be associated with "women's lib" and all that that could mean to the men they worked with daily.

To avoid that stereotype, most denied that there could be difficulties involved in breaking into an all-male environment.

Nancy taught me that some working women worry that men will view them as "hung-up" on women's issues. To counter that assumption, Nancy chose to discard male-female differences entirely. Instead, she resurrected the image of Horatio Alger and believed in it with fervor.

> I didn't feel it would be a disability to be a woman. I never felt that I would be slighted. I've always put a great emphasis on the notion that if you're bright, and if you have an interest in what you're doing, you can make it regardless of whether you're a man or a woman. I never was really hung up on the idea that I was entering into a male-dominated business. I just figured I'd work hard and take it from there.

Helen directs the design department of a large architectural firm. She feels that her expectations of equal treatment helped her tremendously during her first job. Although the women in Helen's family have held professional positions for generations, Helen assures me quickly that this fact does not necessarily make her a "women's libber."

> I never really thought of architecture as a male-dominated field. I don't come from a family of "libbers," but the females in our clan have each been professionals at one time or another. Just last month, my grandmother finally closed her office after fifty-three years as a doctor. I was brought up on the premise that "you do what you want to do and that's it." I never gave the "male-dominated" bit much thought.

Just as women turned to the media for help, they also turned to school for an institutional model of work. Many of their expectations about relationships with men, about rules of behavior, and about rewards and recognition stemmed from high school and college memories.

Two core assumptions were widely shared. First, the women expected that men at work would be their friends, just as men in school had been. Second, most trusted that the system would reward those who worked hard and did well. Few seemed concerned that women had little substantive power in business. Few recognized that upward mobility is rarely dependent on objective criteria alone. Most important, virtually none of the women seriously considered how men might feel about large numbers of female coworkers streaming into their domain.

Andrea and Karen work for competing advertising agencies. When Andrea started work ten years ago, she was nonchalant about the importance of "people skills." Like many other women, Andrea considered herself to be good with people, and thus gave little thought to male-female work relationships.

> The issue wasn't something I thought was going to be bad. I've always had a lot of male friends. I've never really had much trouble getting along with people. My little philosophy was, "Good work will reap its own rewards."

Karen recalls her expectations in a different way. In describing her decision to enter advertising, she remembers that even at the university, subtle forces steered women away from the field. Karen unconsciously chose to "act like a man" in order to compete.

> I never got into worrying that my career would be checkmated or that I would have to compete aggressively with men.
>
> In college, I was in the school of art, and within that school was the school of visual communication. Within the school of visual communication were advertising, illustration, and fashion illustration. Now, in illustration and fashion illustration, women were perfectly acceptable and had no problems. But in advertising design, where I was, the teacher's favorites were always guys. As a matter of fact, it was a big deal when I was complimented on a

piece of work once. I remember being very proud of this. My advertising teacher said to me, "You think like a man."

I agreed to interview Evelyn over lunch in order to avoid her coworkers' knowing about our meeting. Evelyn is worried that if I came to her office, the company grapevine would instantly label her a feminist. In the restaurant, she contrasts her current views about work with those she had in the mid-1960s. Back then, Evelyn felt she could conquer the world. Today, at age fifty-five, she chuckles, remembering that youthful naiveté.

On my first job, I had no idea how long I would be there or what I really wanted to make out of it. I did feel that I wanted to be a professional. I wanted very much to move ahead, and I knew that this was an opportunity to develop some skills in the personnel field so I could get into personnel management. But you see, I saw myself as a manager with a small "m."

I didn't necessarily think about it in terms of male-female issues. It didn't make any difference to me that there were men out there. So what? If I did the best job, I'd rise to the top.

A second myth is the notion that everyone has a real chance to make it big in business. Growing up as they did in the postwar era, the women I talked with heard their parents and grandparents espousing the American dream. Many of their fathers had joined corporations in the 1950s and had become successful. Just as their fathers had believed in the legend of Horatio Alger, women entered the work world of the 1970s and 1980s, blithely assuming that those who work hardest always do best.

Sarah comes from "hearty New England stock" and is proudly committed to traditional values. At forty, she works as the senior editor of a major New York publishing house. Sitting amid stacks of manuscripts and press clippings, Sarah reminisces about how she entered the business.

> The first place I worked there were women who were editors-in-chief—women doing real work. So it never occurred to me that I was limited because I was female. I always felt that the reason I was limited was that I didn't know enough. I don't think that had to do so much with being a woman as it had to do with growing up with a very strong work ethic, with parents who worked very hard and were very successful. I always had the notion that if you worked really hard, you would be rewarded.

Cynthia produces a television news show in a large southern city. She smiles as she recalls working for a gifted mentor early in her career. Under that general manager's tutelage, Cynthia developed new programs and took on new responsibilities. Her approach to documentary news coverage won industrywide recognition. But six months ago, when Cynthia's mentor left the station, she found her advancement suddenly blocked. Discouraged, Cynthia has resorted to calling headhunters. When I ask her to think back to early career expectations, I sense Cynthia is resurrecting a latent part of herself.

> I think that early on, I had no particular expectation about being a woman in this business. It's only as I've gotten older and seen more discrimination that I've realized that the top is not accessible for all women. I always assumed that you could be whatever you wanted to be if you worked hard enough or long enough. I always believed that if you deserved something better, you got it— which may or may not be true. Which oftentimes is *not* true, as it turns out.
>
> That philosophy always worked for me in school. I always studied very hard, made great grades. I belonged to organizations and was always the president or some other kind of elected officer. Hard work always paid off

for me, so I probably never questioned it. College was the same way. I worked really hard and got whatever I wanted. When I competed with other students, I did well. It didn't occur to me until later that there were all these other variables. I certainly never thought in sexual terms. I don't think it occurred to me that my sex would stop me from doing things.

My appointment with Jane, a management consultant, is scheduled for 8 A.M. on her first day back in the office after weeks on the road. Despite the early hour, Jane is outgoing, warm, and candid. Having worked her way up for more than thirteen years, Jane has learned that the reward system in business is nothing like the reward system in schools. Early on, she discovered that in the work world, no raise or promotion comes automatically.

When I was an editor, right after putting in a series of all-nighters with a whole team of consultants, I wrote a proposal for one of the senior officers of the firm. I also wrote a set of presentation materials for a consultant who literally couldn't manage his way out of a paper bag. All these projects happened at the same time, and this senior officer wrote a very complimentary memo to me about my work.

That night I read it and reread it. I said to myself, "Why doesn't he offer me a job as a consultant?" I was talking to my husband, and all of a sudden I saw the light: "Wait a minute—he's not going to offer me a chance to switch from editing to consulting. I have to ask him for a consulting job if I want one."

That was a very important turning point in my own mind, because somehow, all my life, everything had come my way. I was always a good girl in school. I did my work. I got good grades. I got leadership awards. I was on sports teams. I did everything I was supposed to do, and I got honored for it. It all just came. Now, all of a sudden, here was something that I felt I was ready for, and it wasn't just coming.

After work on Friday, I meet with the controller of a southwestern telecommunications company. Kay's eyes look tired, and a quick glance at the computer printouts on her desk tells me why. When I ask her to think back twenty years and describe her first job, her response is quick and to the point.

> I had a very simplistic belief about how you get ahead, which I know doesn't work. But then, I just thought you do the best job you can, and if you're doing an excellent job, then there's just no way that management can deny you promotions. But they can—I know that now. I also know that my original formula doesn't exactly work. The fact is, you've also got to do the politicking.

Tips From the Trenches

Be Realistic

The women I interviewed are eager to pass along what they've learned. As a group, they are worried that female college graduates still hold idealized expectations about careers and still believe that working women can "have it all." Concerned about this widespread naiveté, experienced professional women want to help the next generation avoid the pain they themselves endured.

I asked each woman for her message to those just starting out. The answers came quickly, and they were filled with determination and feeling. Some focused on the need for more pragmatic attitudes before beginning work. Others described the specifics of getting things done once inside a company. In all cases the goal was realism, not fantasy, and the source was real-life experience, not media hype. The women's advice to others is a blend of broad philosophy and practical how-tos.

Sally talks quickly and jokes frequently. Her humor is contagious, her energy invigorating. As she describes her twenty-year climb to the executive suite, Sally repeatedly expresses concern for other women in business. At the end of our interview I ask her to summarize. She pauses, then speaks slowly.

My message to professional women is, number one, don't forget that the decision-making powers in this country are still male. The tendency is to think it's all been done, that women are now accepted. But we're not fully integrated into the business world by a long shot. If women assume that working is a God-given right, they will fall ten steps back.

Number two, a woman must enter into a company—if she has a choice—where it feels right. Because if she does go to Wall Street or somewhere similar, she has to know that she's going to fight day in and day out for ten years. Wall Street is macho. If she wants to be a deal maker, and she wants to be in mergers and acquisitions at any of the big joints, she's got to know that she is talking about really tough territory.

Another thing is that every woman has to pay her dues. One of the hardest things for top-notch MBAs to do today is to meet their ambitions for themselves. Younger people in business don't want to hear about what's going to happen to them in five years, because they think they're qualified for your job, for my job, right now. But there is a maturing process that comes along with paying one's dues.

It's hard for some young women not to let their own personal ambition outstrip them. They need to look at their jobs in two- and three-year chunks. It's great to be ambitious and to say, "I'd like to be the president or the general manager," or whatever, but it's probably going to take some long number of years. Young women need to accept that there are very few thirty-five-year-old presidents of companies. Now, if someone goes into high tech or into certain smaller companies, then different kinds of things are available. But nobody's going to be president of AT&T at age thirty-two. It just isn't going to happen.

Barbara, a Chicago newspaper reporter, agrees that expecting too much too fast leads inevitably to disappointment. As she walks me through a newsroom full of reporters, computers, and battered typewriters, Barbara explains that few people appreciate all the work that goes into publishing a daily paper. Similarly, she points out, few beginning journalists understand how long they must write about humdrum matters before getting a scoop.

Some people look at the glamour of the newspaper business, and they don't look at the hard work that's behind it. A lot of women get discouraged when they find out—"You mean I'm expected to stay after five?" That's what I mean by paying your dues.

Ever since Watergate—it's called the Woodward and Bernstein Syndrome—people think all you have to do is find the right story and you'll be famous and everybody will know your name. They don't look at the fact that Woodward and Bernstein were doing police reports for years before they stumbled across their big story.

So forget about looking for the big investigative pieces. It's the grunt work that has the big stories hidden in it. You're going to go through an awful lot of fender-benders to find a big story. You're going to cover an awful lot of drownings. Know your limitations, and be realistic.

The women agree that the media have placed too much emphasis on moving up and not enough on the joy and challenge of work itself. They advise beginners not to get sidetracked into long-term career planning, but instead to concentrate on the present and to perform well in entry-level jobs. Starting a career with a scaled-down focus does not mean sacrificing ambition; it may mean discovering new possibilities while avoiding unnecessary pain.

Mary Anne's career history taught her to keep options open. Twelve years ago, she created a public affairs program for a midwest manufacturing company. Five years later, she expanded that department to include public relations, corporate communications, and corporate social responsibility. Recently Mary Anne was promoted to a line management position. Analyzing her own career, she concludes that women do best when they start small but think big.

> I always tell young women, "Don't think you have to make lifetime decisions now. Yes, everything you do in life potentially has an effect on what you do everafterward. But only potentially. You're not making irrevocable decisions."
>
> When people are in their twenties, it's a good time to experiment with different possibilities. They need to recognize that what they think may be right today could be quite transformed in two years, five years, or ten. Instead of searching forever for the absolutely optimal job that they'll want to stay with for their entire career, the thing to do is find something that interests them in the short term, and do it. And while they're doing it, they must be alert to possibilities for the next couple of stages.
>
> As you can tell, I'm not one of those people who believes in one-shot planning—basically because it doesn't work that way in the real world.

Anne developed her expertise in computer technology during the 1950s. She has recently worked in several start-ups, and before that she held top management positions in a renowned multinational firm. During her thirty years in business, Anne has watched countless new hires come and go. Throwing a second log on the fire, she settles back in her chair, thinks for a moment, then offers her advice on expectations.

Beginners must recognize that the college degree is nothing more than the first step. It teaches us some things; it's like a tool bag. Unfortunately, college doesn't teach us anything about the business world or what makes things tick. So young women must go in with open minds and must forget any conceit. Just because we happened to be good in college doesn't necessarily carry over. College is just a springboard.

When entering into companies, women must go immediately into what I call "sponge mode." They must absorb everything, absolutely everything. They must observe, absorb, learn, and grow. And they mustn't get higher expectations than what is realistically consistent with their first jobs.

The Harvard MBAs come out of school with this air about them that says, "I'm going to be a vice president in three years." Garbage. Bull crap. People fresh out of school have to take the steps that are necessary to work themselves up to a level where they can perform competently and consistently. At each stage, there is a relationship between the task to be performed and what can come from it. Newcomers can't be afraid to admit they learn a lot by doing any task.

I am scheduled for tea with Rachael promptly at four. I take the elevator to her thirtieth-floor Manhattan apartment and wonder what a seventy-two-year-old woman—a forty-year veteran of Broadway productions—will look like.

Rachael is waiting for me with tea and lemon cookies. She is short and stylish. Her stories about being the only woman theater manager in the 1930s hold me spellbound for three hours. By the time the interview ends, the sun has set and we are silhouetted against the skyline. I ask Rachael to conclude our talk with advice for the next generation. In her words I recognize the unique bond that exists between artist and craft.

I have always felt—I felt it then and I feel it now—that people shouldn't worry about starting at the bottom of the ladder. First of all, they learn more there. They learn their companies. They learn whether they like the work. They learn what the real potential of the work is.

The thing I find so distressing today is that young people get out of school, and they want to be the chairman of the board in two years. They're forgetting that *the work is the reward*. And it is. I swear to you, it is. It's nice to be well paid, but believe me, the work is the most important thing. It's also important to keep in mind that we need the drive, we need the wanting. And dammit, we need the work.

Rachael's eyes blaze as she leans forward to make her point. Her voice drops to a hushed tone. She speaks carefully, choosing her words deliberately. I have never heard anyone talk about work as she does.

You have to love the work because so often it reinforces itself, and it gets better and better. When it's wonderful, I'll tell you, nothing will make you feel as good.

Rachael pauses, then flashes a triumphant seventy-two-year-old grin.

Nothing will make you feel as good. Nothing, nothing —including the greatest sex.

Learn the System

Many women made the point that all college graduates—male and female—face some similar hurdles during the first few years. For example, both men and women must shift their frame of reference from the classroom to the conference room. Both must learn to deal with rituals, bureaucracies, and chains of command. All new hires must study the corporate culture in order to implement acquired knowledge and skill. Those I interviewed suggested two sets of strategies—strategies appli-

31

cable to everyone, and strategies tailored to the unique needs of beginning professional women.

Leslie, a forty-six-year-old stockbroker, and Ronnie, corporate counsel for a West Coast consumer products company, agree that business is anything but a democracy. Each maintains that the neophyte who assumes there is rationality in the workplace will grow confused and unable to act. Both recall that it wasn't until entering the business world that they fully understood how emotional and impulsive management can be.

Leslie, the stockbroker, speaks first.

> My message for young men and young women is pretty much the same. I think a lot of kids have very unrealistic expectations about the work world. For some reason, they think it's democratic. The school environment is democratic, but the working world is anything but.
>
> In school, students have a say, and they speak up. But in business, there's very much a hierarchy. The people making key decisions are often far away from you. I think that causes culture shock for a lot of kids coming out of school. It certainly did for me.

Ronnie, the lawyer, builds on Leslie's thoughts.

> Recognize the absurdity of the whole environment, and don't expect it to be like any system you've encountered before. Primarily, recognize that it's not a democracy. Women especially have mostly had experiences with democratic organizations, and we assume that that's what business will be like. Whereas, in fact, it's a hierarchy with all sorts of leaps here and there in authority and in where the authority comes from. You have to be able to decipher that hierarchical system.

One way to decipher that system is to study it carefully. The women I talked with agreed that despite the recent spate of best-sellers on corporate culture, few people really take the time to observe for themselves the unique customs operating in their companies. For the beginner, that discipline may make the difference between failure and success.

Heidi, the controller at a paper goods manufacturing company, describes how she became a sleuth of corporate culture. In her present job and in previous positions as a CPA and financial analyst, Heidi made a conscious effort to let nothing go undetected.

> We all must figure out how the pecking order works and what the norms of the organization are. They're going to be male norms, most likely, and we women need to know what that culture is early on.
>
> We have to do a lot of listening, and we have to ask a lot of innocent-sounding questions. We need to look carefully at the offices. We need to see who's in what kind of office, and what kind of furniture is in there. Do managers have pictures on the wall? Do the pictures belong to the company, or are they theirs? This matters.
>
> Women need to see if someone has diplomas or certificates on his wall. We need to take a really good look at the surroundings—how posh or how spartan they are. Young women especially need to see what accommodations people at their level and at levels right above and below them have in terms of office furniture, secretarial support, and all those sorts of things.
>
> Every time I go to a new organization, that stuff comes more and more to the top of my head. Like it or not, it really does represent a lot.

Cathy believes that business schools pump up the expectations of students in ways that are unfair to individuals and unfair to companies. The week of my visit, Cathy had oriented four new MBAs in the unit she supervises. Asking me to pretend that I'm part of that group, Cathy gives me the advice she gives each of them.

> You have to really look and listen. It's not too difficult to pick up clues—and this is what separates somebody

who fits in from somebody who doesn't. You can't know an organization until you get there. Spend some time finding out the names of the people who count, and where the bodies are buried. Listen to how things are said. Notice how things are written. There's a culture, and if you don't know it, you're terribly vulnerable.

Women are set back to begin with. We didn't read all the book on the culture. But in a short time, if you're smart, you can get a feeling for it. You get a feel for the language, the way things are done, the way a man drops by another man's office and says, casually, "Can I see you for a minute?" The way they go out and have coffee, the way they buy lunches, the way they present themselves, the way they talk.

If you watch how things are done for awhile, you can get an understanding of how the culture works. It's not based on brightness or smartness. It's based on some people knowing how it's done, and other people not knowing. The people who don't know how it's done are going to be outsiders.

Be fully open to this idea: You've gone to graduate school for two years, and now you'll have your last year of graduate school—in the corporation. Honestly say, "I'm not done learning until I can say I've learned the culture and I really know what it's like."

Maria and three male engineers founded a software development company four years ago. Before that, Maria had worked in the electronics industry for more than fifteen years. With the wisdom and perspective of twenty years' experience, she offers unique advice to those just starting out.

The biggest message I have is to be prepared to learn about people without worrying about whether they're male or female. Understand personalities and whom you're dealing with, as opposed to what sex they are. Everyone's going to have to make compromises, because it just isn't the idealistic world that we all come out of college thinking it is. If we expect it to be that way, we're going to be disappointed.

But we can't give up on our hopes, either. I think that the worst thing we can do is to lower our standards—as opposed to trying to make other people come up to ours.

At the conclusion of our talks, many women told me that the real reason they had agreed to be interviewed was to give the next generation an insider's perspective on making it in a man's world. Over and over, these women described how they themselves had longed for words of wisdom from female predecessors. Because most had received little such guidance, and because most had experienced great confusion, uncertainty, and disappointment as a result, today these women are adamant about reaching out to others. Their final, most emphatic message is that professional women of all ages must support one another far more boldly and systematically than has been the case to date.

Sally, a cable television executive, remembers a time when inadvertently she let a valuable female role model slip away.

My company went with an IBM computer, so I went to IBM for training, to learn how to program. I ended up working mostly with people from the systems analysis division, and they continued to be available for support when I returned to my office. During that time I ended up working with one woman whom I liked very much. I really admired her.

This woman fascinated me. She was about ten years older than I. She was divorced and had a little girl about eight years old. She was a very straight-laced systems analyst type—very organized, with lots of list-making and lots of note-taking. She was also very good at what she did.

I remember she had about three suits. I thought, "This is interesting. This woman must be making a lot of money, yet she has only three suits. She keeps wearing the same drab suits over and over." Then I realized that maybe she just didn't care—that building an impressive wardrobe wasn't a big thing to her. And as I got to know her, there seemed to be a whole other person inside.

One time I walked into the room where we had installed the computer, and she was standing behind the door doing a little tap dance routine. I said, "What are you doing?" And she said, "I have my tap dance lesson tonight, and I haven't practiced in a week." I remember thinking, "There is a whole other person here. Absolutely."

Well, I didn't get to know that woman as well as I would have liked, because at that point I was shy and really naive about who I was and what I wanted to be. I regret that I didn't get to know her, because she could have taught me so much, and I could have gained a very special friend.

Margaret, a black attorney, sits in a large office surrounded by trophies and public service awards. Though her accomplishments are impressive, Margaret's style remains soft-spoken and down-to-earth. When I ask her to imagine that she's addressing the women of tomorrow, Margaret's eyes widen and her face lights up with a broad, hopeful grin. In a few short sentences, she captures the sentiments of hundreds of pioneers.

Help each other as best you can, and don't be afraid of each other. Don't plan year by year what you're going to do, and where you're going to be five years from now. Attempt to have unlimited horizons. Tend not to be hemmed in by what you see, because when you start setting your goals, they're based on what you see. And you don't even know what the future holds for you.

There's a whole world that will open up if you let it. But when you begin, do your very best at whatever you get into. And don't hesitate to get into something. Don't say, "I don't want to get into this because I don't want to be doing this five years from now." Get into something that you think is interesting now, and do as credible a job as you can do. People will recognize you for the job you've done, and then other things will open up.

Every time a door has been closed—and there have been many doors closed on me—windows have opened.

2

Establishing Credibility

Life Under Scrutiny

When they first started work, the women I interviewed felt they were not taken seriously. Instead of meeting acceptance, they found men skeptical of their abilities. Quickly they discovered that before they could prove themselves as individuals, they had to disprove the assumption that women do poorly in business.

From the day they arrived, the women realized they were being noticed and studied. Most had never imagined how much they'd stand out. Being visible brought different reactions. Some believed that the limelight had afforded them special opportunities. Others, the majority, felt that being noticed really meant living under scrutiny. In response, most women developed the need to perform every task thoroughly. Perfectionism flourished, and the women worked late.

High Visibility

Marilyn looks back on a twenty-year career and recalls her first days at the company.

39

Being a showpiece is a bittersweet feeling. On the one hand it makes you feel good and proud that you were the one selected. But on the other hand, you feel like a token. You always question the motivation: Was it because I was young and attractive and nice and got along well and displayed the same role I had played with my father—which was one of being relatively docile and Daddy's little girl? Or was it truly because of my strength as a manager?

Being a showpiece involves all the pressures of any visible role. You feel that you're always being watched and you can't make any mistakes. There's no room for failure. I've always felt—and I still feel—that I have to be much better than any man at my same level.

Two related dynamics caused the women discomfort. The first was the obvious pressure to achieve. The second—the underlying tone of sexuality—was more subtle. It was difficult to perceive. All the women really knew was that men's eyes were upon them. The atmosphere was charged and the stakes seemed high.

Cathy admits that being observed causes great anxiety. As vice president of marketing for a large West Coast bank, she frequently addresses loan officers, vendors, and executives. Part of her discomfort in front of an audience comes from the pressure to deliver an impeccable speech. But another part comes from Cathy's sense that hundreds of male strangers are checking her out at once.

I feel a lot of stress in doing public presentations. I always feel so different from those around me, and it's very hard for me as I walk down that long aisle to the podium. I think, "I'm the only woman in this room, and I look different. Period."

Two weeks ago, I was sitting in an auditorium at the Hilton, and there was this whole row of senior executives—and me, smack in the middle. I was the only one with a skirt on. All I could think was that members of the audience could look at all these pants, and then at these legs. It's very intense being the only woman there.

When I first met Ginger, creative director at a Madison Avenue advertising agency, she reminded me of Mary—of Peter, Paul, and Mary fame. A tall, energetic blond, Ginger talks in colorful language that accentuates her humor. Though the industry has recognized her talent, Ginger believes that it's good looks and sexuality that have made her career.

It would dishonest of me to say that I was promoted on the basis of my skill and my craft alone. In fact, I was promoted on the basis of having some skill and some appearance. But I never used my looks as a weapon; I truly did not.

Still, there definitely were moments that would send me reeling. Once something happened at a major presentation. It was an internal review of the work that was about to go out the next day. The project involved a lot of work, a very substantial amount. After my presentation, my boss turned and said to me, "Well, that's all very nice, dear. Just make sure that you wear a tight white sweater tomorrow."

That just knocked me down. Until that moment, I don't think I'd ever been truly conscious of being a woman in business. That crack really hurt. It brought me up short. What it finally comes down to is that he thought the work could be sold only by virtue of the appeal of the body that sells it. So he told me to wear a tight white sweater. I just couldn't believe it.

The women looked around and saw that their young male colleagues were also scrambling for recognition. They acknowledged that any professional's first tasks are to prove his or her ability and to try to fit in. The difference, as the women perceived it, was that male coworkers were expected to succeed, while they, the females, were expected to fail.

41

In the short run, this meant that young men were allowed to make mistakes—their difficulties were seen by those in authority as part of learning the ropes, a natural part of being new. The women felt that their challenge was something far more demanding. If the dominant assumption was that they couldn't perform equally, then anything less than perfect work would confirm that belief. The women not only had to prove that they could do it, but they also had to disprove latent traditional views.

Men set up tests of the women's abilities and then watched to see how they would fare. Most women knew at once that they were being tested. They were aware that credibility was on the line. The length of the testing period ranged widely, depending on the industry, organization, and individuals. Meanwhile, all the women felt that they were on stage and under surveillance. They experienced the dual pressures of work and critique.

Helen started in land development when she was only twenty-four. As we sit in a back office cluttered with blueprints, she describes her first six months at the firm. Back then she'd been surprised at the number of contacts developers must maintain. At first, her firm's associates—contractors, architects, and tradesmen—all balked at having to do business with an inexperienced "girl."

> The contractors will always test you. I don't care who they are—plumbers, electricians, whoever—they're going to test you. They'll try to pull a number on you right away.
>
> You have to be clear in the first half-hour that you know exactly what you're talking about. If you don't know what you're talking about, they know it immediately, and then you're in trouble. But I always treat them with respect, and I feel that for the most part I've gotten a similar response back. The testing is tough at the beginning, but once you've passed, you're on your way. You're guilty until proven innocent.

Minority women pointed out that proving themselves to men at work was much like proving themselves to whites anywhere. The survival skills they had learned growing up in a white society prepared them well for being "the different one" again. Patricia, a black anchorwoman, recalls what her mother advised thirty years ago.

The pressures of being a woman in a man's world are no different from the pressures of being a black in a white world. Where I lived as a child, the schools were integrated about the time I moved into the third grade. So I already had some coping skills by the time I went to work. I had been through the worst of it during the transition from the segregation period to the integration period. In the back of my head I can still hear my mother say, "They expect blacks to fail. You've got to be better. You've got to be the best."

Working with men is no different from working with whites and going to school with whites when we were going through that trying period. It's as if they dance around you and say little things, and the way they'll treat you depends on your reactions to them. That testing and trying never stops. It never stops.

When you get a new co-anchor, for example, you've got a new process all over again. When a new white male anchor came in recently, he was given top billing on the show, even though I've been here longer. So I went to management and said very nicely, "Why is it that he's being introduced first and I'm not?" Traditionally, with only male co-anchors, when the new man comes in, the one who was already there gets top billing.

I was told, "Well, his name is shorter than yours. It's easier to say 'Bob and Patricia' than it is to say 'Patricia and Bob.'" I didn't say anything. It wouldn't have done any good.

But I haven't given up. In business, in television, the trying never stops. Just the way it never really stops in a racially integrated society, it never stops in a male-female society at a job.

Men's Stereotypes

The women reported that part of gaining credibility was establishing the fact that they did not fit commonly held stereotypes. Having overheard men's conversations, they worried about being labeled "bra burners," "bitches," "ball busters," and "sirens." I listened to their concerns and discovered that the stereotypes they feared fit into two distinct categories.

The first were generalizations about female temperament. These were the assumptions that women are, by nature, "too emotional," "too nice," or "too unstable" for business. The second set had to do with occupational ability. These were beliefs that subjects such as finance, electronics, and plumbing are inherently beyond the scope of a woman's intelligence. Each person I interviewed had encountered some stereotypes. Many of them were subtle; others were not.

Wendy is a senior vice president. Part of her job is to present complex financial data to the corporation's all-male board of directors. After attending quarterly meetings for three years, Wendy assumed that she had gained the board's respect. When she discovered that to them she was no more than a stereotype, she was devastated; she went into shock.

> I was having lunch with one of the board members and he said to me, "There's something I've wanted to tell you for a long time." I said, "What is that?" and he replied, "The board perceives you as being tea-and-cookies." I looked at him and asked, "What does that mean?" He said, "They don't know the real you. You've got to start coming across a little bit differently."
>
> Now, when I'm performing my job, I'm all business, and I can be very tough. But the board doesn't see that, because with them I'm only there to make a presentation. There's no arguing, no confrontation. So I sit and talk

about something with them, and they apparently don't feel that a woman—particularly a soft-spoken woman who polishes her fingernails and wears silk dresses—can be effective.

When I heard that phrase "tea-and-cookies," it depressed me at first. But it also made me very angry. I'll tell you honestly, I wanted to scream, "That's bullshit!" In fact, I probably did.

I got past the depression when a friend reminded me, "You are a woman. Act like one, and don't do anything differently." And so I didn't. Being a woman doesn't necessarily make me only "tea-and-cookies."

Another set of stereotypes that operate in the workplace are those based on family roles. Many women I interviewed were convinced that male colleagues first viewed them as mothers, sisters, and daughters, and few found this surprising. They recognized that men who have rarely worked with female professionals rely on their family relationships as a frame of reference for learning to live in a coed world. The women admitted that they too participate in family stereotyping. Some said they view their peers as brothers and cousins. Many were conscious of seeing men in authority as fathers.

As a management consultant, Jane has the opportunity to observe all kinds of organizations. When I ask about stereotyping inside the corporate world, her face lights up in instant recognition.

Just the other night a bunch of us had a conversation about our office. It seems that consulting firms have distinct family characteristics. Our firm likes to think of itself as one big happy family. When I started out, the roles were especially clearly defined, and there were just twenty of us.

All the role-playing that goes on! It's like being on a family vacation with teenagers, the father, and the son. We have two fathers in the group, actually, and a rebellious

45

teenager—and, of course, the daughters. There are very distinct ways that we women fit into that group. Most of us are seen as daughters. Whenever there's stress in the office, these roles come out.

The women warned that as soon as a female professional is cast in the daughter role, her credibility wanes. First, the role tends to widen the power differential between her and the boss. Second, a woman viewed as Daddy's girl is likely to be envied and criticized by peers—both male and female. Most important, the role itself prescribes behavior: The good daughter does not challenge, but readily obeys. She does not act independently, but conforms to parental dictates. At all times her performance is at a safe, predictable level. Above all, the good daughter agrees that Daddy is someone she will never outdo.

To be viewed as professionals rather than as daughters, the women made conscious efforts to avoid this confining role.

Debbie works in a new manufacturing company. As is true of most entrepreneurial ventures, the firm reflects its founder's personal style. In the midst of describing the CEO, Debbie abruptly swivels in her chair, checks the area around her cubicle, and continues speaking in a near whisper.

It's not like a business here. It's more like a family. Everyone does everything. The phone is ringing all day, and you're trying to get work done or you're trying to catch the boss to get decisions from him. It feels as though you're always vying for Dad's attention among all the other people who need him at the same time you do. There's something about this place that keeps you a child. You can't really make any major decisions.

Stereotyping was associated with anonymity. It waned as each woman established her reputation and style. Like many I interviewed halfway through their careers, Nancy is not worried about stereotypes today. After ten years as a manager, she has learned that competence and consistency lead to success.

She believes that being herself has worked to her advantage. Once labeled "too sweet," then dubbed "the bitch," Nancy throws up her hands and asks with a twinkle, "Given the choices, what's a girl to do?"

Early in my career I ran into the stereotyping of the woman who always needs to be the nice one, smiling and accepting and nurturing. And I was that stereotype. I really was. I had this tape that said, "No matter what somebody says to you, just smile and take it." So when I'd be giving a speech, I'd be smiling. I could be talking about the most serious thing in the world, and you wouldn't know it from my body language and posture. That was the first stereotype.

More recently, I've been classified as the battle-ax. People who know me well don't see me that way, but there are people either outside the department or two or three levels removed who really are afraid of me. I don't think it's because I'm a bitch. I think it's because I'm a stickler for quality.

When I first found out that people were saying I'm the stereotyped woman-manager-bitch, it was very hard for me to get used to thinking that not everybody liked me. Finally, I had to say, "Screw it. Not everybody's going to like me." When I finally accepted that fact, it was a relief. I was glad, really, because quite frankly, I didn't like everybody else in the company either. And I didn't want the burden of being liked by everyone. I didn't want to end up going to lunch with people I didn't like. Why was I playing that game? I don't know. Finally I quit doing that. If that's bitchy, too bad.

Perfectionism and Stress

Many women had to go through the process of proving their competence each time they changed companies or were reassigned. Facing a new group of colleagues, the women braced themselves for tests they knew would start again. To speed up the process, they drove themselves fiercely for the first few months. They hoped that a high volume of good work at the outset would be enough to satisfy the men and themselves as well.

But contrary to expectations, the women discovered that reality rarely worked out as planned. What they had not predicted was that the pressure to perform took on a life of its own. Schoolgirl wishes for recognition were reactivated. Memories of straight-A report cards became vivid once again. The women struggled as much with internal drives and self-criticism as with evaluations from their supervisors and peers. The psychological fact of being new on the job was that perfectionism escalated, it didn't go away.

Marion, an attorney, sums up the interaction between the internal and external worlds.

> I think you're more visible as a woman. You're more on center stage, so you have to perform. That in itself creates a pressure. Also, I have certain standards of my own—I like to do the best I can. So I think the push comes as much from within as from without.

A related phenomenon was that women learned never to show publicly that the going was rough. Intent on disproving the "hysterical woman" stereotype, for the first few years they kept feelings to themselves. Despite their anxiety and cumulative exhaustion, the women were determined not to let on. As I listened to individuals repeat the same cycle, I saw that the more desperate they felt, the more they denied. In New York, Chicago, and Los Angeles, I heard three different versions of a very similar tale.

After two jobs as a financial analyst in the suburbs, Laurie has finally made it to Wall Street. When I ask about pressure, very abruptly she changes her tone. Part of her stress comes from being a woman; part of it comes from Wall Street itself.

As Laurie describes a typical morning, she clenches her fists and her knuckles turn white.

> Wall Street is fast-paced and very aggressive. There's a morning meeting every day. You go into this big boardroom where all the top honchos sit around, and when it's your turn, you speak into a little squawk box, and your voice goes out to 4,000 brokers all over the country. Everyone reacts to your opinion. The brokers listen in, and they ask questions as you're speaking. You're talking in front of all your superiors, all men in white shirts and red ties and blue suits. The spotlight is on you.
>
> The first time I spoke it was scary as hell. I was panicked. You sit there, and you see people shake. I used to write things out. If I was going to say "Good morning," I used to actually write out "Good morning." In time you learn that you have to have a little more confidence—you have to *portray* it, I should say. One way or another, you'd better learn how to look self-assured. You can never show that you're scared. You have to overcome that, and that's a major difficulty for me.
>
> Even today it's still terribly scary. When that spotlight is on, you have to show that you are confident in your opinion, that you have conviction, and that you don't doubt what you're saying at all. That's the air you must present, and that's very, very difficult. There's tremendous pressure.
>
> Also, you have to be ready to defend yourself. In all my years in the business, I have never heard anyone say they're wrong. They say, "These were my assumptions, and because of this, this is what I believe." But you never admit that you're wrong or that you doubt yourself at all. Never, ever.

Elizabeth is treating me to breakfast. We sit in the dining room of an old New York hotel and discuss the details of public relations. She recalls that for five years she struggled to meet consistently high standards. But after suffering a depression at the age of 26, Elizabeth redefined her measures of success.

> I was definitely a perfectionist. When I first got into the agency business, the feedback I was getting from my supervisor was so erratic that, as a perfectionist, I was being destroyed by it. I used to labor over projects for hours. Even though the person who was receiving my materials—the client—was probably saying, "This is pretty good," my boss always focused on the negative. He never gave me direct, positive feedback.
>
> I was taking much of this as a personal attack on my capabilities, and I was devastated. I would say to myself, "I'm worthless. I'm a piece of shit. I can't do this." It was very difficult for me.
>
> When I felt I was letting myself down, I was shocked. I'd always gotten what I wanted—I got good grades, I was accepted for a special program abroad in college, I always got the man I wanted to date. So when this happened, I couldn't believe I was floundering.
>
> Since I've always been fairly energetic, I decided to work out insanely. I'd run five miles every night because I knew I was under a lot of stress. Even though I worked out all the time, I wasn't sleeping well. I was very depressed, which scared me because I had always been an up person.
>
> Finally, I did get to the point where I went to see a counselor, because I felt that I was putting demands on myself that I just couldn't meet. Then I realized it wasn't that I couldn't meet these demands. It was that I was working in an extremely unhealthful environment.

I must pass by three security guards before I'm allowed to enter the aerospace company where Sharon works. When I ask how she got used to living under tight security, Sharon shakes her head. Dealing with security and classified documents is all part of a culture that promotes efficiency and control. Everything must appear to be in order. Emotions are never allowed.

I'm going through a serious family problem right now with my niece and nephew, and it's causing me a lot of anguish. I try to keep it outside of work as much as I can, but recently I had a phone call that just destroyed me, right then and there.

I knew I couldn't cry at work. It was like a voice saying to me, "You can't cry, Sharon, you can't be an emotional woman. You simply can't have that feeling right now." There's this stereotype that says, "Women can't handle it. Women break down. Women cry." Well, I was determined not to let that happen, not to let somebody say of me, "See, I told you so."

Before I had an office mate, if I ever felt like crying, I used to shut the door and I'd just cry—get it out, get it over with, and I'd be fine. I'd go right back to work. But with an office mate it's difficult. When I received that phone call, I had to get out of there immediately, but I didn't know how. I thought, "Oh, God, I've got to walk past all these people to get to the women's room, and they're not going to know why I'm crying. They might think I got yelled at, or that I couldn't handle a meeting."

I had all those fears, so I just sat there. My nose got red and my eyes stung. Finally I got up and made a dash for the restroom. I sat in there for almost half an hour, trying to get myself together so I could go back out, go to work, and not let anyone know I felt sad.

All too often the women's isolation and perfectionism led to self-doubt combined with self-blame. Some identified with the men who questioned their abilities. When progress was slow, they wondered what they'd done wrong. The psychological danger was that over time, many women felt unable to trust their own perceptions. They were never quite sure what was going on.

Marion thinks the problem stems from a lack of outside feedback. When she's alone but visible, she forgets that other lawyers' wisecracks are just part of the test.

During one trial, I would make an objection to a question, and I'd hear snickers throughout the audience—this was with twenty-five male lawyers present, and that's a lot of lawyers. I'd hear snickers, and I'd get comments. It was just endless. I would open my mouth to object, and someone would start in with, "Are you a member of the New York Bar?" And I'd say, "I don't see what relevance that has." And they'd say, "I'd like to advise you and your client that it's a misdemeanor to practice law in New York without a license. I'd like to know if you're a member of the New York Bar."

It was harassment, actually. I don't think all that snickering would have happened if I had been a man. In fact, I'm sure it would never have happened. At first I had myself insulated. I thought I was prepared. I would start out, and at my first objection, I'd get some snickers, and I'd ignore them. After the second one, I got more snickers, and by the end of the day, I was sitting there thinking, "Is what I'm saying really a valid objection? Am I a fool? Is something wrong with what I'm doing?"

Jessica, too, berates herself. Though she's established a citywide reputation as a litigator, she still feels devastated when she makes even one mistake.

There'd be lots of times when I'd go out and flub. There would clearly be times when I didn't do such a hot job. So I'd come back to the office, and immediately I'd kick myself. I'd go over the situation time and again. I'd try and try and try to understand it. I would kick myself and say, "God, how could I have ever done that?"

Some women understand that they are their own worst enemy, and see how they may have contributed to the pain inherent in breaking in. Recently, Lisa was recruited by the CEO of a Fortune 500 company to head up the implementation of an innovative strategic plan. Despite her credentials and twelve years in management, Lisa recognizes the old anxiety of starting a new job. Now that she's experienced the cycle several times, she's seeing a pattern and is trying to change.

> My toughest critic is me. I beat the holy dickens out of myself. I'm learning to do that less and less, though. Still, even the worst form of discrimination wouldn't be as bad as what I do to myself. As a child, the way I got loved was to be perfect. I had to have my little ankles crossed and my little hands folded and my little hair perfect and my little dress just so. And of course, if possible, I had to get all A's.

In remembering their early years, most women concluded that the hardest part about not being taken seriously was never quite understanding all the reasons why. They knew that the factors were related and complicated, but they could never tease out the precise roles that gender, age, and inexperience played. This fact made them wary of alleging discrimination, and it forced them to tolerate the ambiguity of their worlds. Debbie, like many others, has given up trying to analyze frustration; she's become more of a pragmatist than she knows.

> Being a perfectionist and wanting to build a wonderful department that everybody respected and that I too would respect was terribly, terribly difficult. Time and time again, I would make a suggestion and it wouldn't happen, for whatever reason. It might be that my boss wasn't strong enough to push my ideas through, or that I wasn't, or that this particular corporation just wasn't sophisticated enough to accept the fact that they needed a well-developed human resources function. And maybe some of it was due to the fact that I was female. I don't know. And looking back, I realize I'll never know.

Tips From the Trenches

Streamline the Process

With willpower and time, the women passed their tests. Little by little, men recognized their talents and began to respect their judgment. Long hours and hard work had finally paid off. Looking back on that early period, most women chose not to dwell on painful memories—they preferred to summarize what they had learned. Eagerly they offered suggestions on how to speed up the "proving process" and, equally important, on how to make it more humane. With better information and a well-developed strategy, they argued, professional women can protect themselves emotionally while proving themselves to men.

Marie, a high-tech vice president, tells what works for her.

> You want to know what I do to get men to take me seriously? I overwhelm them with my knowledge.

Marie is not alone. Every woman I met echoed her claim that in the end, there is no substitute for competence. Time and again the women told me stories of how they had won over cynical colleagues when they had supplied correct answers or provided new ideas. While they warned that knowledge alone doesn't guarantee success, the women believe that solid training and technical skills will in the end impress the majority of men.

I asked what one thing all women should keep in mind when first going to work in an all-male office. To my surprise, the answers I received were consistent and succinct. Whether speaking with Marie in high technology, with Diane in consumer products manufacturing, or with Suzanne in interior design, repeatedly I heard the same advice.

Marie speaks first.

> The only thing that really works is to be right. Someone wants the right answer, and you have it. Any woman in business must hone her abilities. Her self-respect will be

based on that, and it will come through to other people. If she takes herself seriously, people around her will take her seriously too. Competence is so rare and so valued that in a way the more competent you are, the less you need to assert it. In the end, competence always shines through.

Diane's words reflect fifteen years of management experience. Working strictly with all-male teams in finance and operations, she quickly found out what really counts.

It still seems that the bottom line is to do the best job you can. That gets you through more than anything else. Doing well is so important. You make allies when you consistently do well, and it softens people up like crazy. Competence is so much better than anything else. Just be very, very good at what you do.

Suzanne started as a secretary on Seventh Avenue. Today she is a partner in an internationally known design firm. She's convinced that she was promoted because she kept a clear focus and produced high-quality work. In the crisp style of a minimalist, she minces not a word.

Outperform everyone. Put your nose to the grindstone. Don't worry about the future, or tomorrow, or any of that. Worry about what you've got in front of you right now, today. Bust your ass, and do it better than anybody. Because if you don't do that, none of the rest of it is ever going to matter.

The tricky part is that quality work is a necessary but insufficient ingredient for a woman proving her worth.

Those I interviewed had learned this the hard way. Fifteen years ago, most had assumed that delivering the product was all they had to do. Back then they had labored over projects and turned out good results, but felt frustrated when men still doubted their skill. Gradually they came to recognize the need for self-promotion. They saw that skepticism would linger until influential leaders saw what they could do.

The women began to strategize. Some learned to read their bosses better and to tailor their efforts accordingly. Others developed techniques for establishing a reputation company-wide. All found that they had to make deliberate efforts to speak up and to make sure their ideas were heard. The women launched proactive campaigns.

Sharon is two years out of business school. When she first took a job in the aerospace industry, her goal was to master corporate finance. With a grin, Sharon tells me she has since shifted that goal. Today her top priority is marketing herself.

> I go out of my way to get the men I'm working with to talk to me. It's a challenge. I push back. I know this is just another barrier I have to overcome. I know this is something I need to do.
>
> Everywhere I go within this company there are very few women. But I don't feel lost anymore, because in most of the meetings I've established myself. It's when I go into a new meeting—with men whose reputations I know but who don't know me—that I feel I need to overdo it. I need to oversell. I need to make damn sure I'm not a wallflower.
>
> I see to it that I'm not invisible because I'm "the woman." I contribute. I ask questions. I'm no longer intimidated because they're more senior. I don't let them know I'm so junior, and it works.

Elizabeth uses her public relations skills inside the firm as well as with clients. Writing promotional copy has taught her the subtleties and power that language conveys. Her statement, like its message, is forceful and direct.

> A woman must do her homework, and once she's done it, she must be sure to speak up. And she must be one hun-

dred percent sure of what she's talking about. In the initial stages of our careers, many people have already formulated an opinion that says, "She doesn't know what she's talking about." So it's especially important for a woman to know that she's right. When giving her opinions, she needs to state them in a way that shows she's convincing—a way that shows she firmly believes in what she says. I tell the women working for me not to say, "I think." Instead, they're to say to the men, "This is the way it is."

Evelyn reports to an all-male senior management team in an industrial products company. When preparing for meetings, she divides her time in two. Half of it goes toward organizing her data. The other half goes toward analyzing the group.

I believe the only way for a woman to survive with any self-respect is to speak up, to engage in repartee, to question. What I come away with is that we women need to know more. We must have more information. And in order to be equal, we must be better. I truly believe that.

When I meet with men in my company, I don't go into the room without all my ducks in a row. If I suddenly get called into a man's office, and he doesn't tell me in advance what the subject is, you can be damn sure that I've got the eighteen possibilities neatly lodged in their compartments in my head. I've got it all figured out. Even if it takes me an extra five minutes to walk over to a man's office, I'll have my answers prepared when I get there.

I find that as women we can't knuckle under, but neither can we attack. We've got to be "players." We can argue, but we can't challenge their male egos. That is the core of what I'm trying to say.

Becoming a player is rarely an easy task. It involves a woman's ability to share responsibility and to work collaboratively with men. It requires that she be sensitive to spoken and unspoken norms. It forces her to strike a balance between her own style and the style that the culture respects. In the chapter that follows—Learning the Informal System—the women detail their experiences in trying to fit into men's informal groups. Here they emphasize the crucial role of these intangibles in building credibility and ensuring early success.

Janet captures the essence of the issue.

> There are forces beyond performance evaluation that can cause a person to keep or lose a job and to build or destroy a career. Those forces have everything to do with the subjective realm and nothing to do with the objective. These are things like personality conflicts, how you get along, chemistry, and feelings of acceptance or rejection.
>
> The way people see you is so important. If people see you as a bad egg or a thorn—and not as a team player—they don't want you around. At that point, it doesn't matter at all if you just did a good job and your budget came in on target. It doesn't matter at all if you just made a million dollars.

Several women found that when they hit an impasse and were worried about credibility, honest confrontation produced the best results. Heidi asked that her boss redefine her job, and her evaluations soared. Natalie sat a hostile colleague down and solicited his advice. Lisa figured out a way to befriend six anxious wives. In short, when the women took more initiative, their self-esteem rose. They regained a feeling of control and experienced relief.

Chain of command is a reality, Heidi argues emphatically. A woman's boss is pivotal, and his influence can be profound. After years of second-guessing what each new boss found valuable, Heidi has adopted a more direct approach. It gains her credibility while it puts the men at ease.

> Learning to manage a boss is a matter of feeling that person out—what he's looking for and what the expecta-

tions are. This is important from a strictly job-related perspective, but also from the perspective of things like appearance, how we relate to other people in the organization, what our boss's expectations are for our roles on certain projects—those sorts of things. We have to find out what the boss feels is important for our roles, as well as our responsibilities.

To learn all the informal codes, we women have to observe behavior. We have to get a feel for how a department interacts with other departments, and how the people there interact with one another. In the first several staff meetings here, I didn't say a lot because I was watching. I was trying to get a feel for the personalities, their interactions, the roles people played, and how they dealt with one another.

It would be difficult to do an "a, b, c, d, e" on how to manage one's boss—a lot of it comes down to observing and asking questions. I now say straight out to my boss, "What role do you want me to play in this project? What are your expectations of me?" I believe that women and men all need to be more open and to communicate better. If there's something any of us doesn't understand, the best way of finding out is to ask directly. Usually bosses appreciate that because it demonstrates our interest in what they want. Normally, they don't hesitate to respond, because they want us to perform in a very specific way. It's in their own best interest.

Natalie works for a real estate developer in the Deep South. In the beginning she tried to hide her personality when she was at work. "All that changed on a business trip," Natalie remembers. Guts and a conversation altered her career.

I had one project director that I could not get through to, no matter what I did. One time he and I wound up going with some executives on an open house in another office in Colorado. We all went out to dinner, and when we got back to the hotel, this man said, "I think I'm going to go to the bar and have a nightcap. Anybody want to join me?" Well, I just assumed everybody would go, and so I said, "Sure, I'll go." And immediately all the others started in with, "Well, I'm tired," and "I think I'll pass." I groaned to myself, because I knew this guy really didn't like me.

But sure enough, we went to the bar. Finally I looked at him and said, "You know, we've always had a problem, and I don't know why. I try really hard to work with you. Tell me, honestly, what is it about me that grates on you? What is it about me you don't like?"

And he said, "You really want to know the truth? Well, when we go into meetings, there are all the guys, and then there's you. Whoever is chairing the meeting goes around the room and asks everybody what they think on a certain subject. When they come to you, you always say something that contradicts what everybody else has said. And all of a sudden we realize that what you said makes a lot more sense than what we all just said. It makes us look stupid. The problem is, you're always right. Couldn't you ever be just a little bit wrong?"

I said to him, "Let me try two ideas out on you. First, what do you do before you walk into that meeting?" He said, "What do you mean?" I repeated, "What do you do?" He said, "I don't do anything. I go to the meeting." And I told him, "Before I go to a meeting in this company, I research for thirty minutes what we're going to discuss, and I make sure I've covered every possible thought, because I know I'm going to be asked. I know too that when I'm asked, if I don't know what I'm talking about, you guys are going to look at me and say, 'Well, you know, she's a dumb woman. We told you she shouldn't be here.' So I do my homework. I don't say those things in the meeting because I'm any smarter—it's just that I've spent a half-hour thinking about the topic, and you've just decided to think about it as you walk into the room."

Then he said, "Well, that's true. I guess I never thought about that." I continued, "Besides, how would you feel if I was always wrong? If I always said things that didn't make any sense or were totally off-the-wall? You'd think I was the typical 'female dummy.' You'd think, 'Why did they hire this stupid woman? She doesn't know anything.' Then do you think you'd want to work with me?"

His answer was "Hell, no," so I said, "Well, how do I win in this situation with you? I'm in a no-win." He looked at me and started laughing. Then he said, "You know, you're right. I just never thought about it that way. I guess my ego was in the way, and I couldn't let it get past this situation." And from that moment on, we were the best of friends.

Lisa's tips are especially helpful to women who move up faster than men. Now a senior executive in an industrial products firm, Lisa recalls the years she worked at a financial services company. In those days, a bright young woman was threatening not only to colleagues but also to wives. Lisa chuckles as she remembers her anxiety. What sounds like a cleverly crafted scheme was her way of being direct.

When I first took over the department, I took the other department managers out to lunch to say, "Hey, I don't know anything, and you guys are the gurus. What do I need to look for? Where can I get into the swamp and the quicksand?" They were all terrific, and very helpful.

Then, about a year later, I became their boss. These were the department managers who'd thought it was cute that this young girl was running a department—but now it was probably not so cute that I was their boss. It dawned on me that if my father came home to my mother one day and said, "I now have a boss who's a girl, under thirty, who's from the corporate lending side of the company (which was enemy territory) and who's a Stanford MBA," he'd be very upset. I also knew my mother would want to know just exactly what this young lady looked like.

"I've got to do something fast," I realized, "because I'm going to give these people my all, yet they don't know me from a hole in the wall. I've got to pull this thing together quickly."

I decided to have a cocktail party at my apartment. I hand-addressed the invitations, and on each one I put the wife's name and wrote little things like, "Patty, I'm so looking forward to meeting you." I had my boyfriend there, and I made sure I dressed with my blouse buttoned all the way up—nothing low-cut. I memorized their children's names—I even had a crib sheet in my pocket, and every now and then I'd run into my bedroom to check it. I purposely spent all my time talking to the wives, talking about kids and volunteer work and I don't know what.

Basically I did all this because I wanted them to see that I was a human being. Because when you say "a woman MBA," a lot of people immediately think "hard, son-of-a-bitch woman." I wanted to get rid of that image. I also wanted to get rid of the idea that I might be silly or dumb—or that I might be a siren.

With different people from different backgrounds, all those labels bring up images that don't relate to me. I thought if I could get the wives to see that I was OK, then if their husbands came home and said, "That goddam bitch," the wives might say, "She's really nice. How can you say that?" And I found out later that that's exactly what happened.

All I did was be me. I realized that with the women I had only one shot. I wanted to be sure that when the going got tough and the men went home, their wives—rather than reinforcing the negative—would be reinforcing the positive.

To tell the truth, when I did this whole thing, I hadn't thought it through to the degree I'm telling you now. My gut just said to do it.

When the women I interviewed for this study dared to break out of their roles and approach men as people, the tension abated, and they passed the harder tests. Often the realization that they could discuss the issue openly came only after months of fruitless expenditures of energy and few tangible results. Looking back, they recommend addressing the dynamic earlier and head-on. For Nancy, soliciting help directly was always the safest bet.

> Asking a man for help when you sense that he's skeptical of your abilities can work miracles—especially with older men, who aren't used to working with females. I'm not too proud to say to those guys, "Look, you've been around a lot longer than I have, you know the people a lot better than I do, and you see things from a different point of view. Tell me what you think I should do in this situation." Almost always I'm immediately a comrade, as opposed to a threat.

Not one woman failed to mention the importance of perspective at the outset of a career. In closing, each one urged that all professional women starting out keep in mind that they're part of history, and that challenging tradition takes stamina and time. Paula, an architect, sees the larger picture and offers this advice.

> Always take time for yourself, no matter how much it takes out of you. Be sure to take time. Also, keep a variety of friends in and out of your field. Don't get too tied in to the people you work with and deal with all the time. And be sure not to disassociate yourself from women—not necessarily for discussing "women's issues," but just to keep in contact.
>
> I think people in general are going to need a lot more ways to deal with the increased complexity and demands of the work world. This applies to men as well as to women, and it especially applies in the beginning. The first few years can be terribly tough if you're not extra careful.

Marion's message is hopeful. Gaining credibility was a long and trying process, but it happened because she held on.

> Take it on faith that the first five years are very, very difficult, that the first one is particularly hard, and that your first job will probably not be the ultimate job. There truly is a lot of experience to gain, and the only way you can become experienced is by keeping at it. As far as the difficulty of those first few years goes, it's hard to decide how much of it has to do with being a woman and how much of it has to do with being inexperienced. The two progress together. And the experience gets better.

Learning the Informal System

It's Still Who You Know

> After we wrapped up the meeting, we went out to lunch—nine men and I. I remember feeling excluded, but it was interesting to watch. They were simply oblivious to my presence. That's one thing that kind of surprised me. Nobody fawned over me, nobody gave me special treatment, nobody tried to engage me in conversation about "womanly things." They just launched into their conversation without me. I remember sitting there, eating my shrimp salad, and thinking, "Well, they're off."

When women face the challenge of establishing credibility, few give much thought to the social side of work. Though they notice men eating lunch, playing golf, and going drinking together, early on most women ignore the meaning of such events. Only later, when they try to join in, do women discover new barriers. Quickly they learn that two worlds exist simultaneously—the formal world of business, where roles and tasks are spelled out, and the informal world of business, where friendships and loyalties reign.

This chapter tells the story of how the women came to recognize the importance of informal ties. It describes them watching bonds develop among men in their offices, bonds that get strengthened over poker games, in the locker room, and at lunch. It depicts the women's efforts to be accepted a second time, this time not on the basis of measurable performance, but rather on the basis of friendship and trust.

Given that the women I met had had little preparation for this experience, it's not surprising that few expected to be excluded from men's informal groups. One by one, they faced the reality. Some were unaware of informal networks until they'd worked for several years. Others, like Melinda, discovered them in a job interview, where she learned that a man's comfort level with his male colleagues can determine hiring decisions—even if it means going against the law.

> The first time I felt excluded was when I was interviewing with a large law firm. After many interviews there, I was finally escorted in to see the senior partner, who was about eighty-two years old and sitting behind a desk. It was clear that this man still ran the firm. I sat down across from him, and we began to banter back and forth. Everything was going along well. All of a sudden, he looked at me from across the desk, then he looked at his watch, and said, "Well, your twenty minutes are up. I've really enjoyed talking with you, but there's no use wasting your time or mine." I said, "What do you mean?" And he said, "As long as I'm head of this firm, we ain't hiring any niggers or women."
>
> Yes—this is a direct quote.
>
> I remember thinking that maybe there was a punch line coming, because I had never, ever heard such a comment before. I just stood there, and the guy who was sitting in on the interviews with me—who had obviously heard this before—didn't even bat an eye. He hadn't prepared me for this at all.
>
> I stood up and said, "Well, that's fine, because I wouldn't want to work for your firm." And I walked out.
>
> Interestingly enough, I have now talked to other women who have had the exact same experience. At first I thought

it was all a joke. I really thought there would be a punch line coming. But I looked at him again, and I realized that no, this was an eighty-two-year-old person who truly believed what he was saying.

More than anything else, I was angry. Number one, it was a firm that I hadn't planned to interview with, because, from my research, I didn't think it had a big enough name. Also, I hadn't heard all positive things about the firm. So it made me mad that I'd not gone with my instincts and said no to them to begin with, and had wasted an entire day. It also made me mad that I couldn't jump across the table and punch that man in the nose.

I was given example after example of how the women were subtly excluded from informal circles within their organizations. Some incidents occurred in the office, others on the way to the airport, at lunch, or in out-of-town hotels. Off-site, women seemed to be left out of activities, and at the office, they weren't a part of men's impromptu talks. When conversations were suddenly terminated or when invitations "got lost," it was clear that some parts of business still were off limits. It was clear that the informal world had not gone coed.

Suzanne has two children and works a fifty-hour week. She has neither the time nor the interest to pursue activities outside of work. Still, she longs for professional companionship, and she's jealous of the camaraderie she sees among the men.

I always say that being a partner in this firm is like being a girl who's joined a fraternity. The guys have their secret rituals. They have all their men stuff. They stand next to each other at the urinal and talk business. They hunt. They go to clubs that don't allow women—they'll schedule a meeting at a men's country club, and we'll get there, and they'll realize I'm not allowed in.

There are all these ritual things that they do to build relationships—personal relationships that enable them to work better together. Women have a tough time developing such relationships and really getting in. Sometimes I think I should go out and learn to hunt pheasants with the troop. But I don't want to do any of that stuff. What I do want is for them to relate to me at work the way they relate to each other.

For most of the women, though, the more they found out about the importance of informal activities, the more they recognized the challenge of trying to break in. The task seemed especially hard when they realized they had limited or uneasy access to other places where men conduct business—places like golf courses and tennis clubs, local bars and steak joints, Jaycee banquets and Rotary Club events. Nothing tangible prevented the women from joining men in these settings, but what they found unsettling was a strong covert message. That message was simple: You do not fit in.

Sometimes the women felt a similar tone at the office. In her ten years at a telecommunications company, Kay has worked with one female colleague, and the rest of the time she's worked with men. Finally, she's proven her competence, and now she's accepted as one of the team. While working, Kay gets along well with her colleagues. After hours, she finds she's out on her own.

I have a picture in my mind of three men in our office standing at a hallway intersection, talking. The office closes at five-thirty, and this may be six, so things have gotten slightly more casual. These three men are talking, and another man goes up and slips—slips!—into the conversation with no problem at all. I walk by and the conversation comes to a screeching halt. No one says anything until I've gone past. The idea that I might try to join the conversation? Forget it. Never! Ever, ever.

Challenges Off Site

Incidents occurring out of the office are more difficult to handle, the women agree. At conventions, some are not told about meetings. On retreats, they may not be asked to dine with the group. On business trips, they are assumed to be uninterested in after-work festivities, and so, uninvited, they spend evenings in their rooms. As these patterns developed with increasing frequency, many women grew puzzled. They couldn't understand why the situation got worse when they were away from routine office life.

The answer may have to do with latent sexuality and the need on the part of all involved to deny it. Without structured work to channel their energies, colleagues feel attractions in a much more conscious way. In off-site settings, the dynamic is intensified; the more heightened the intensity, the more explosive the results. Some men would rather exclude women entirely than deal with the flirting and teasing that may evolve. Because of their worries about potential scenarios, those planning social events opt to leave females out.

For the women I talked to, exclusion was the flip side of visibility. Instead of enduring an uneasy spotlight as was the case in meetings, once out of the office, they often felt ignored. Lawyers, managers, and reporters all described similar reactions. They, like those in other professions, spoke of feeling angry, insulted, and sad.

Some women grew determined to have the men accept them. Others chose to associate with only women's groups. Collectively they struggled to understand the dynamics and to determine why, once again, they had to fight so hard to get in.

Michelle thinks it's difficult to separate the formal and informal parts of her job. I interview her on a holiday, when no other stockbrokers are working downtown. We sit in a room crammed with desks, printouts, and terminals, signs of activity from a frenzied week. Here, the physical proximity of so many workstations requires that relationships go smoothly; people can't afford not to get along. Despite all the closeness, Michelle feels isolated. Though she's a top broker, she's outside the group.

> As a woman, you're left out. The men don't want you to go drinking with them after work. And certainly it is rather strange if a woman goes to the local bar where these

guys are going to down twenty in a night. It's just not appropriate.

You're not invited to lunches during the day. In the three years I've been here, I don't ever remember my boss, Richard, asking me out to lunch, yet he'll ask all the other brokers out. I think he feels strange around me. I'm not saying he hasn't helped me. He has. But he always does it with a kind of a "don't come too near" attitude. He doesn't relate well to women. He makes that perfectly clear. He would no more ask me out to lunch than the moon would fall out of the sky.

Here's a beautiful example. I once won a contest for producing $100,000 worth of a mutual fund. The prize was "dinner with your boss at any restaurant in town," paid for by the firm. That meant you could go whole hog. But Richard wouldn't go, so he had to do something to make up for it.

I have a young broker friend, Dave, who happens to sit next to me. So my boss came over and said to Dave, "You and Michelle are friends." Dave said, "Yes," and Richard went on: "Well then, you take her." So Dave and I went, because Richard wouldn't. I was so angry. Richard's whole attitude, and the general attitude of the older men in this business, is simply, "Fine, if we can't whip you, if we can't drive you out, then just keep your distance. Don't come too near. Don't bother me."

The younger guys are different. They're growing up as a part of this "aggressive woman thing," so they can accept it. They've gone through college at a time when men and women have been equals, and the women have sometimes beat them out. They're in businesses where they're used to having women equals and even women bosses. Their whole attitude toward women is a lot different from that of the older guys.

Women recognize that when male colleagues play sports, usually their friendships deepen at once. Older men golf and go fishing in the mountains. Younger men play racquetball and jog after work. Women I interviewed know that each time they're excluded from company sports events, their colleagues grow closer, while they remain out.

Debbie lives in a state known for natural beauty. She expected that corporations would use recreational resources in a variety of ways. Yet she was surprised when she joined a start-up company and learned that only male managers regularly got to fish.

> Every May, the entire management group goes on a fishing trip up north. The trip ends up costing the corporation about $100 per employee. They get a day off with pay too, by the way. It was interesting when I became a manager: What would happen in May?
>
> That spring I remember having a discussion with my boss and saying, "Well, I don't imagine I'm going to get asked to go on the fishing trip." Sure enough, beginning that May, the men would go fishing, and the company would give each woman manager $100—without a day off, of course.

Linda works for a major oil company. Having begun as a secretary and moved up to a management role, she has strong opinions about an industry dominated by cowboys and cigar-smoking tycoons. Linda attributes her success to an unusual mentor who advocated consistently on her behalf. But an off-site trip with spouses seemed to turn the tide.

> At one point, we were all supposed to be taking a trip to California, to our Los Angeles office, and the men had decided it would be fun to take their wives. So several of the vice presidents were busy making plans.
>
> I went to my boss and said, "Do you think it would be OK if I took my husband? The invitation said 'Your spouses are welcome,' so I'd like to take him along. Would that be OK?" Immediately my boss said, "Well, I don't know.

He's not your wife." I said, "That's right. I don't have a wife—but I do have a spouse. Can I bring him?" He replied, "I don't know. Do you think he'd want to go?" "He probably wants to go more than most of the wives want to go," I answered. Still my boss said, "I don't know. I've never dealt with anything like this. What do you think Jane Fonda would say?" I said, "I really don't know, Lew, let's ask her. I'm sure Jane Fonda would think it was fine." As it turned out, the spouses didn't go. I never knew for sure whether they didn't go because this issue came up or whether none of the wives really wanted to go after all.

But my boss's response really struck me as funny. I guess it was the disappointment of finding out that even someone who always tried to be fair and realistic about women in the workplace—even he had prejudices. It never occurred to him that my husband was a spouse.

Melinda tells me how she once dealt with a law firm golf game. Because she's now a partner, she feels free to speak her mind. But even at the outset, she always relied on humor. Each time Melinda's been excluded, she's responded with a joke.

About five years ago, a memo came around from one of the partners saying that they were going to have a golf outing about 50 miles from here. It was going to be for "golf and poker." The memo was addressed to all partners, so I got one. Right after I got it, the fellow who had sent the memo came running into my office. I think he was embarrassed because it was such a male-oriented event. He was trying to explain everything to me when I said, "No, no, you don't need to worry, because what I'm going to do is to have a counter party. I'm going to invite the female associates to go to Rich's, where we're all going to have high tea and wear white gloves." So I sent a memo around inviting everybody to come and do my high tea thing. It was delightful. All the women came.

The Generation Gap

It is the older men in companies who seem most uncomfortable in the presence of women. The women I interviewed expected this reaction, recognizing that men in their fifties and sixties have worked for years in all-male offices, and some have had to make tremendous professional and psychological adjustments to accommodate women. Most men highest up work with few women regularly, and socialize with female staff members even less. Older men who find dealing with women awkward, naturally tend to exclude them from after-work events. Though the dynamic is understandable, its implications are serious: It isolates the women while it keeps senior managers unaware of their competence and skills.

The women agreed that establishing informal contacts with older men presented by far the greatest challenge. They recognized that over the years the men had grown accustomed to their clubs, their dining rooms, and their friends. But the women felt frustrated when senior men excluded them; those men held the power to make or break careers.

Dorothy is a fighter. I interview her one evening just after she arrives home from work. It's already after eight, and she tells me she's been working long hours for many years. Despite her exhaustion, she still seems undaunted. As a veteran banker, she knows what's required in the struggle to get ahead. When I ask Dorothy to describe the bank's informal culture, she grows very quiet, suddenly lost in thought. Finally, she admits that the higher she goes, the more difficulty she faces as she tries to fit in.

> My informal relationships all depend on the age of the man I'm with. The older he is, the more strained the relationship is, and the more uncomfortable he is around me. The younger he is, the more unconscious he is of sex differences. When I used to work in the credit department, a group of us went out for coffee together every day. We were all analysts—men and women both. I never thought anything of it. It was just an exchange of gossip and fun

things like that. But since I've been promoted to this division, the three most senior men go out and never think to invite me along. I'm out of it now, because I'm higher up.

Tina is a writer, an English major who never planned to work for a corporation. Five years ago she answered a blind ad for a copywriter, and within a week found herself on the corporate communications staff of an industrial products firm. Tina talks candidly about how she became acclimated to an industry with so few women. She decided to befriend the men her own age.

> Informally, it all depends on which group you're interacting with. I think that men my age are much more able to accept a woman as an equal, because they've just had a lot more experience relating to female professionals. Men who are in their fifties just slip into their old stereotypes, even though intellectually they know they shouldn't—because now they're liberal or something.

Cathy worked in politics before entering the corporate world. Her background gives her a unique perspective on the power dynamics she witnesses each day. At thirty-two, Cathy has already figured out that because she is cut off informally, her chances for leadership in the company are severely curtailed. For the present, she enjoys her job in marketing, but she plans to leave the business world and run for local office if her leadership opportunities remain limited.

> There's a boys' network on top, and they have their limousines, and they have their things they do, and they have the clubs they belong to—the Pacific Union and the Bohemian Grove. You can bet that there are no women there. All of that is true. Do I feel excluded by that? Yeah, as a package, it's overwhelming. I just feel it's a brick wall that's there.

74

Paying the Price

The obvious effect of exclusion is that when professional women are not invited to parties, picnics, and after-work drinks, they rarely get the chance to know their colleagues as friends. Having strong allies at the office could have relieved some of the pressures and provided these women with coaching and support. Similarly, as long as most company events remain noncoed, men lose the opportunity to develop new female friends. Though the women pointed out that sometimes they're invited, those occasional casual luncheons and dinners remain the exceptions, not the rule.

As the women described their psychological reactions, the word they used most was "lonely." Having worked hard to prove themselves at the outset, they had looked forward to a time when they would fit in. When they weren't included at functions or couldn't join in conversations, most experienced a second wave of disappointment. After one particularly upsetting incident, it took Marion months to turn depression into hope.

Being ignored is like feeling you're a gnat; you ask a question, and you get brushed off. In this one case, two of us were taking a deposition. The witness and the other attorney would exchange comments back and forth, but whenever I'd say something, I'd get a very cursory, perfunctory answer. Then they would go back and continue their thing. I felt as if I were sitting in on someone else's tête-à-tête.

As for my reactions? I'd have to say that they ran the usual gamut. First I got depressed. I got that feeling of being the woman lost in the profession. You just know that if you were a man, your statements wouldn't evoke the same reactions. In addition to depression, I also had feelings of insecurity. I was taking it out on myself initially. But then I moved into the anger phase. I think that now it's cooled down to something in between the two.

> This kind of thing is a real problem. Maybe it really is "their problem," but law is also "their world." And I'm in that world. I have to learn to cope so that I don't feel lousy myself, and also so that I end up getting positive reactions from the people around me. I really want to be effective as a lawyer.

Bernice is a tax attorney, a partner in a prestigious downtown firm. For seven years she strove to become an expert, and now her office walls are covered with diplomas and certificates, the world's recognition of all she has achieved. I am surprised when Bernice, outwardly exuberant, shares with me feelings she keeps hidden inside.

> I think it's lonely to be a woman who is told by everyone that she has the aspirations and the drive of a man. Once I found a greeting card—actually, I think I bought four of them. The card said, "I don't know if it's lonely at the top, but it's hell in the middle and scary at the bottom." I really don't think that a lot of men appreciate that being here is really different for a woman—and just how terribly lonely this place often is.

In addition to the psychological costs, women found that being left out of social interactions often had harmful effects on their work. Soon they recognized that the line between the formal and the informal realms is arbitrary. Friendships influence decision-making, and comfort level wins.

Some women felt awkward and had difficulty concentrating when someone subtly pointed out that they were different from the group. This usually occurred when a man swore unexpectedly or told a crude joke and then made exaggerated apologies to the women nearby. Laurie has tried all possible methods of handling such moments. She wants to remain calm and to put the men at ease. But once, when she spoke up and voiced an objection, her isolation became even more extreme.

It's very difficult breaking into men's informal groups. If you're too cold and aloof, the men won't want to be with you because you're not the typical fun, sensitive, vulnerable woman. If you let it show that you are in fact vulnerable, you break the strong "professional woman" image that you have to portray at work. There's a very fine line that you have to tread. It's subtle.

Another thing is that there's a tremendous amount of traveling in this job. While you're on the road, you meet a lot of people and you go out for dinner and drinks. There, too, it's difficult to be accepted, because you can't show you're too much fun. You can't be one of them. You don't want to be one of the boys, really, because if you are, you immediately take the professional woman image away. You're always balancing on that subtle line. I find that to be difficult.

One time two years ago, I was feeling really uncomfortable when I was the only woman in the restaurant, and the men were all telling dirty jokes. We'd been at some kind of seminar. Anyway, the jokes the men were cracking were totally uncalled for. I felt they were doing it purposely, to make me feel uncomfortable, to tell me I didn't belong.

I remember finally saying, "Well, that one was really uncalled for." And suddenly I had ten men turn around and stare at me in disbelief. The joke was in fact very bad. It was also crude and inappropriate. I remember thinking then, "My God, did I say something I shouldn't have said? Should I have just been meek and kept my mouth shut? Or should I have been assertive, opened my mouth, and said what was bothering me?" After that, the men complained that they couldn't get away with anything. They couldn't be comfortable with me in the room. And of course I want them to be comfortable because I'm supposed to be sweet and nice. As I said, this is all very, very difficult.

Edna believes that this pattern occurs in all companies. Since she now works exclusively with managers, she sees it every day. She has noticed that older men are the most uncomfortable when someone uses obscene language in the presence of a woman. But when men rush to apologize, often in excess, they don't understand that subtly they're putting a woman on the spot.

> An instance came up not too long ago when a really fiery man was working himself into a frenzy over a particular project. There was a group of guys standing around, and I was just sitting there working at my desk. This one man was getting more and more aggravated, and then he suddenly blurted out, "This fucking thing . . . ." But then he turned to me and said, "I'm really sorry, Edna." I said, "What do you mean George? I say that all the time when I'm mad. You don't have to apologize." He knows that he shouldn't be worrying, but he's walking that fine line between what he knows is OK now and what he was taught not to do. Oftentimes with swearing or dirty jokes or sexual topics, they shut up when someone like me comes in.

The most critical way exclusion hurts a woman's work is when it removes her from decision-making spheres. Emily reports that in southern California, corporate policy is set on tennis courts and yachts. Watching mortgage bankers go off for outings, she anticipates that policy changes will be announced the next day. Being left behind has become so familiar that recently it forced Emily to rethink her career.

> Even if women knew how to play the power game, the men here wouldn't let them. That was one big reason I didn't take the last promotion I was offered. I knew that even if I was a senior vice president, they'd never include me. I'd be even more isolated. At least in my world now I have a staff, I have a team, I have a family. In senior management, I'd be totally by myself.

The men don't let women play at big-time decision-making at meetings, basically because the decisions are rarely made there. They're made in the bathroom. They're made over at the golf course. They're made at tennis. They're made at "my house" at cocktails. They're made after hours, here and there. Women can't really make decisions because the men will never consider taking us to the gym.

Julie negotiates defense contracts for an aerospace company. Part of the negotiation process involves presenting manufacturing data, prices, and bids. Over time, Julie has developed a reputation for clear, objective analysis. She has also learned that on the subjective side, there are some aspects of business deals that numbers can't predict.

I can tell that the men on the other side of a negotiation don't want to deal with me directly.

They want to deal with a man. They don't feel comfortable with me. One time I had a customer from New York who was coming in to negotiate a fairly large contract that I had been proposing for my company. The other side brought in three representatives—all male, of course—and management dictated that I would handle the negotiations for our side. The three men showed up, and I went into the room with them and with our contracts administrator, who is also a male. I led the negotiations.

We were right in the middle of the process when their head guy stood up and said to my contracts manager, "I need a pack of cigarettes. Could we take a walk?" Then the two of them got up and left the room. They came back half an hour later and had concluded the negotiations.

Well, I tell you, I felt terrible. I felt like that I had been abused and pushed aside, that I was of no value, that nothing I had said was important. I felt worthless being there.

But the most ironic thing happened later. That night management said, "We need to entertain these men. We've

79

concluded a very successful negotiation, and we want to take them out to dinner." So the corporate manager, the vice president, and I were selected to take them to dinner. I was the only woman, and I was clearly there for entertainment.

Basically, the company wanted somebody there to make the men feel good. They wanted me to make them feel comfortable, to enjoy their jokes, and so on. The company really likes it when I entertain the customers. Management always comes to me, because the customers like going out with women. Naturally, our customers always are men.

They love to flirt with me. They want to put their arms around me, they want to dance, they want to dance close, and then they drink too much. It becomes a very sticky situation: The whole time you're trying to maintain a professional demeanor, yet at the same time, you're expected not to keep things *too* professional. Above all, remember, you never want to alienate the customer. It's a very hard game to play. It puts me in a very awkward position.

When women do get included at dinners, drinks, and lunches, their suspicion that the real action takes place outside the office is generally increased and usually confirmed. Mandy explains that in public relations, many deals are closed in hotels and bars. Because she picks up new information each time she joins colleagues, Mandy's upset to think how much more she may have missed.

You lose access to information when you're excluded. I remember being on a business trip, and we arrived at the conference location at noon the day before the conference was scheduled to start. My boss and another man in the department immediately went into the bar at twelve-thirty in the afternoon.

Well, not only do I not drink in the afternoon, but I was in a place where I would have enjoyed either seeing the city or being outdoors or doing almost anything other than sitting in this very dark bar for the entire afternoon. Anyway, these two men proceeded to start drinking, and I was just sitting there, sipping Perrier and trying to figure out why I was spending the entire afternoon in the bar.

The only way I could rationalize it was that I was getting access to information that at some point might become valuable. At the time, frankly, it didn't seem all that worthwhile. But any time you're excluded, you miss out on discussions. Some very valuable information can be shared over a drink.

The more they observe the men's networks in action, the more women understand just how tight those networks are. Whether the organizations are exclusive social clubs in Chicago, New York, or Dallas, or fraternities or Rotaries in Omaha or Des Moines, informal associations play a key role in most businessmen's lives.

In her law office in the South, Melinda thinks aloud about the assets male attorneys bring to her firm. The men have friends—potential clients—who are relieved to entrust their problems to someone they know well. In contrast, forty-year-old Melinda realizes that her old college roommates are off in middle America, most of them married and working in the home.

The thing I feel strongly about is that I wasn't plugged in from the start. I never figured out the networking thing when I was in college. I look at my male counterparts. They're my age, and all of them have close friends from the old football team who now live in San Francisco, or somebody they went to grad school with is now CEO of a corporation.

I simply don't have those kinds of connections. My sorority sisters are all married with 2.3 kids, and they live in Orlando. They're wonderful people, but I certainly don't have that networking thing. When I came into the

81

practice of law, a couple of women kept saying, "We all need to get together and have lunch." And I thought, "Well, this is wonderful." So we'd have lunch, but we'd all talk about our Friday night dates, and I'd think, "This isn't exactly what this is supposed to be, is it?"

A strong male network is something I didn't have access to. In law school, I made some truly good friends. But I was in law school at a time when most of the people were coming back from the Vietnam war. Most of them were married with families, and it wasn't the same bonding that I would have had with the single classmates who were struggling in the library until three every morning. Everybody went home to their wives and kids when I was in law school. I do keep in contact with five or six of the people I went to law school with, but it's not the same thing.

Social exclusion hurts women's careers most because it limits their exposure to managers at the top. Without a relaxed atmosphere in which to meet leaders, female professionals have no access to policymakers other than through their work. From the executive's standpoint, if few women are present at company outings, there is little chance for them to spot a possible protégé. Lacking informal ties, women's choice of mentors is limited, and without opportunities to build valuable friendships, their chances for making it are greatly reduced.

The executive dining room is a metaphor for power within an organization. When people dine together regularly, they get to know one another in almost a familial way. Friendships solidify quickly over steak knives and caviar, but for many women there are few opportunities to share in that process. First Brenda, in the automotive industry, and then Ginger, in advertising, talk about the messages those dining rooms convey.

I was in a building once where the executive dining room was on one floor and the regular employee cafeteria was on another. I pushed the executive dining room button in the elevator, because I was at a level that qualified me to eat there. But a gentleman on the elevator told me I had pushed the wrong button. I looked at him, said "Watch me," and winked.

That incident told me then and there that I had to become more visible in that dining room. I tried to get other women—the few who were qualified to eat there—to join me at least somewhat regularly. We needed to have a presence there so men didn't ignore the fact that at least a few women qualified to eat upstairs.

As time went on in the agency, everything got all fired up. There was a men's dining room, and I and some others lobbied to have the thing made coed. It caused such an uproar! At one point, the men even thought we were going to go and storm their dining room. According to policy, we were only supposed to go in on Ladies' Day—Wednesdays. I just kept saying, "Hey, this would be a much more profitable operation if it were coed. Men and women enjoy having meals together."

At one point, because they thought we were going to storm their sacred territory, the senior management team actually went and locked arms and stood there in front of the door of the thing for half an hour before they realized that it was a false rumor. I mean, we had jokingly talked about it, but that had been it. So they closed the dining room. It was reopened about six months later as just a regular dining room.

Tips From the Trenches

Study the People

The women offered concrete suggestions for dealing with exclusion, but emphasized again that no set formula works in every case. One strategy many recommended is for women seeking jobs to investigate carefully how potential employers have treated females in the past. Jill remembers that both times when she looked for work she made a special point of finding out how well women attorneys fitted into a firm. When it finally came down to making her selection, this was the factor that dictated her choice.

My first firm was one that didn't really exclude women from their informal scene—at least not in the group that I dealt with in the corporate and insurance areas. Women were definitely part of the group, and I never really felt excluded. In part, it may have been due to my own comfort in dealing with men. This is something I'd always done. I figured that if I was going to be social at all in my daily work life, I'd better fit in.

I purposely chose both my first firm and then the firm up here because of a distinct feeling I had about them— their lack of strict formality and their ability to deal with women on a social level. I think that you can very easily find a firm that's essentially stuffy, where women wouldn't fit in at all. This was an issue that I looked at very closely when I was interviewing. In fact, I narrowed my choices down to only two firms that I felt I could feel comfortable in. Those were my only choices.

Sometimes men will make inadvertent comments that point up the delusion that women don't belong. Heidi believes that the best way to handle those situations is to keep the rejoinder spontaneous and light. Because her responses seem off-hand and friendly, her colleagues get the message without losing face.

I remember one time we had a strategic planning retreat, and I was the only female there. We stayed overnight at a hotel in Chicago. At breakfast the next morning, I was sitting at a table with several other people. One of our accountants sat down, took one look at me, and then blurted out, "I told my wife there weren't going to be any women here." So I said, in the same shocked tone of voice, "I told my husband there weren't going to be any men here."

Basically, I've found that when these things come up, it goes better if you just joke with the guys. If I'd been at the point where I still took it all seriously, I'd have been in big trouble. But as long as you just roll with it, you sometimes just have to laugh at the whole situation.

When I give a talk to women coming into the work world, all of them still seem to be taking these kinds of comments so seriously. They all say to me, "Can't you see what's going on? You've got to stand up and fight." I think to myself, "Look, you've got to decide what you want to fight for." Do I want to fight to change the whole culture of this company, or do I want to effect change among the employees? I have consciously chosen to effect programs with employees. I didn't want to get hung up on the cultural aspects of what was going on. I figured that just by the fact that I was changing programs, I would inevitably affect culture somewhat. I didn't want changing the company's culture to be the main thing, because the minute it is, the guys get defensive, and you've lost.

All types of maneuvers were suggested for breaking into conversations. Some were straightforward, others were downright wily. The women agreed that the way they approach the men depends on the membership of each particular group. Cynthia has learned that the important thing is perseverance. Taking the initiative is always up to her.

You feel very awkward, and you wonder what on earth you're going to say. My normal response is to want to get away. But the fighter in me wants to make them deal with the fact that I'm staying there, and that I don't know what they're talking about. Sometimes they'll just keep on talking, and won't pay any attention to me. But sometimes they will. If you stand there and ask a question, they can't stay in that mode forever. You try to break up that little cluster. But it's pretty rare for one of them to turn and try to ease you in. I think this is something you have to do yourself; you can't ever expect one of them to.

Janet and Tina disagree on tactics. For twenty years, Janet has pretended not to notice what's really going on. When men leave her out of casual conversations, she simply denies that this is what's happening. She approaches them nonchalantly, offers her ideas, and soon finds she's established herself on the inside. Janet is convinced that if women let on that they're feeling rejected, the exclusion will escalate to a greater degree.

> I feel like red flags are waving, but you can't let it get to you. You try to pretend that you don't know it's going on. Sometimes, if you pretend that, you seem nonthreatening enough that they'll start to include you in the conversations. If they ever do perceive you as having worthwhile input, I think they'll convey information to you. But if you show that you feel hurt and excluded, they'll just continue to do the same old thing. You get a sense of "Hazardous areas ahead!" and "Be very careful of what you do!" Don't make jokes about it, and don't acknowledge it, because if you do, then you're trying to break into the inner sanctum, and the ranks will immediately close in front of you.

On the other hand, when Tina feels left out, she lets the men know right away. The trick she uses is to keep a light tone. Since most stressful incidents occur away from the office, she recommends a less formal style. Raising the issue needn't always be confrontational. Some men get the point right away, and then with real sincerity invite the woman in.

> These conversations rarely happen in business situations. They happen mostly at dinners, at lunches, to and from airports—places like that. I think the best thing to do is to steer the conversation away from what they're talking about—or else make a joke about it. Just point out, in a very lighthearted manner, that you'd like to be included

in the conversation but that you have absolutely no idea who John Havlicek is!

The women felt that sometimes the opposite was true—that they were included in social situations as an extra added attraction for men doing business. Then when they had a hard time entering the conversations, they resented having been required to attend. Janet says this phenomenon occurs frequently in public relations, and in her early years, business lunches were hell. Now, after seven years, she knows how to handle them. Janet recommends that women plan in advance the topics they can discuss easily with men. To be sure she's ready for last-minute meetings, she makes a list and keeps it in her purse.

I feel that I've often been invited to certain meetings because I'm a woman. It's usually a prospective client, and management wants to show them that we do have women, and here's one of them. When I'm with a client, I usually talk about their industry and the kinds of work we've done in that industry, but the problem is that, at lunch, you tend to get away from that kind of talk. We've already done the business talk in the office, where I feel pretty comfortable being one woman among five or six men. But then, when we go to lunch, the business rules end and it becomes social.

I think it's social talk among men who don't know each other very well that tends to turn to sports, to business and industry, to banking relationships, and to lawyers—all things that I simply don't know much about or have much of a feeling for. I always feel uncomfortable in social settings away from business. So I usually try to come up with something else to talk about that I can contribute to. The way I figure it, in a luncheon conversation you never talk about anything for too long. But I know that I need to plan a specific strategy in advance—what I can talk about, or what the client might think is interesting, or what we could talk about together. Expecting it to come naturally is generally a disaster.

Taking the time to build a network of contacts in and out of the organization was the strategy women found ultimately most helpful in overcoming isolation. Some recommended volunteering for company activities, such as sports teams or task forces, just as a way to create alliances outside the office. Their sense was that informal events with a stated purpose and structure were far easier to manage than were cocktail parties and outings where the agenda was unclear.

For others, professional organizations provided the best opportunity for getting to know male colleagues informally, again through structured events. Away from office politics and united by a set of common interests, they established relationships with men in the broader community and deepened those friendships over the years. Participation in women's organizations was also seen as an important source of companionship and support, as well as a way to promote equal opportunity and increased political clout. Even those who described themselves as shy and introverted agreed that taking the initiative to carve out a network of associates was the proactive strategy they relied on most.

The women I talked to were gradually starting to reap the benefit of all their efforts. Slowly, sometimes after many years, they had begun to feel included as part of company alliances, and had already seen how that affected their work. Diane feels that in the end, gender is a secondary issue; she believes that people want to associate with those they know they can trust.

> I do agree that if you're excluded informally, it will hurt you. I'm very aware that it is an issue, and an important one. I know personally that it's from my informal friendships and relationships that I have a much better sense of what's going on in this company. There are several major *faux pas* that I could have made or have managed not to make—or have helped my boss not make—just through the informal grapevine.
>
> People may respect other people for their professional purposes, but they also like to work with people they feel comfortable around. If they have a choice between two

equally competent people, I don't think it's going to be male-female so much as "Whom do I feel comfortable with? Whom would I enjoy working with?" that will determine who gets a promotion or a particularly good assignment. I think a woman would be very foolish not to realize the importance of informal networks and to try to plug into that.

Ellen's business contacts are now international. Her work for an energy company takes her all around the world. Though she relies on financial skills for getting the job done, she knows that in the long run, success depends on something else.

No matter how much you think business is done in a theoretical and logical structure, it's really done on the basis of "Do I know you? Have I dealt with you before, and if I have, have you kept your word?" I ask myself if we're back to a handshake and a man's word, and my answer is "That's it exactly; it's never been different." It's whom you know and whom you know you can trust. It's the people involved, and it's not the numbers or anything else.

4

Understanding Sexual Dynamics

Chemistry at Work

When I began the interviews for this book, I was surprised to find that women were reluctant to discuss sexuality. I had expected that most would welcome the chance to talk in confidence about sexual dynamics in the office. What I discovered instead was that even though most had experienced some form of harassment, few wanted to admit that it remains a problem. The women are tired of dealing with come-ons. They want to be left alone to do their jobs in peace.

But as their stories vividly show, sexuality is rampant in the professional world today. As I listened, I saw how people—both men and women—who act responsibly in most realms can still regress to adolescence when sexual feelings get aroused. Just as in high school, males do the initiating—this time with flirtatious comments and an occasional touch. Females anticipate the overtures and respond with ambivalence and sometimes a smile. Problems develop when this subtle interplay starts to escalate inappropriately. Productivity suffers when adults play teenage games.

Beyond the issue of productivity lies the question of legal rights. During the summer of 1986, the United States Supreme

Court issued a landmark ruling with wide implications for sexuality in the workplace. In considering a case of alleged sexual harassment, the Court found all employers liable for the behavior of their supervisors. Title VII of the Civil Rights Act of 1964 provides individuals the right to work in an environment free from intimidation, ridicule, and insult. In interpreting Title VII and accompanying guidelines, the Court determined that unwelcome sexual advances, requests for sexual favors, and verbal or physical conduct of a sexual nature can all be considered violations of federal law.

The decision means that if a working woman can prove that men's comments or actions have created a "hostile environment" that interferes with her performance, she can legally be considered a victim of sex discrimination and can sue her employer for damages. Whether or not her job is overtly threatened, if she feels that the physiological pressures are interrupting her work, she can make a legitimate claim of sexual harassment.

Clearly, the economic implications of the Supreme Court's decision are vast. Already the issue of sex discrimination is costing American industry millions of dollars. And current total figures tell only a fraction of the story.

Court-ordered damages rarely reflect an employer's indirect costs, such as the salaries of in-house legal counsel and employee relations personnel. Nor do damages always measure absenteeism, turnover, and decreased productivity among women who allege harassment and men who stand accused. Most important, aggregate data are based only on cases that have actually been filed. They don't incorporate the countless incidents that go unreported, yet create anxiety and turmoil for everyone involved. Though the Supreme Court has opened the door for increased litigation, many professional women will still choose not to sue.

Sexual Time Bomb

I had a situation in the corporate office where my boss, who was the vice president and was supposed to set the example for all of us, became involved with one of his subordinates.

Supposedly no one knew about this. But in fact everyone knew about it, and it created a lot of tension. The first clue came when, shortly after my boss joined the department, he promoted this particular woman, who had just been demoted by somebody else. Several similar events occurred, giving people the very definite impression that a relationship was going on.

All of this caused a lot of tension. Even though my boss tried not to give preferential treatment to this woman, there was obviously subtle favoritism going on. Their relationship created tensions outside our department, too. Soon the whole company was talking.

The biggest irony was that because there was so much stress in the office, my boss decided we all needed to take a couple of days off and go on a "team-building" retreat in the mountains. What he didn't understand was that much of the tension in our department was directly related to his supposedly secret relationship.

One of the people in the group tried to bring up the relationship in the team-building session, but my boss denied it completely. It was all so strange, because on the one hand, he was trying to get everyone to be a cohesive unit, and he was professing total openness and honesty. Yet on the other hand, by denying the relationship, he was being dishonest with his staff. Of course, by that point, everyone knew what was going on.

An amazing amount of energy went into talking about my boss's affair. People love to gossip. In a way, it's fun and interesting. Back then, people gossiped about how the vice president would drop his girlfriend off at the back door and then drive around to the executive parking lot—petty things like that. People were placing lots of phone calls, saying things like, "I saw Janet and Bill in the grocery store together."

Later, things got worse. This same vice president, who

was still my boss, had another affair with a different woman, but this time it happened right in front of everyone's eyes—at the departmental conference. It also occurred right after he publicly announced that he was now living with the first woman, who previously had been his subordinate. So now, here he was, involved with a second woman, this time someone at a higher level than he was, and someone at the parent company, to boot.

Of course, when things like this happen, everyone stops and wonders, "What does it really take to get ahead around here? What are the real criteria that people are looking at?" I mean, here is someone who is vice president, who is supposedly setting an example for the rest of the organization. What kind of message does his behavior send? What is this corporation condoning?

Most of the women I interviewed had been approached sexually by one or more men at work. Some acknowledged that since they too had been excited by the chemistry, consciously or unconsciously they had communicated that interest. In the majority of cases, however, women were adamant that they had done little to provoke inappropriate behavior, and they're resentful that such behavior continues unchecked.

The following incident is typical of hundreds I heard. Marilyn outlines the cycle of emotions women experience when they are first sexually harassed on the job.

Once I was out to dinner with a large group of coworkers, and all of a sudden I felt this hand on my leg—just like you read about in books. I sort of kept moving over—which gets tough after a while when you have ten people at a dinner table. We were having dinner in a hotel. As we were leaving, the man said, "Why don't we stop upstairs?" I was absolutely shocked. He said, "You know, I really like you, and I could do a lot for your career."

My first thoughts were, "My God, what's going to happen to me if I say no? I could get fired." And so I found a way of saying no that would be easily accepted. It was, "Look, I'm really attracted to you, but you're married, and I'm Catholic, and I don't believe in that sort of thing." You have to protect their egos. You have to find a more politically acceptable solution than slapping someone in the face—even though that's what I was inclined to do. I would have slapped him if he hadn't been in my direct reporting line in the corporation.

Later, when I was by myself, I cried. I was so upset. I was so hurt to think that he thought he could do that to me. What went through my head was, "It's because I'm single," or "It's because I'm too friendly," and finally, "How dare he?" I asked some of my friends, and they told me that these kinds of propositions were very common to the corporation, that I shouldn't be so upset about it, that it would happen a lot more, and that unless you're a dog or old—which at that time meant over thirty—it was going to happen a lot.

And they were right. It did. But I never ceased to be amazed that men would try to use that power over you.

Marilyn's story shows how the term "sexual harassment" has come to stand for a complex pattern of emotions and events. The pattern begins when a psychological spark develops between men and women at work. It can range from a one-way physical attraction to a two-way feeling of closeness that stems from shared projects and later becomes personal. In most cases, it is the man who translates the feeling into action. His behavior may be subtle, overt, or even bizarre.

Women's responses tend to follow a pattern. First comes a feeling of shock and disbelief. Next, the worry of bruising the man's ego and endangering one's job. Aware of the man's status and position, women fear that rejection could lead to anger and could have repercussions for their careers. Immediately following harassment, most women need to find out if others have experienced it, too. They approach peers and friends for a kind of reality check—a chance to calm feelings of confusion, hurt, and rage. If, over time, harassment continues, many try to deny it as best they can. Feeling powerless to affect the dominant culture, these women avoid individual men and try to pretend it'll never happen again.

The women in this study all hold professional positions. Whether managers, editors, or sales reps, they inhabit that part of the work world that prides itself on expertise, subtlety, and style. There, sexual harassment is especially hard to detect and easy to deny. Its subtlety occurs in part because corporate cultures reflect middle- and upper-class norms. People at the top have come from families where words, not actions, are used to express emotion. In adulthood, that emphasis on verbal skill continues. Sexual attraction in the management ranks is conveyed more by comment than by touch. But the clever, witty language that marks a professional can make the underlying message sometimes quite oblique.

As a result, many people in professional jobs want to believe that male-female tension and potential harassment "are just not issues here." The wish to deny is powerful. Paulette, a thirty-year-old corporate attorney, is certain that no sexual chemistry lies hidden in her firm. As I listen to her protests, I notice with what vehemence she makes her point.

> The people I've dealt with so far are sensitive to sexual harassment issues. Certainly everybody around this office is. If anything like that ever happened here, there would be an immediate uproar. I think people realize that this kind of thing is completely unacceptable. The clients I work with are also sensible enough to realize that this is not to be done. The women they are dealing with are professionals, and they must deal with them professionally, and that's it.

The fact is, though, that sexual tension in organizations is both widespread and intense. Sexual intrigue surfaces everywhere, from inside the conference room to inside exclusive clubs, from the opening moments of an interview to late-night drinks after work. Regardless of rank or position, all types of men approach professional women sexually—from presidents of companies to clients, customers, and peers. Often it is someone unexpected who drops an innuendo. Sometimes even subordinates dare to make a pass.

Sexual dynamics can color all aspects of a woman's work experience. Emily, a mortgage banker, talks about their implications for long-term careers. She feels that until women accept that they are still viewed in sexual terms, they'll never understand or overcome the awkwardness they feel.

> The only thing that really makes the men in my office feel good is sexuality. Their interest in business is fine, but the number of women who find them attractive is much more important to them than how many issues they got through at the board meeting.
>
> How can I tell that? Because ninety percent of the time they seem to be thinking about sex. For example, I can be sitting in a room, and I'll notice my boss looking at my legs, so I'll look at his legs—I have to get on his level to keep things light. He's always making off-color remarks or comments, regardless of who's in the room. Frequently, his greeting for the day is, "The reason you have a smile on your face must be because you 'got some' last night."
>
> Initially, it bothered me. But then, once you realize that most of them would never do anything anyway, you start to relax. Half of them don't mean anything by it. It's just that sexuality is the only thing that makes them feel good about themselves. Sexuality is really their only means of satisfaction.

The women I interviewed hold men at the top responsible for setting a tone. They're certain that senior managers who tell crude jokes, make lewd comments about employees, and report with regularity on their sexual exploits are likely to tolerate harassment in the ranks. Jennifer reports that in Silicon Valley the executives she knows make sexual references all the time.

She doubts whether men understand that these preoccupations affect productivity and morale.

> I was in a meeting the other day, and our president made a bunch of comments about how, if we did something, he was going to buy us all a drink and a whore. And I said, "Well, that isn't going to help me much." And he said, "Oh, I forgot, I thought we were all guys." You know, I think they've gotten to a point where they just relax about having a woman in the group. I don't think it's even an issue to them.

Jennifer's anecdote illustrates that jokes about sex can bond a group of men together. Fran learned in advertising just how tight that bond can be. When an account officer embarrassed her in public, Fran was shocked that not one man spoke up in her defense. She realizes that even if the men had wished to show disapproval, doing so would have meant risking their membership in a powerful all-male group.

> Sometimes men make obnoxious comments to me, but they end up making more of a fool of themselves than of me. I can give you an example. I once worked on an account that required me to go on a trip to Europe with a group of men. I was the only woman on the trip. At that time, I was twenty-five. We all went to lunch at a very elegant restaurant. The account supervisor was known to be a womanizer. Usually, I avoid people like that. But at this particular lunch, everybody was talking, and the head account guy made some very overt crack like "Well, I'll bet you all thought that I was just here to sleep with Fran tonight." Or he may have said something even worse, like "I'm here to screw Fran," or something like that.
>
> I got very flustered and didn't know the appropriate response. But then, when I looked around, I realized that nobody else was laughing. It was like everyone was looking at this man and thinking how foolish it had been for

him to say that—not necessarily about a woman, but about me, because everybody at the table knew that I was not the kind of woman who was going to put my sexuality in front of my professionalism. So, in a way, I didn't feel so bad.

But in another way, I was horrified. Even though no one was laughing, I still thought, "Everybody's going to think I don't take my career seriously." I was also thinking, "What do I say? Do I joke back to him? Should I try to top him? Should I try to buy into it? Should I make him look good?" Actually, I was very concerned about stroking his ego, because he was my professional superior. He had a title and was much further along in the organization. Part of me was thinking, "That's my job, to make sure he looks really good."

Several women told me that even during job interviews, sexual attraction had played a crucial role. As Heidi remembers such an incident, she turns her face away so as not to meet my eyes. Eighteen years after an insulting experience, she cannot recount the story without resurrecting the shame.

I did go through an interesting experience one time when I was being interviewed. The man who was interviewing me tried to get me to go out with him right after the interview. He suggested we continue discussing the job in the bar over a drink, and I felt that I was being put in a bind. I wanted to know as much about the job as I could, so I was eager for that, but the whole bar scene is a little uncomfortable for me.

Though he professed to have legitimate reasons for talking with me, I was reluctant to have a drink with him because I got the feeling that maybe the job wasn't really what he wanted to discuss. Sure enough, when we sat down at the bar, he started talking about his wife and how they have an agreement that he can go out whenever he's out of town. I remember that I said, "That's very interesting, but it's not job-related." I excused myself somehow and quickly left the bar.

You know, we've all heard about those kinds of incidents, but when it happens to you, it's shocking. It puts you in a position of feeling degraded, because you know that the same approach would not have been taken if you were a man. Yet I was concerned that my reaction to his advances would have a negative impact on my getting the job. I didn't want to make him feel that it was anything personal, but I wanted him to know that I wasn't interested in dating anyone I work with, period. And I certainly didn't want to get the job because I had dated the interviewer.

As it turned out, I was offered the job based on my credentials. When I initially went to work, I did discuss the incident with the man who was in charge of the office. I didn't want other women to be subjected to that kind of approach. I thought the interviewer's behavior was very unprofessional and reflected poorly on the organization. The man in charge did deal with it—I believe the man in question was no longer allowed to go on the interviewing trips.

Believe me, an incident like that puts you in a very, very uncomfortable position.

Some men use humor as a way of initiating contact. Lucy says that when men comment on her appearance in the middle of a meeting, she loses her train of thought, though usually not for long. Later, when she arrives home, the comments affect her. Only then does the anger surface. Only then can she cry.

Mostly, what bothers me is the subtle stuff, especially the tone of teasing. Nobody's ever come at me and made an overt proposition, and I've never had any problems with people touching me. The only way a lot of these guys feel comfortable relating to women is in this teasing, sexual kind of way. They often make comments about your body, about the clothes you're wearing, and what they think you'd look like in various situations. In the middle of talking business, they say things like, "I'd love to see you in a bathing suit." This type of thing is really unnerving, and it makes me angry. I've never asked for that kind of remark.

Julie, a manager in the aerospace industry, sees a shift in how the sexual game is played in her firm. Now that the law prohibits harassment, the behavior is more subtle, the psychology more intense.

Recently, I've been getting more subtle sexual innuendoes. Like the men sidle up and rub shoulders with you and say, "Boy, I really like the way you look today." The men are getting smart. They know they can't make overt comments and body motions, because they can be called on the carpet for sexual harassment. And women are getting to the point where they don't put up with it any longer.

Sometimes, you get a guy like my old vice president, who's been sent away to Siberia for two years because of sexual harassment. He was pretty direct. If I dropped a pencil and bent down to pick it up, he'd make comments like, "Oh, could you bend over again? I really like looking down your blouse."

When he'd say things like that, I'd have a dual feeling. First of all, I knew for sure that he wouldn't be saying things like that if he were standing in the men's bathroom looking at the size of a male subordinate's organ. So why did he feel he could take liberties and say things like that to me just because I'm female? It made me feel hurt and angry. On the other hand, because he was the vice president, I had to laugh it off and make some crack back, like "Gee, I didn't know my blouse was unbuttoned that far," or "I'm going to have to get a safety pin," or "I should start wearing turtlenecks to discourage guys like you." I had to deal with it on a whimsical, comical note and pretend it was really my fault, because he's the higher-up.

I can't always tell if what I say works. Sometimes I'm afraid I provoke them further. I honestly don't know. I haven't quite figured out the secret to dealing with comments like that. On the other hand, there's a little part of you that says you can't help but be flattered when somebody notices you. So it's really a mix.

The women talked candidly about their role in the dynamic. Though hurt by experience, Suzanne still has trouble resisting men on the the job. Over the years she's recognized the pattern. When she finds that a project turns her on intellectually, her urge is to transfer the turn-on and apply it to a man.

At my first job, I had a relationship with a much older, married man. I fell madly in love with him. I was married to my first husband at the time. I divorced him, hoping that the relationship with this man would work out, but it didn't. It was just devastating to me. He eventually left the firm, and I stayed. Then I married my current husband. We've been together for ten years.

During the last year, I've been working with the new managing partner of this firm. He and I have been friends for nine years—really good friends. And it started happening again: I began getting these really strong personal feelings for him. We spend many hours in the office together, travel together, and share a lot of common interests. He's divorced right now; I'm not even separated.

I'm thinking about what repercussions getting involved with him would have on my career. I'm asking myself, if I decide to get a divorce and marry this new managing partner, would it cost me my job? Would it cost me respect among the other partners? Would people say that I "slept my way to the top"? It wouldn't be the truth, but who would ever know? Could I handle all the pressure? I mean, I live my whole life in this office.

Natalie finds that when a male colleague understands her pressure, she feels drawn to him for emotional support. But as soon as she feels a glimmer of attraction, she remembers her husband and gets uncomfortable at work. After dealing with this cycle over the years, Natalie has decided to avoid it altogether. Now she goes to women when she needs support.

> I think that a lot of times I get attracted to someone at work, not because I think he's the best-looking guy in the world, but because I need someone who understands what I'm doing and who shares some of the same problems. I find it difficult to have my husband be the person I talk to about work. He works in a totally unrelated field, and even though we have a very good home life, he doesn't exactly understand what I do all day. So sometimes I find myself getting attracted to a guy at work just because we work so closely together, and I need to talk to someone about the problems I'm having there.
>
> When I really get down, and feel that I just can't stand the problems at work anymore, I would much rather have a woman peer to talk to. If I talk to one of the guys in the office, then I'm going to be very vulnerable and possibly cry. And when my emotional guard is down, that's when I have trouble with my feelings about the men I work with.

June works as a manager in network television. She knows that in the entertainment business people are especially conscious of image and good looks. Nonetheless, June feels annoyed when colleagues remark about her body and her clothes. Although she sees that the teasing is "their problem," she's tired of wisecracks that distract her from her work.

> I go out of my way not to be treated like a seductress. I try very hard, but you always come across some men who look at any woman as a sex object. These are probably the most difficult to handle. They just do not take you seriously at all. They're more interested in the shape of your body or the color of your eyes, and they'll blurt it right out. I've had men say in the middle of my financial presentations, "Gee, you have beautiful eyes." That kind

of behavior is totally out of place and totally uncalled for. I try my best to keep things like that from happening, but sometimes they just do.

Most of the women believe that men who harass them are suffering from serious psychological distress. Though this insight may not alter a woman's own feelings, it does help her see the need for limits early on. In her second year of legal practice, Jill was not ready for the bizarre antics of a client. Her naiveté kept her from understanding how firm she had to be.

Early in my career, I got a card from one of my clients. It was an art card of a nude woman, and on the inside he had written something about our getting together and all the things that would happen when we did. I remember feeling sick—and being shocked, since he hadn't said anything to me during our work together. I thought, "Lord, this man is a nut." Then he started calling me, and I kept having to put him off. Once I told him that I never wanted him to call me again. After that, I just ignored him.

It was an embarrassing situation. I didn't tell anybody in the firm about it. I was especially worried that the partners would think this man's advances detracted from the good job I had done. Going a step further, I thought this situation would cause the firm to restrict my dealings with clients. If the partners believed I was encouraging clients in this way, the firm could also be concerned that clients would become angry about dealing with me and might ultimately change law firms. I certainly didn't want that to happen. So to the extent that I could, I handled the incident myself.

That was a long time ago, before the whole sexual harassment thing came up in the news. Back then, I think it was more hush-hush. In those days, the best thing you could do was talk to your friends—your women peers. When you did, you found out that it was happening to them too.

The point when I realized I didn't have to remain quiet about this came much later, when I was a mentor to a woman lawyer here. She told me about a client who was propositioning her after she had done good work for him. I was a partner by that time, and I decided to bring this situation to the attention of the partner whose client this person really was. I simply said, "We can't have that kind of thing happening here." The partner, a man, agreed with me. He then dealt with it by talking to the client.

Unfortunately, not all women receive that kind of backing. Evelyn tells how the sexual concerns of an executive in her company eventually caused a stir. But long before the incident gained notoriety, Evelyn was doing battle all by herself.

Our president is a very sharp and direct manager. One day he called me into his office and said, "We were discussing your salary recently in the monthly executive staff meeting." (This meeting is like the Pentagon or the Supreme Court—eight men, all large, gray-haired, wearing glasses and gray suits.) He went on, "And as a result of that discussion, we were talking about you." Now, I didn't think that my salary was up for discussion at that particular point, so I just sat there and waited for the punch line. He said, "You really have done the best job anyone's ever done in your function." I sort of smiled and kept waiting. He continued, "But someone at the meeting said—and I don't want to name names—but someone said that you were somewhere and you—I'm sure you didn't mean anything by it—but you touched a man." Then the president said, "Now, I really like your style, and I don't want you to change it at all. But I'm just telling you this because it was brought up at the executive staff meeting."

I said, "I don't know what you mean. Touched a man?" I mean you can touch somebody anywhere. I knew I hadn't done anything wrong, but I wanted to know what he thought I had done. He said, "Well, you know, I guess it has to do with your ethnic background, that you touch."

Later, I told my immediate boss what the president had said, and my boss was devastated. He's genuinely concerned with issues of sex discrimination. So he had the story corroborated by another man who'd been at the meeting. The next thing you know, the man who had brought up the whole touching thing called me, out of the blue, and asked if he could come see me. I agreed, so he came to my office and shut the door. He admitted that he had brought the issue up in the meeting, and said that he really had nothing against me but had meant to be helpful. I was angry, but I was willing to deal with it humorously. I said, "That's all right, Ed. Here, let me shake your hand." I shook his hand and I purposely put my hand on his shoulder as I walked him to the door. I said, "It's all over now."

That was about three o'clock in the afternoon. An hour later, the president came to my office and wanted to know what my next steps were going to be. Basically, he was scared of a lawsuit. They never said it, but I knew that's what they were afraid of.

Honestly, I'd been so caught off guard because I do tend to touch people casually. It's just something I do, though now I think I'm a little more guarded. The next time I talked to the man who had raised the issue of my touching, he had to tell me an "old boy" story to make amends. The story had to do with somebody's secretary who was dressed in a very sexy way—a real yuck-it-up kind of story. He was apologizing by treating me like one of the boys, and I didn't know whether to laugh or cry. Here he was trying to talk to me like I was one of the guys, and yet what was he doing? He was using a woman again as an object of ridicule, in a sexual way.

The women all stressed that in dealing with harassment, a key consideration is the man's position in the organization. The political ramifications of reporting on a fellow employee depend to a great extent on the individual's reputation and rank. Women worry—appropriately—about their long-term futures.

They know that their decision to file a grievance will be judged differently, depending on whether the accused is a subordinate, a peer, or someone higher up.

Many believe that the most awkward situation occurs when the boss himself makes an advance. Mindful of the corporate dictum that says, "Make the boss look good," women are hesitant to break that tradition and risk appearing disloyal. Some think that supervisors sense this dilemma and manipulate the circumstances to maximize the fear. Wendy tells how her boss harassed her, then tried to ruin her reputation when she implicated him by quitting her job.

> One day, I went out for drinks with several of the men I worked with. There were my boss, six or eight others, and myself—I was the only woman in the group. Anyway, my boss looked at me from across the table and said, in a very loud voice, "I'd like to fuck you right here." I was just paralyzed. I was crushed, and I didn't know what to do. I couldn't believe he had said that to me, especially in front of all those men I work with.
>
> I don't really remember what happened after that, except that I went home and talked to my husband about it. The next day, my boss said, "If you won't sleep with me, I will make life very difficult for you." And I knew he would. At that point, I realized I'd have to leave the company, so I began looking for another job. It got even worse when I left. My old boss called my new employer and said, "If she ever sets foot in this office again, I'll kick her out." He said a lot of awful things about me. My new boss said to me, "What did you ever do to make him as angry as he is?" So I told him.
>
> At first, I thought of taking my former boss to court. Then I thought, "No, it's just not like me to do anything like that." I mean, why should I jeopardize my reputation in the industry for this one harassment incident? If I had taken him to court, I'm certain potential employers would find out about it. They would ask, "Have you ever sued?"

I figured my image would be tainted by something like that.

Elizabeth grew up quickly her first year out of school. Now she sees her youth and inexperience caused her to overlook signals coming from her boss. As she describes a traumatic evening, strong feelings return, and she cries. She explains that the tears reflect not just the incident, but also the impact that has lingered ever since.

I was hired by a man who seemed in the interview to be a wonderful guy. After about four weeks on the job, he said, "I'd like to take you out to dinner to talk a bit about the projects that we're going to be working on." I didn't think anything of it, so I agreed. That night, I called my mother and said, "My boss and I are going out to dinner next week." She asked, "Where are you going?" I said I didn't know, and she said, "Be careful." Now, my mother had never worked in an office in her life. I asked, "What do you mean, 'Be careful'?" All she would say was, "Just be careful."

The day we were supposed to go to dinner, my boss told me where we were going. He'd chosen a very cozy French restaurant that I knew was a romantic place. We got there, and he had three double martinis. I'm sitting there thinking, "What's with this guy?" In the midst of the meal, he reached over to hold my hand and said, "You probably know by now that I have a really special feeling about you." I just sat there, speechless. I must have been around twenty-four years old at the time. I looked at him and finally said, "No, I didn't realize that," but I didn't let go of his hand—which, when I think about it now, was really absurd. He was obviously trying to make a move on me, and I was absolutely dumbfounded.

I had heard about these kinds of things from time to time, but I never thought I'd be the victim of something like this. Finally, he drove me home. We were sitting in his car outside my apartment, and I looked at him, thinking "I don't give a shit. I don't need this job." So I said, "I think you're trying to get me to say or do something that I have no intention of saying or doing. And I think it's really shitty." With that, I got out of the car and ran into my apartment. Now remember, this guy was the senior vice president of the agency. Even so, I thought, "I don't need this crap."

I knew I was risking my job, but at the same time I didn't think he'd fire me because everyone at the agency knew I was doing a good job. In the long run I was right— he didn't fire me. But that night I ran into my apartment and began crying my eyes out. I remember thinking, "So this is what it's really like." I was bitter for a long time after that. I went through a period of being unhappy that I was attractive. That's when I learned that I had to change the way I approached people in the workforce, and the way I talked to people on the job. I concluded that you have to be somewhat guarded at all times. I guess I'm still very, very bitter about what that man did to me.

No realm of the work world is exempt from sexual chemistry and potential harassment. The women I met said that men outside their organizations approach them just as regularly as do those they work with every day. The tricky part about dealing with men from the outside is that usually they represent business for the firm. It's one thing to alienate a disturbed in-house manager; it's another to jeopardize a possible income stream.

As head of the training department for a soft-drink manufacturer, Nancy works with a network of distributors, as well as managers and staff. One day, without warning, Nancy met a challenge. She was asked to conduct business beside a customer's bed.

I had one bottler tell me, when he picked me up at the airport, that all of his training equipment was at his house.

So he took me out to this house, but there were no people there for me to train.

I said, "Well, where is everybody?" His answer was, "Let me show you where the equipment is." Of course, the equipment was upstairs in the bedroom. As this guy was giving me a tour of his house, I kept thinking, "What am I going to do? Remember, Nancy, this is our customer." I knew I had to handle him very delicately, because I didn't want to offend him. I felt a little nervous, but not scared— I was mostly worried about offending, since he's an important customer, and my company treats all of our customers with kid gloves. Also, customers have so much power with the company that all you need to do is get a reputation of pissing off a customer, and you're dead. So I wanted to make sure I handled it with tact.

I never said to him directly, "You're coming on to me," or "What's going on here?" Instead, I just addressed the fact that we were supposed to be having a training session. I finally said, "Why don't you just call the others and have them come out here for the meeting?" He looked at me and said, "What?" I said, "Well, we're going to have a training session out here, right? You got all my letters, didn't you?" He said, "Oh yeah, right." Then he called his supervisor, took all the equipment downstairs, and believe it or not, we ended up having our training session in his dining room.

I didn't take what he'd done as an insult. I took it more as a flaw in his character. He lived in this gorgeous mansion of a house, and he was obviously a bachelor. He probably would have been a fun guy under other circumstances, but I was there to do a training session for my company. I just said to myself, "Too bad this guy isn't used to working with professional women. Small-town man—what does he know?"

Jessica was stunned when clients first propositioned her. Gradually she saw that there had been misunderstandings. When

Jessica gets excited by the challenge of a legal case, her enthusiasm is contagious, but it confuses some men. When clients themselves feel sexually attracted, they mistake her love of law for interest in them.

> In my experience, and from talking with other female lawyers, I'd say getting propositioned is quite common. It usually starts with an invitation for drinks, and before you know it, seemingly out of nowhere, the client will lean over and ask you to go to bed with him. When something like this first happened to me, I was shocked.
>
> I immediately asked myself, "My God, what did I do?" I evaluated my behavior: Did I do anything to provoke this? Did I come on to this person? Or was I just getting excited about my job, and he took it the wrong way? You know, you can be happy and pleased with the work you've done, and a client can interpret that as personal excitement about him.
>
> I've talked to a number of other women lawyers about this, because when it happens to you, you want to find out if it happens to other women as well. I had no idea that my professional performance could have sexual connotations and be interpreted as leading someone on. But I found out that my enthusiasm about my work can be misinterpreted, and I'm not the only woman who has this problem. It happens to a lot of us.

The women found that they were ostracized completely when coworkers believed they were sleeping their way up. The faster Maureen was promoted, the more silences she met, and the more isolated she became. When finally she began reporting directly to the president, she was cut off completely. With her arrival in the executive suite, new rumors flew.

> I was the only MBA in the company, so I got a lot of exposure to the president. He was a very autocratic manager and made just about every internal decision. Well, I

ended up working for him, and it got very complicated. People were saying that I was sleeping with him, and he would do things to encourage those rumors. He was constantly propositioning me. Several times he set up situations where we would be alone together. Once I was at a trade show, and he planned dinner when nobody else was there, so it was just the two of us. He was always asking me to go out and have a drink with him, suggesting that we take a trip together—things like that.

Another time, he called me into his office and gave me this bag that had a big bottle of scotch in it. I took the bag back to my office. It was about three in the afternoon, and I sat there, scared to death. I didn't want this bottle of scotch, and it made me feel that there was something going on that I didn't know how to control. At about six o'clock, after everyone else was gone, I walked into his office, put the bottle back on his desk, and said, "I don't want this. If you want to reward me for a job well done, give me an increase, or something like that." I was so scared.

I know there are cases where women are forced into situations where their jobs are at stake. I was lucky. After I turned the president down repeatedly, he said, "You are very valuable to this company. If that's the way you feel about it, I'm not going to jeopardize your contributions to this company. Let's just let it drop."

If I'd been a clerical worker and he hadn't stopped making those advances, I think that maybe I could have walked out and gotten a job somewhere else. But once you've started moving up, you can't do that. You can't just walk out.

All this time, there were insinuations that I had moved up because I was sleeping with the president. Our controller resigned when I was made vice president, because he said I didn't deserve it. What other people in the company didn't understand was that I was frightened. I wasn't afraid of my job responsibilities or of mixing with those higher-level people who were all men. I was frightened by the sexual advances of the president.

Ruth also attests to the power of the rumor mill. When she decided to switch legal specialties, she worried that her reasons might be misunderstood. When colleagues suspected that an affair prompted that decision, several confronted her with angry, bitter words. When protesting did no good, Ruth gave up trying. Her statement of fact couldn't alter their beliefs.

> The reason I became an immigration lawyer is that the man who was the officer in charge of the immigration office here liked the way I handled a case. He said to me, "You're wasting your talents being a commercial litigator. I'm going to make you want to be an immigration lawyer." And he proceeded to do that. He is a charismatic, dynamic man. He has moved up very quickly in the Immigration Service and he's in an extremely powerful position today. But the thing is, people in my firm and people in his organization thought we were sleeping together. And we weren't. There is a sexual chemistry there—a definite attraction that made us want to talk and become friends, but all the rest of it is simply professional.
>
> I took a lot of heat for our relationship in my own firm. I got called on the carpet several times. I was humiliated and angry that they thought I got good results because I was sleeping with somebody. I was terribly annoyed that they wouldn't look at my work before they passed their judgments.

The women all believe that marital status plays a major role in sexual dynamics. Julie senses that men in her company treat married women with far more respect. She watches men harass single women frequently. Her recommendation is to interrupt the teasing the minute it begins.

I believe that the atmosphere at work is really different for a married woman. The men don't make the same snide remarks or suggestive comments to a married woman that they do to a single woman. The single woman is treated much more loosely and not nearly as professionally. If you're single, the men treat you as if they're saying, "Well, you're just here, honey, because we like the way you look." Whereas with married women, the message is, "We hired you because you have skills."

Now if a married woman acts single, she's going to get the comments too. But if she has pictures of her kids on her desk and brings her husband to the baseball games, the dinner meetings, and the company parties, she's treated a whole lot differently.

How can a single woman minimize some of the sexual come-ons? If she's really concerned about the comments and she wants to put a stop to them, she has to let the men know that she wants the comments to stop. It's best to tell the men who are talking that way that you don't like it— right from the beginning—rather than let the comments go on. Just make it understood up front that you don't like it. Take the risk.

Patricia has worked at the same television station for seven years. She's been there single, then married, and now as she goes through a divorce. As soon as a change occurs in her personal life, men in the newsroom shift their behavior in response.

The come-ons you get when you're married are more subtle than they are when you're divorced. When you're married, the men know your husband, and they aren't going to be disrespectful of another man. It's not that they respect *you*—it's the man. You're seen as his property. When the man is no longer your keeper, you're treated as though you deserve no respect.

When I got divorced, one man said to me, "I'm sure

your unit needs servicing." And I said, "Oh, no, does it really?" Newsrooms tend to have romances, with reporters dating people in the same area. When you get divorced, there's a kind of macho thing among the men, like, "Who's going to be the first one to get her?", because everybody—or so the rumor goes—has a newsroom romance. All of the men want to put little notches on their belts. And that's the basic difference. When a woman's single, the men have got to get notches. When you're married, out of respect to your husband, they don't bother you.

Shirley works as a data-processing manager. In many ways, her career has become her life. When she joined the company, she had no time for dating, so she got involved with men she knew best. After several affairs ended uncomfortably, Shirley got discouraged. Then she made a decision she has stuck with ever since.

I have a rule: You don't play where you eat. I think that's one of the hardest things for single women to learn when they first go to work. Single women naturally wonder where they should go to meet people to go out with. You have to socialize, but you don't want to go to a singles bar and just pick somebody up. You want to meet somebody and get to know him before you go out with him, and you think you can do that in the workplace.

Well, it's all right for a man to meet a woman at work, because it's perfectly acceptable for a man to sleep around. But it is definitely not acceptable for a woman to sleep around. If you go out with somebody from the office, and it gets around that you slept with the guy, you're automatically labeled a whore. And you sure don't want any links between "whore" and "manager."

At any given time, a large number of professional women are separated or about to be divorced. When Lois took her children and moved out from her husband, she tried to change jobs and relocate, but she met resistance right away. Today, she is remarried and works as a programmer, but memories of discrimination are with her still.

> It's much easier being a working woman who is married, because then you're safe. If you're married, you're not seen as someone who's looking for a date. Being married adds credibility. You're seen as a good, honest, solid citizen.
>
> Being separated is the worst. When I was first separated, I applied for a job in an advertising agency in Chicago, and they basically said they were going to hire me. In those days, you could be asked about marital status in job interviews. When they asked me what my marital status was and I said I was separated, they said, "Oh, well, we're very sorry, but you can't have the job. We could take you if you were divorced, or if you were married, or if you were single. But if you're separated, you're either in tears or in court all the time, and we've found that it just doesn't work out."
>
> Today it's OK to be divorced, because so many people are, but being separated is still something that nobody understands.

Tips From the Trenches

Take Control

Most women I interviewed had been able, over time, to deal with men's subtle comments in an increasingly effective fashion. Many had developed a repertoire of responses and knew when to use each. Repeatedly they emphasized the need to spot a come-on early and to choose, on a case-by-case basis, whether to confront it, make a joke, or ignore it for the moment. Women's anxieties dissipated as they thought through the issue. Their confidence grew as they knew where they stood.

Jane, a CEO, warns against how-to prescriptions. Her success on this issue stems from one-on-one wins.

> I think that women have to be intellectually prepared to accept the fact that the professional world really is a minefield, and they must say, "OK, I'm going to face some sex discrimination because it's ingrained in these guys' heads." When discrimination happens to you, it hurts. Emotionally you want to blow up, but intellectually you know you'd better accept the fact that discrimination exists and say, "OK, I'm not going to take what that guy did to me as a personal affront, because he was raised to react that way."
>
> What you really have to do is deal with discrimination on an individual basis. Sometimes I jokingly say I feel like Mae West—so many men, so little time! It's one man at a time. If you can convince each man you work with that you really are a professional and you really are terrific, then he might think that the next woman is not so bad.
>
> Men and women are different. When I say something, it sounds different from when a man says it. I have a different timbre in my voice; my voice has a different sort of authority in it; I look different. But different can't always be considered to be bad; the differences have to be recognized for what they are.

After twelve years in banking, Lucy feels she has handled it all. Her strategy is to sense political dynamics and to pick her response accordingly. "In some ways," she tells me, "survival is endurance. Their goal is to engage you; your goal is to break free."

> How I handle those situations depends on the individual. Sometimes if you come back with, "I'd like to see you in a bathing suit, too," and laugh, you can get through it

and everybody else laughs, and that's all there is to it. With some people, ignoring them and just continuing with what you're doing works best. After a while they get tired, because they're not getting any response. Usually when such comments are made, I feel annoyed, because this behavior is impeding my progress and interfering with what I'm trying to do. Then, later on, usually when I'm back home, I get angry.

The women talked about the need to project a sense of professionalism and disinterest in all matters relating to sex. They feel women can discourage men's attention by controlling the messages their bodies and words convey. Claudia tries to assure an all-business stance in federal court. To ensure her effectiveness, she'll compromise her style and hide strong feminist views.

How can I say this? It's not my advice politically, but just as somebody trying to make an honest living: My advice is to be good-natured but also be sort of curt, if you can combine those two sensibilities. Just try to shut it off as quickly as possible. Don't get pissed off about it, because usually you have to deal with that same guy in the future, and it could get tense. You have to be somewhat "shut down" and let these little sexual innuendos slide right off your back. Politically, I think you ought to tell him to go fuck himself. I think this kind of behavior deserves an angry response; unfortunately, I don't think that's practical.

Rhonda wants to minimize the put-downs. She seeks to prevent teasing before it begins. In years of architectural practice, she's evolved a formal style. It permeates her business as well as her design.

I always pick up the phone using my full name, and there's a little murmur in the office about my doing that.

But if you take two people—a man and a woman—the reactions are different. A man will get a respectful response to a call automatically, but I'll get, "Hi, honey. This is Bob Johnson at Midland Steel," or even "Hi, Rhonda honey, how are you, sweetie?" I really can't stand that. I don't know these men, and here they are treating my name with a familiarity that isn't warranted. I answer the phone the way I do in order to set a formal tone with these guys. And it works.

Sarah thinks back over her career in publishing. Though her business is words, she ascribes to the power of nonverbal communication, too. To some extent, male-female tension is two-way, she argues. Women who want to control it in their professional lives must determine whether their posture, tone, and gestures invite the behavior they protest.

I never communicated that I was even possibly available. Not that I was hostile—I think I always let the men know that I thought they were nice.

And I think my unavailability has been liberating for a lot of the men here. There's an enormous amount of stress that comes with the stereotype that men are supposed to be tremendously virile and sexy, endlessly available, and able to perform at any level at any time. Not only are they supposed to do their jobs and hit a baseball, but they're supposed to be a great lay.

When a woman flirts or indicates in some way that she may be sexually available to a man, it puts tremendous pressure on him, because he feels he must oblige and come through. And if he doesn't want to, or isn't interested, it makes him feel guilty and therefore angry. Frankly, I think this is the source of a lot of rage and difficulty in the whole sexual situation at work.

If you seriously, truly, really mean you're not sexually available, everybody relaxes. Then you can go on to deal with what you're supposed to be dealing with. But if you as a woman indicate, either consciously or unconsciously, that you're sexually available—or sexually interested—it immediately puts a man in the mental space that he has with his wife or his lovers. Then he has to deal with you as a domestic woman, and you definitely don't want that in business.

I think that for a lot of women this process of subtly coming on to men is not conscious. I think it's often the way they dealt with their fathers, which was to be flirtatious or innocently seductive. Many women have never learned another way of relating to men. After many years in this field, I've come to the conclusion that women have as much difficulty relating to men as men have relating to women.

Certainly there are plenty of men out there who can only see women as sex objects. But if you're walking through the door in a silk blouse cut down to here, what message is he supposed to get? Where is the sign that says, "I'm a serious grownup"? You're simply not wearing it. Often the heaviest signals come through body language. I see women all the time who are wearing pants, and will put their feet up on the desk seductively.

It's all basic baboon stuff—you know? It's highly provocative, and what's more, it is usually completely unexamined.

Jennifer and Melissa are traditionally good-looking—tall, lanky blondes who could model with ease. Since both are also single and looking for partners, they share a temptation to mix pleasure with work. As I compare Jennifer's voice in California with Melissa's in New York, I hear contrasting styles but similar goals.

Jennifer is quick, witty, and direct. When she's confronted with come-ons, her frank approach works best.

Trading favors definitely does go on in the computer business. I get propositioned by customers all the time. I just don't worry about it, even though a lot of customers flat out tell me that if I'll sleep with them they'll give me the order. And our company sells one- and two-million-dollar-ticket items—I mean these are not small orders.

Usually the way I handle a proposition like that is to say, "Well, that's an interesting business proposition, but your order's going to have to be a lot higher." That usually puts a stop to it, to throw it back at them with a joke.

The very worst thing you can do is to ignore the proposition. The truth is that we are all sexual people. If you're big on top, men are going to notice. If you aren't, men are going to notice that, too. People are simply much more interesting than business.

When I get propositioned at work I generally try to take it at face value. If a man's interested in me sexually, I tell him whether I'm interested in him or not. Usually, we can get off that subject quickly and back to the real business at hand. I try to address it honestly and then move on.

Jennifer's looks and the hustle of her business have presented her with more challenges in five years than most face in a career. As she reels off the incidents and how she chose to handle them, I am struck by the wisdom of someone so young.

Most men will make their approach very subtle. It will be a very low-level kind of tickler. If you just recognize it and react to it, it never comes back again. Like the other day, after a meeting, somebody came up to me and whispered in my ear, "Do you wear underwear?" I whispered back, "I may never wear underwear, but let me tell you one thing—you'll certainly never know." My response was sort of a joke, picking up on his line, but it was also shutting him off. That guy never bothered me again.

Another time, when I was on a business trip, somebody said to me, "Don't you ever get lonely out here traveling all by yourself?" I said, "Sure, I get lonely. But that's why I bring my teddy bear. He keeps me safe." I'll say something dumb like that, but most men get the message.

The thing to remember is that most people don't want

121

to embarrass themselves. The only time they'll embarrass themselves is when you ignore their subtle signals and require that they yell out their message. If you don't respond to someone's come-on, it's only going to get worse. Then it gets obnoxious, and you're going to be embarrassed, and the other person's going to be embarrassed, too.

Unlike Jennifer, Melissa is soft-spoken and shy. For a long time, she ignored the rumors surrounding her, though she was startled to learn others' fantasies about her life. But once, when her reputation for integrity was at stake, Melissa changed her style and challenged what was almost a lie.

One time they brought the Midwest sales manager east to become the New York sales manager. It was a bigger job with more staff and more money. He wasn't necessarily a difficult man, but he wasn't used to working with women other than secretaries. After he'd been in his job in New York about one week, he came into my office, closed the door, and said, "If I ever find out you're sleeping with anyone you're calling on, you're fired. And I want you to know that from the beginning." I said, "Oh, OK."

It wasn't until I got home that night that I became enraged. I mean I really did flip out. And for me, at that time, that was something! It was early 1973, so I had only one year of selling under my belt. I walked into his office the next day and closed the door. I could see him getting nervous. I said, "There are some thirty-odd men on the New York sales staff. To how many of them have you said what you said to me?" He answered, "I wouldn't have to say it to them." I said, "So the new rule is for the woman." I told him I found that unacceptable, and I walked out of his office.

I sat in my office the entire day waiting to be fired, really thinking that this would be it. But I was also feeling proud of myself, because in those days what I had done was very hard to do. He came in later that day and apologized. He said, "You're going to have to bear with me. I'm not used to this—you make me very uncomfortable. I don't know quite how to deal with you." That episode established a smidgen of respect for me on his part.

While women advocated flexibility in dealing with teasing, their recommendations against in-house affairs were unanimous and strong. Indeed, of all controversial topics discussed in our interviews, none drew such a loud, resounding response. The women pointed out that when a man and a woman in the same organization become involved, usually the female has less status and rank. If the corporate culture frowns on in-house relationships, generally it is she, not he, who sacrifices a job. Later, if the affair doesn't pan out, the woman loses not only a paycheck but also self-esteem.

Emily advises women to consider these realities before acting even once on what may be a fleeting urge. Though she dislikes it, Emily knows that in business, the double standard is as prevalent and powerful as it is in the rest of life.

I once had a relationship with somebody in a company I worked for. I was willing to take the risk, because I really cared for the person. But the pressure of hiding the fact that we were having a relationship eventually became too much, and we broke it up. You have to ask yourself, "What's more important, my personal life or my career?" But if the word gets out that you're having a relationship, the woman always goes. I've never seen a man go.

You've got to remember that when a woman gets sexually involved with a man, the man is conquering. He gets the notches in his belt. The woman is seen as the person giving in. And inside a company, the man is almost always rewarded by his peers. They pat each other on the back and say, "Good for you, you got her." The woman gets penalized for allowing him to have her. It may sound terrible, but the double standard still exists.

Women empathize with the stress that such a firm policy can place on an individual, particularly if she's going through a lonely time of life. Single women may have no time to meet men outside the office. Divorced women, unaccustomed to being available, may enjoy being propositioned by attractive, successful men. Even so, the women in this study reiterate their warning carefully: Getting involved with colleagues means risking a reputation and a job. If Andrea has a tryst with a fellow salesperson on the road, the national grapevine may destroy her in a moment's time.

> I really think women have to conduct themselves far more carefully in business than men do, no matter what. Basically, women must be absolutely aboveboard in the office and at company functions. There's such a double standard out there. I don't think women can go out and have a good time the way the guys do and still be looked upon as someone to be promoted. Maybe that's just what I'm experiencing here in the Midwest. It might be different back east or on the West Coast. But here there's no room at all for a woman's fooling around.
>
> It makes me angry that if I meet someone and I really want to have a fun time with him, it affects how I'm looked upon by the company. If I fooled around it would be all over the company in a matter of hours—not just in the home office, either, but all over the United States, because the sales reps have quite an active hotline going. I would never have been approached for this upcoming promotion if I fooled around. I know that for a fact.
>
> This is really about never letting your hair down, never letting them see that you're really a fun person or that you can be one of them. It's sad, because I find you can't be yourself a lot of the time. You have to be a certain person that the company expects you to be.

Edna's final story drives the point home hard. She cites the case of a colleague who slept with the CEO. A one-night stand changed that woman's five-year relationship to her company. Later, she had to join a different industry; she had to establish a new career.

> I believe people shouldn't get involved with people at work. When they do, their professional friendships and alliances change. I think adding sexual politics to business politics builds another layer of confusion and distortion you don't ever need.
>
> There was a woman at my other firm who did sleep with the president of the company. She also got promoted. She was a tremendously capable woman. I firmly believe she got promoted because she was an outstanding, competent professional. But she never knew why she got that promotion, and it still haunts her today. She never knew whether she got promoted because she slept with the president or because she was competent. She finally left the company.

More impressive than their strategies were the women's changed attitudes. In earlier years, teasing had been disarming. Sexual harassment had thrown the women off track, had stripped them of confidence, and had made them feel confused. But by the time of our interviews, most had adopted a different perspective. Though resentful of rude behavior and angry at management that allows it to persist, the women have built up psychological defenses. Harassment no longer appears to interrupt their purpose. It no longer seems to threaten self-esteem. Their initial hesitation about discussing this topic is not a sign of avoidance. Instead, it represents change.

> At one time or another, I've been propositioned by two of the six executives in this company, a couple of times by employees and managers who work for me, and more times than I can count by customers or field people. It's happened frequently enough now that it doesn't bother me.

The first time it happened, it bothered me a lot, because then I felt that they were discounting me. I thought that to them I wasn't a whole person anymore. I was just the person in the centerfold. I felt then that somehow their interest in me sexually meant that I wasn't powerful or that I wasn't being professional.

Now, I just think it means they think I'm attractive. And I like that. I don't lead them on, because that's unfair. If I'm not interested in them, I'm not interested. But being a sexually alive person doesn't mean you're not powerful, and it certainly doesn't mean you aren't capable.

5

Scrutinizing the Power Game

The Ethics of Power

Working women are thinking about power and ethics in new and serious ways. For the majority of those interviewed, life in corporate America has brought grave disillusionment about how power is used, who has it, and why. Each woman I met had considered the topic seriously and was more than eager to talk. One mentioned that finally, finally we were addressing the great taboo.

For many, discussing power was both the most meaningful and the most painful part of our conversation. Answering my questions on this subject prompted freshly lit cigarettes, coffee refills, and second glasses of wine; it also brought the most bitterness and the most tears. With noticeable anxiety, women recounted story after story of politics, corruption, and employee abuse. Over and over, they declared how shocked they had been at the behavior they'd witnessed and how they had never expected to encounter so many examples of aggression and greed.

As women examine their companies more closely and learn about what it really takes to succeed, many are growing worried about the future. For the first time in the past twenty years, increasing numbers of professional women—including some of the most talented leaders—are seriously scrutinizing how their organizations have operated to date. In doing so, they are raising fundamental questions about ethics, identity, power, and choice.

In traveling across the country, I noticed that even though this reassessment is profound, it remains in private. Women agonize individually, often unaware that others share their concern. After hearing the hopes, dreams, and worries of 125 of these women, I recalled the words of a designer who summed up the trend one winter afternoon. Perched on a stool next to her drafting table, the young woman swiveled and looked me in the face. In a shy voice she whispered, "You know, it's kind of awesome. Women today are questioning, questioning—questioning everything, questioning it all."

Personal Power

Brenda, Sarah, Louise, and Courtney have never met. They live in different cities and work in different industries. All four are successful women in management. Each has an area of expertise, more than twelve years' experience, and substantial responsibility in a major corporation. To hear their definitions of power, one would think they had collaborated.

These four represent a growing number of professional women who define power in terms of character and the ability to use personal strength in facilitating shared goals. In Lee Iacocca's terms, these women see the importance of "strong" egos, and the dangers of egos that are "large" and presumably weak. Most important, they understand the connection between a leader's psychology and power that is shared.

Whether the voice belongs to Brenda, the black human resources specialist in Detroit, or to Louise, the chief executive officer of a manufacturing enterprise in New York, the message conveyed is always the same: Power comes from working with and through many different people. Hearing these women voice humane and pragmatic objectives, I recognize that a movement toward participatory management has already begun.

The role of women in this wider movement remains unclear. What is certain, given the echoed concerns, is that women will continue to challenge old assumptions about centralization and control in the months and years to come. From what was told me in confidence, I suspect that a subtle revolution may well be under way.

It is growing late in Detroit and my mind drifts, wondering if the snowstorm outside has become a blizzard. Here, in a vast, silent automotive plant, Brenda, too, is quiet as she ponders the issue of power. Absently she picks three Hershey kisses from her glass bowl on a regulation company table. Twirling them in her hand, she takes a deep breath and begins.

> An outside consultant I worked with once told me that I was a very powerful person. I asked him, "How can you say that? You know what my position is here, you know what my level is in the company." And he said, "No, you don't understand. I'm not talking about your authority, I'm talking about your personal power." He really made me take a look at what kind of power plays a role in success.
>
> I had heard that feedback before—that I'm viewed as being somewhat powerful here—but he made me understand what it really means. He was suggesting that power is an ability to lead, to communicate with all kinds of people, at all management levels, and to basically believe in oneself and act on one's beliefs. I realized that if I had to choose between having personal power and having authority, I would choose personal power. So it made me feel great when he told me that's what I've already got.

As I talk with Sarah, a senior editor in publishing, I find myself marveling at the complexity of her thought. No matter what topic we discuss, her ideas are complicated, yet her style is direct. I look around Sarah's office, noticing stacks of books, magazines, and newspapers piled high in every corner. I grow curious about power in her field, for it seems that this is a world where respect for knowledge supersedes all. Sarah's comments show the reality; I know her world less well than I thought.

> One of the things I've learned in the last couple of years is that there is something very distorted about our typical perceptions of power. After many years of working with this company, I have come to realize that nobody gives you power. It resides within you. Corporations don't magically give power to individuals—individuals either assume it or they don't. Acquiring power is an option that is available to people who choose to take it.
>
> I have observed great potential power in people who, for one reason or another, have failed in the eyes of the corporation and have been fired. Some of these people never recover. Sadly, they believe that the magic of power is in the corporation rather than in themselves as individuals. I don't agree with them. I don't think power belongs to institutions. It belongs to people.

Louise is the president of a large manufacturing company, the wholly owned subsidiary of a renowned multinational firm. Having climbed the corporate ladder for more than two decades, she assures me she's seen everything in the way of political games. Louise traces her career from the age of nineteen. From moving up the ranks, she learned what it was like to have talent and skill but little control. As she remembers her frustrations, her face grows hard. It softens when she describes how she manages today.

> I think too many people come into organizations with a title and assume that power comes with that title. But you must empower others before power comes back to you. Power is something people give you in relation to how you make them feel about themselves. I don't think a lot of people understand that. I think power is misused in

companies where you have autocratic CEOs, where employees are ruled by fear, where there is a less-than-participatory management style. Real power comes when you're strong enough to make your employees feel good about themselves and their work.

I saw the misuse of power, or at least the symptoms of misuse, in my first company. For one thing, the CEO would call meetings at the drop of a hat, no matter what anybody else was doing. He was rude and insensitive, and he didn't care about his employees' concerns. He needed the ego gratification of feeling that he was all-powerful, so he made his own schedule and wasn't concerned with how his whims would affect the rest of his employees. He was working on his own agenda and didn't worry about anybody else's. I think his use of power was destructive. It created a tremendously disgruntled workforce. The vice presidents and I used to sit around and grouse about it, and you know it's counterproductive to spend a lot of energy grousing about the way a boss or CEO operates.

So one of the things I'm trying to do here is to have everybody understand what the organization's objectives are, where we're headed, and how we're going to get there. I believe that if my employees know where we're going, and everybody's charging to get there together, it's a much easier way to run a business. My style takes a lot more of my own personal time because I spend a lot of energy reinforcing the culture. Four times a year I go to each of our regional locations and speak to the entire workforce. I let them know how we're doing. I answer their questions, and I show them how we're progressing toward our mutual goals. I am very visible and try to remain on a first-name basis. I don't think the time I spend doing this is wasted at all. On the contrary, I feel it really goes to fuel the positive aspects of our business.

Courtney is a pragmatist. Her sentences, like her gestures, are sharp and precise. Watching her move quickly, I am not surprised to hear her define power as "the ability to get things done." Unlike the philosophical statements of others, all of her comments focus on tactics and techniques.

> I've always had a lot of power, even without titles, because I've always found out whom I needed to know to get the job done. This means I don't have power by authority, I have personal power. I trade IOUs back and forth with people, favor swapping, that kind of thing. And I was lucky to have had important mentors early in my career, people who were high up in the corporation. These mentors made me powerful, because from them I had information that would help me do my job better. I also had information that other employees respected, which made me more powerful in their eyes. I sort of had tentacles all over the place.
>
> In effect, I created my own job. I took on projects that nobody else wanted to do, things that people didn't know about or didn't think were important. I never took somebody's job away from them, but many times I saw that something extra should be done. In those situations, I said to myself,"This is just lying here, and it could make the company lots of money," or "This is a real problem; let's fix it." And then I'd go do the project or fix that problem. I just kept doing more and more and more of the work until soon I had a whole lot of responsibility.

Learning the Game

Women contrasted their definitions of power to the political operations they witness every day. In a small town in Ohio, America's heartland, Heidi summed up the dominant view.

> Unfortunately, people see power like a pie, so that if you take away a piece of it, they have less. That's my view of the game—a competitive struggle to get pieces of the pie. But to me, that just isn't valid. I believe that the more you spread the power out, the more you really have.

There was general agreement among the women on the characteristics of power in their organizations. Usually it is viewed as a scarce commodity gained through competitive battle. Once achieved, it must be protected, for others will try to steal it away. The women watched these power plays and marveled at how passionately people jockey for money, status, and position. Most view the dynamic as a draining of energy, a needless diversion from the work they have to do.

Sandy, a corporate loan officer and veteran of power games, worries that such attitudes will leave women out and curtail their advancement. In her opinion, all professionals must be realistic; they must recognize how irrational and primitive power wars can be.

> The business deal is a matter of exchange. You have to learn how to handle the rules of the small exchanges between individuals in order to get the big rewards in the big operations. The tricky rules, the very political rules are the ones that are basically power rules. There's power of ability, which is good work. There's power of your position. There's personal power. There's obviously sexual power. And you have to know which of those to use, and how, and which ones are appropriate in which exchange, and which ones are not going to win out.
>
> I've always said that the thing that our manager in this department now—who's a woman—has going against her is that she tends to assume that business operates on a rational level, so she expects everyone to be reasonable. She's tremendously frustrated and almost offended and hurt when people don't make decisions on a rational basis. I believe you have to assume irrationality before you can even begin to decipher what the business exchanges are really about.

Cynthia and Anne work for Fortune 500 companies. Between them they have more than thirty-five years of experience. In speaking with each, at different times and locations, I heard strikingly similar refrains. Cynthia, a controller, has access to budgets. She knows precisely how money is spent. With anger mounting in her eyes, she speaks slowly. She points to budget items and analyzes the inequities both men and women face.

> Rank hath its privileges. That's definitely the case here and, frankly, in every organization I've been in. But it's especially interesting to watch the hierarchy in a Fortune 500 company. There are budget cuts going on now that have our department down to the bone. At the same time, the company has chartered jets for business trips because a commercial plane may leave thirty minutes too late or thirty minutes too early or get in twenty minutes too late. Accounts payable reports to me, and those people get so frustrated because they see all those things going through, and meanwhile, they're sitting on ratty furniture in crowded conditions. The fixed accounting people see all the building changes that go on for no apparent reason while they're stuck in little-bitty rooms. To me, that's abuse—it really is.
>
> There's a woman who works up the hall from me, and we sit around and say, "Well, when we run this organization, things are going to be a helluva lot different." For one thing, it would be more egalitarian. I understand that you've got to have some hierarchy in order to manage 4,000 people—you can't have each employee reporting to the president. But at the same time, there are many things that could be done to make these people's lives more comfortable and wouldn't cost the company much money. But they aren't being done, simply because we're not important. We don't have the rank.

Several times in her interview, Anne's voice shakes and her eyes well up. It is the most poignant hour I have spent with any of the women. Anne, a brilliant computer scientist, once spearheaded a division. After rising to the top, she could no longer tolerate political abuse. She left the corporation.

Sitting in a three-day planning session for the company's annual goals, I was the only woman, and I felt invisible. I felt that they didn't care whether I was there or not, and mine was probably a courtesy invitation. I felt as though I had no role to play in the overall forward movement of the company, and yet I knew that I did. I felt that they were all automatons in their jockeying for their division's positions—that this was a three-day jockeying party. And that's exactly what it was, everybody stroking everybody else, trying not to make a fool out of themselves and, if possible, trying to subtly make a fool out of the guy next to them. It was a totally plastic scene. These guys had to be gentlemen for three days when they had just come in from the combat zones. Everyone on the team was an enemy of someone else. It nauseated me that it was so impersonal, so false. It's a monopoly game that doesn't have any rewards associated with it, but everybody plays because it's the only game in town. Yet I felt that they were keeping me out of the game entirely. I remember sitting there watching and thinking, "Well, there's only one key that fits the power restroom."

Women struggle to understand why and how office politics play such a major role in their organizations. Some, like Michelle, the Wall Street broker, see power games, favoritism, and psychological abuse reflecting "the system" and what it rewards. Others, like Sarah, don't analyze structures, but instead lay responsibility at the feet of individuals—men who abuse their power rather than use it constructively for the benefit of all.

As I listened to women expressing both viewpoints, I saw that few consider economics separate from values. Rather, women today are concerned about which ethical principles and assumptions underlie which business decisions. Michelle, as always, minces no words.

I hate the way power flows in this organization. It's a medieval system that dictates that if your father happens to be the head of a major financial institution, or if you're wealthy, you're given a good position. It's a typically feudal system that says the more you bring into the firm, the more you're going to get. Now, you do see big producers who've made it in other ways. In fact, our biggest producer has made it entirely on his own—as I have. But the structure is built on money, background, and what you bring in.

I've seen young guys come here, and just because their father was president of this or that, or the head of a bank, they were immediately placed in positions over men who have been here a long time or who have made moderate amounts of money. That's the way it works. It's accepted, and no one can do anything about it. Sure, you hear grumbles and gripes all over the place, but no one can do anything about it. It's a rotten system, but the firm has to make money. So they're all out there vying for the sons of bankers and the sons of presidents of large corporations, because obviously that's where the money is going to come from. Sure, people resent it. Not just women— everyone resents it. But that's the way the system is.

As our talk about power becomes personal, Sarah grows agitated. Her brow furrows, her mouth draws into a tight line. Talking about politics abstractly was easy, but applying it to daily life upsets her. Finally Sarah sighs and tells me her main worry: She has serious misgivings about the CEO. Though the company continues to do well financially, employee morale has hit an all-time low.

Power, like money, has no moral value in and of itself. It's neutral; it's not a good thing, and it's not a bad thing; it just *is*. What takes on moral weight or value resides in the consequences of its use.

For example, the CEO of our company has done an extraordinary job in the few years I've been here. He went from a vice president to CEO and turned what was once a medium-size company into a huge, huge corporation. Since he's been CEO, we have tripled in size. Now, this man has intense professional magnetism. He is also a man of great personal charm. However, he controls the economic fortunes of virtually everyone in the company. And he can, when someone displeases him, absolutely shred someone's self-esteem. The fact that he has the power to do that is neutral. The fact that he chooses to do it is shocking.

How to Play the Game

It soon became clear that executive women know what it takes to play the power game. While publicly acknowledging that politics is vital, in private those I interviewed saw it as destructive and a wrongful use of time. Some noted that many male colleagues share their frustrations, attitudes, and ethical concerns with women in the organization.

From these comments, I sensed that a new coalition is developing inside corporate America. An informal alliance, a New Girl–New Boy Network, is based not on gender, race, or age, but rather on talent, mutual respect, and values. Within all types of organizations, men and women are coming together in support of common beliefs and moral commitments. Their concerns about rampant power and politicking soon may have profound effects on the places where they work.

When I asked the women to spell out the rules of office politics, they talked nonstop. They told me how they had watched incredulously as competent adults spent hours rechecking party invitation lists, writing memos to cover themselves, and keeping careful watch over who lunches with whom. Some women believe that office politics is really socially approved aggression, an intricate set of rituals that detract from productivity and instill in employees a latent sense of powerlessness, fear, humiliation, and shame.

Anne is one of the highest-ranking women I met. On a rainy Friday night, she reminisces at a farmhouse in the country. She sips her brandy and talks in subdued tones, her eyes fixed on the fire in front of us. With the same analytic ability that brought her national recognition, Anne turns her fine mind to political concerns.

If you took the whole upper stratum of my company—the president, the chairman, and their staff—they're all members of "the team." But if you get beneath that, then the vice presidents are either anointed or not anointed, on an individual basis. It's the informal system that is so critical. It's not the formal system at all. You can't tell rank by title, or by salary, or even by job function. But you can tell by what happens after hours, by who meets whom, by who can get an audience with whom. You can see the coalitions, and the coalitions are well thought out. There's a great amount of effort directed to the question of "Who's going to be my buddy tomorrow?"

To be anointed, first of all it takes acceptance, and the acceptance comes from buddying around with those who are already in. There are some who are already in who don't really carry any additional weight—they've made it, but they can't bring anybody with them. Then there are those who have tremendous influence on the others. Anyone who is a candidate for getting into "the team" is extremely careful about the meetings he conducts, the people with whom he conducts them, the meetings he attends, the people with whom he eats lunch and with whom he travels to visit one of the plants, whether he's on the company jet with A, B, or C, or whether he flies commercial. Also whose wife is in what health club with who else's wife, what committees outside the company people are working on—all those different types of things go into it.

When I think about how much energy this involves, I feel nauseated. It's the biggest waste of time I've seen in my life. I divide politics into two pots: voluntary and involuntary. Involuntary politics is what one has to put up with, has to play, just to get the job done. I mean, you obviously interface with other people—you're dependent on them; you have actions, interactions, and reactions. Those things have to go on. So you do what is necessary in the interest of getting the job done.

But the voluntary politics is the brown-nosing stuff. That puts self before job, or self before function. That is the "How do I get ahead by stroking somebody or by letting somebody else know I have this piece of information?" syndrome. It can be offensive or defensive. That's the politics that I detest, I absolutely detest. And that is precisely the sort of politics that gets played every day in many of our large corporations.

Diane believes that her best preparation for corporate life was becoming a teen-age athlete. Unlike most girls, she was exposed to teamwork and rules. Both help her now in comprehending political games.

Neatly groomed in her regulation blue suit, Diane sits poised behind a large walnut desk. After an hour's discussion, she leans back and grows silent, deciding whether to address more controversial ideas. Suddenly, her whole demeanor changes. Her words come out in spurts, and her speech seems pressured and tense. Finally she reveals the real story: Last week she was told she's gone as high as possible on merit alone. Whether she gets promoted again is strictly a political decision. It's a turning point in her life, yet it's beyond her control.

There's a lot of gamesmanship here. Business is very much like a game, and there's always a person who's ahead, the winners and the losers, and the concept of "the team"—who's going to carry the ball on a project and who's going to follow up. I think all of this is really tough for women to understand. I don't think every man working for a corporation has a clear sense of the game either, but I do think that, in general, women haven't been exposed to it as much. Those women who have made it to a certain professional level perhaps have, though a lot of the rest of us haven't, and I think we'll hold ourselves back if we don't become more aware. There are just certain things you don't say or do to certain people. For example, if it's something as simple as giving a reception for customers, there are certain people you make sure you ask, for politics' sake.

Shirley began in the data-processing industry years before it boomed. She had watched high-tech companies rise and fall, and twice had lost her job in takeover moves. Over the years, she has learned to protect herself. She knows the details of all corporate games. Speaking in her office outside of Boston, Shirley introduces me to Route 128, Silicon Valley East.

People say, "Everybody plays the game here." It means that you understand where everybody else's power is in the pecking order. You've got to play the game, but you also have to get your work done. You try to figure out how you can do that within the pecking order. You've got to be very aware of what's going on politically. You spend at least fifty percent of your time finding out what other people are doing. You've got to cover your bases. You've got to protect yourself. If some guy says something to you in conversation, and it's a point that you want to make sure you can hold him to, it means you must send a memo to him confirming your conversation, with copies to his boss. You've got to remember to do all that. Otherwise, if you've mentioned to your boss that this guy's supposed to do something for you, but you don't have any paperwork to back it up, you're in big trouble.

After interviewing Shirley on the East Coast and Glenda in the Midwest, I marveled at how savvy each had become. Glenda, two years out of college, concludes that "politics is everything" in the industrial products company where she's employed. In contrast to Shirley, who thinks politics is survival, Glenda worries that gamesmanship fosters deceit.

140

A lot of people talk about office politics. To me, it means doing what it takes to get your job done. That may mean not making waves if the person you're dealing with is more powerful than you. In that case, you may have to find another way to get the job done. On the other hand, politics means *making* waves if you're more powerful than the person through whom you're trying to get something done. So in the end, politics means being phony.

Glenda's fears about becoming phony are shared by many women. Some worry that they have grown sneaky, indirect, and paranoid in order to survive. Others wonder if the atmosphere in their companies has affected them in ways that they still don't even know. For single women, a major concern is whether the style needed to make it in a cutthroat environment is the style that prevents them from forming close personal ties.

Susan, an MBA, offers advice for success in Big Oil. Later, a conversation with Sandy shows that the advice is relevant in the financial services industry, too. Susan's strategy ensures that her department will triumph; she makes certain that all staff get coaching in how to play the game.

I train my people in politics. I think there are two types of politics. There's the dealing with the bureaucracy. That's things like whom you send memos to, whom you "cc," and whether you call someone first so he's not surprised when he gets the memo. That's the kind of politics I call corporate savvy. Then there's another kind of politics, the unwritten kind: Whom should you inform? Whom should you try your ideas out on first? Whom should you consider when you're making a decision?

The second kind of politics is very difficult to explain. I think this is the rule of thumb: Never be candid. I'm usually a very candid person, and I know my openness has hurt me in the past. For a long time, I felt that people should know the truth, but I've moved away from that notion. I've realized that I'm a square peg in a round hole here, and that it would be best for me to get smart about politics. I have enough background so that I can succeed in this environment. It's not me versus the corporation anymore.

Sandy works in one of the bank's satellite offices. In the middle of a sentence, she gets up, gestures toward the skyline, and points to a glass tower two blocks away. "That's our head office," she explains. "You really have to see it to understand what happens." Sandy stares for a moment at the city below her. She returns to her desk, lights a third cigarette, and tells me a pointed political tale.

When I called this man to arrange an appointment, he said, "Why don't you come up here? I'm on the seventy-eighth floor." He was sending definite signals by saying that. First of all, "Come see me here" meant I had to go see him on his turf, which is kind of a power play in business. If you come to my office, it means that you're in the vulnerable position. It's like being the visiting team in a football game. And also by saying, "I'm on the seventy-eighth floor," he was making sure I knew he was on the executive floor of our headquarters. This was supposed to make me very impressed, and therefore I was supposed to go along with what he had to say. I was to be swayed by the sheer power of his position.

Most upsetting to women is watching employees receive verbal abuse by people hungry for power. Dorothy, a thirteen-year veteran of corporate finance, defines office politics as "all about put-downs." Having watched men play ruthlessly with one another, she understands the real stakes of the game. Exhausted after a long day, Dorothy plops down in an easy chair, takes a sip of beer, and with a metaphor, summarizes the central power play.

In many public forums, men are trying to find a weakness, trying to make you display a weakness. And that's done not only to women—the men do this to each other. This is the standard mode of operation. So if you want to be in the group, you have to put up with that, you have to be always on your toes and always sharp and always ready to defend—but not in a way that seems defensive. To play in their ball game, you have to be just as good at their game as they are. You have to be willing to put up with a lot of flack as part of your test. It's so much like the army.

The three women who speak next recount how they first witnessed raw displays of power. When the incidents occurred, each felt a mixture of annoyance and surprise. Whether in consulting, banking, or stocks, they discovered that humiliation always works the same. Wendy, a senior vice president, leads with a classic story.

This new guy we hired happens to be very political and very much driven by power. After he had been here a week, he came to me and asked if he could talk to me privately. I said, "Sure," though I didn't know him from Adam. The first thing he said, straight out of the blue, was "I want your job. There's not enough room in this organization for the two of us." And I said, "Is that right? Really? Tell me about this." It was something I had never encountered before—someone coming in and telling me he wanted to take my job away from me.

I probably laughed, but I know I was offended. I had come to this company to help turn it around, and we'd gone through the worst part of all that—we had, in fact, turned around, and we were making a profit. He was hired after the worst was over, yet he was telling me that I wasn't needed? It was very shocking.

Men are not the only ones to get swept up in politics. Jane's story shows that when women view relationships exclusively in power terms, they too become aggressive, vying for control. When Jane turned to her husband for help in understanding the behavior of a colleague, she, a consultant, got political consultation right inside her home.

> I had a situation a number of years ago where the head secretary for the division head was feeding information into the pipeline to pit me and a guy against each other. It wasn't until the guy and I got our heads together that we found out we were getting the wrong information from the same source. I remember talking to my husband about it that night, saying, "Why would she do that to me?" And he said, "Why would she do that to you? Don't be naive. She's threatened by you. The only way she can guarantee her own safety is by pitting Paul against you. If Paul doesn't use that energy against you, he's going to realize that she's not competent and come against her." It was a very important lesson for me.
>
> I was a very good girl, very task-oriented, and I got rewarded for my performance. By that point, money and promotion had come without my having to ask for them. It never occurred to me that people played games. It never occurred to me that people stabbed you in the back. Learning that was a sad but important breakthrough.

Everything is more dramatic on Wall Street. With billions at stake, brokers, investment bankers, and analysts agree that the atmosphere is electric with political energy. While awaiting my interview with Laurie, I stand at the base of the World Trade Center and watch dozens of pin-striped suits scurry by. A sense of urgency is prevalent. Self-importance and tension fill the air.

Later, talking with Laurie, I learn that recently she had been humiliated by a typical power play. "In my work," she explains, "money is power, and power is everything. Without a large salary, I'm nothing at all." I stare incredulously at this competent young woman, and once more I see clear evidence of the human costs, the psychological duress caused by power games.

While I was out ill, I found out a company from L.A. was coming into town about three weeks after I expected to return to work. So my secretary helped me schedule a luncheon. I would see the chairman of the board of this company at eleven o'clock in my office, and then a meeting was scheduled for lunch. I had set up an appointment with about seven other brokers—men—in my firm for the luncheon. I told them I wanted to keep it to just the visiting chairman, plus myself and the brokers who worked three floors up.

But when I invited the brokers, I got hedged answers. "I think I can make it, I'll let you know" was what I heard from each of them. About a week before the luncheon, I tried to make it a little more definite, and I got five "probablies." Meanwhile, I called the L.A. company and said, "Yes, we're definitely on. There'll be seven of us at lunch."

A day before, I went upstairs to confirm, and I got three "definites." So I made a reservation for five for lunch downstairs at a ritzy hotel—you know, flowers, filets, gold silverware, the works. The finest.

The lunch meeting was scheduled for 12:15 and around that time I went downstairs with the chairman of the board, but no one showed. It was 12:15, then 12:30, 12:40. I excused myself to call my secretary, who called the brokers, and each of them was out to lunch. Now, I'd been in the office all morning, and there'd been no phone call from any of them, and not even the courtesy of a message at the table.

I was furious. I was embarrassed and insulted. I apologized left and right. I felt terribly torn, because though there was no excuse in the world for the lack of courtesy these people had shown, I wanted my firm to remain on good terms with this company.

Those people—those brokers—feel that they're above remorse, that they don't have to give the details of their time to anyone.

I don't know if it would have happened the same way if I had been a man—or even if I had been a woman at a higher level in the company, and making big bucks. I'm a young analyst, but I'm not a junior. Anyway, I wouldn't do what those brokers did to anybody, whether I was making $300,000 or a lot less. But that's the attitude of the type of people who said they would attend the luncheon. They only value big money.

In sum, professional women resent office politics for two reasons: It hurts people psychologically and it takes energy away from work. On the positive side, many women are determined to minimize politics in the environment they control. Whether that be a small department, a division, or an entire company, these leaders are intent on creating alternatives to competition and backstabbing. In the following comments, an architect, a public relations manager, and an advertising executive agree that shared power, not top-down control, is the way to minimize political infighting.

Once the decision-making chain is set into play in an organization, there's continual vying for the ear of the person who has the power to make that decision, the one who gives the final OK. Vying for that ear means saying, "Let's go play a game of golf," "Let's go have lunch," "Let's have you over for dinner." The goal is getting the ear of the person, getting to know them, and above all, getting them to like you so that you have more credibility with them. And people will jump over other people's backs to get to that ear—all this so that they will have more power. It's all a game. But if you sit down and think about it, you realize we're all working for the same purpose. Why can't we just relax and do our work on a rational basis, as a team?

I hate politics. Nothing is more diseased. I think it's the single greatest disease in the industry. You might as well face the fact that your people are not working an eight-hour day. They're working a four-hour day, a four-and-a-half-hour day, because at least two to three hours are spent being concerned and burdened with all the garbage that's going on in the office. I may be very Pollyanna about it, and I know I'm not able to eliminate it—it's inherent; it comes with the whole professional world. But everywhere I go, I seek to minimize it, at least.

I don't like politics. I don't like game-playing. I just want to jump in and get a job done. So whenever there's a hint of game-playing, I get out of it. I think playing the game diverts energy from getting the job done. The waltzing around doesn't appeal to me. I would rather know where I stand.

A Woman's Advantage

In most situations, my opposing counsel is a man, and even now I want him to like me. That's contrary to the way you're supposed to work here, which is against this other person. Whether he likes me or not shouldn't be an issue at all. I think that because aggressiveness is tolerated and encouraged in men, they're used to doing it. They're expected to do it, so most of them don't feel uncomfortable with it, and the whole thing of being liked is just not an issue for men. I remember that as a kid I'd go home and say, "So-and-so doesn't like me." And my mother, rather than say, "Screw her!" or "Screw him!" or "So what?" would say, "Now, tomorrow you go in and tell this person that they look very nice or that they've done something very well. Give them a compliment. Then the person will like you." I was never really allowed to have anyone dislike me. No wonder this is so hard.

Until recently, women like Marion believed that a traditional female upbringing caused nothing but problems in the work world. People used to point out that women value relationships, but business rewards competition. Women strive to be polite, but corporations seek managers who are tough. Women shy from bragging about their accomplishments, but promotions go to those who get the most and best PR. Given these old assumptions, consultants have advised that the only way women could make it in business was to relinquish traditionally feminine aspects of their personalities.

For over a decade, seminars and books fueled this notion, promoting materials designed to teach women "power behavior" modeled after men. In workshops across America, professional women studied how to be "assertive," not aggressive; to dress "for success," not for ease; and above all, to play politics for oneself, not to include others. From this vast educational outpouring, thousands of working women tried to take in new values, holding them next to traditional ones in an uneasy, internal truce.

In the past five years, however, a new trend has surfaced. Women who once mimicked male attributes are now turning inward, examining their assumptions, values, and strengths. No longer willing to dismiss femininity, women are viewing it as essential for full, rich careers. Whether this shift stems from economic security, from experience, or from a fundamental disillusionment with the status quo, it is clear that in the 1990s American women are celebrating renewed self-confidence and personal power. They are intent upon integrating the masculine and the feminine. Emily, like many others, thinks of a family when she thinks of her staff.

> I find developing my employees the most exciting part of my job. I take my biggest pride in the letters I get from former employees saying how happy they are and how they've gotten where they are today as a result of working with me. I would say that's the biggest satisfaction. It's wonderful to see them go on to bigger and better things as a result of something I might have taught them or some opportunity I made sure they had.
>
> I have a very open management style. Compared to the styles of other managers, mine is much more open and

casual. I have a lot of interaction with my people. It's more like a family than an office.

In Silicon Valley, things move fast. Start-ups rise and fall, and the pressure is intense. Jennifer believes that not everyone is suited to the harsh competition, the pace of production, and the tempers that flare with million-dollar deals. Because the payoffs are immense, the power games are cutthroat.

Jennifer describes how she's accommodated and how she's survived. In meetings, she gets as angry as the men surrounding her, but she also runs a department that is personal and small. As she combines her upbringing and her MBA training, Jennifer creates a new form of management and a new political style.

My mother grew up in a southern household, and I knew the word "grace" very early in life. I was taught that a person should try to be gracious and to always find a gentle way of achieving something. But many times in real life, in business, there's not a lot of grace to go around. Not all problems are graceful ones. Not all situations have gentle solutions. Sometimes you have to put your soul on the line and summon the emotional energy to just walk through a brick wall. Being tough is a necessary criterion of success.

Business is not about brains. Brains are important, but they're not the difference between winning and losing. The difference between winning and losing is having the guts to go make it happen. If that means getting angry or having people not like you or taking a few bullets in the ribs, then that's what it takes, because your job is to go make it happen.

I've learned to yell in meetings. The way I was brought up, it would not have occurred to me to yell at anybody, period. I still have a hard time getting angry. But when I do, I think to myself, "I'm just doing this to meet this person halfway." It's a concession I'm making, a change in my behavior that is an adaptation to the culture and lifestyle of the people I work with. I prefer not to yell, but

149

if that's the only way I can communicate to someone, I'll do it. It's funny that anger is what sometimes makes people comfortable. And I'm willing to make compromises in my behavior. I'm willing to make an effort.

But there are certain lines I simply will not cross. I won't be unethical. I don't intend to change my basic moral values. But if somebody wants me to yell rather than whisper—shoot, I can yell. It's not a big deal. It's harder to feel the anger, but sometimes people don't know you're serious until you get angry.

Once Jennifer shifts the scene from the boardroom to her office, her voice gets softer and her blue eyes grow bright.

The fact is that I do tend to make a stronger trade-off toward doing what's right for the individual, or for developing the people in my group, than I do for the company overall. I will continue to make that trade-off because, in the end, I think that is actually what's right for the company as well.

I don't yell at my people. We don't get angry in this department. We tend to communicate on a personal basis. I tend to concentrate more on social solutions or social relationships than on strictly business issues. To me, it's not enough for people to agree with each other. I expect people to have some level of friendship and mutual respect. My group is sort of seen as a social clique. We have parties, and we do a lot of things together after work. When we have issues to knock out, a lot of times I'll take people off-site, and we'll deal with things informally.

I don't know if my management style comes from my upbringing as a woman or from my satisfaction in having a lot of positive emotional energy bouncing around the department. I only know that I work hard and invest a lot of energy in making my group operate on a very personal level.

The women I met are overcoming the once-touted conflict between being professional and being female. Lynn, a television newscaster, now seeks recognition and no longer feels guilt about it. Jo, a trial attorney, speaks up more easily, though sometimes in court it's still hard to do. Both Lynn and Jo are feeling relieved—thankful that the deepest conflicts are past. Each is carving out a style that is feminine and competent. They are integrating two elements into a whole.

Lynn speaks first about what she's learned in television.

> I think being brought up female has influenced me a lot. Girls don't have that sports interaction that is "team play." Boys learn how to hand-off and delegate. I always used to feel that I had to do it all. I felt uncomfortable asking other people to help me out, especially secretaries. I also felt very uncomfortable at self-promotion—another thing men are much more comfortable with.
>
> To brag seemed egotistical. I felt it was unnecessary. I felt that being recognized by every professional organization in the city, and being recognized nationally as a top anchor, would win me recognition at the station. But I learned that if you don't call attention to your accomplishments, they're certainly not going to do it for you. They don't want to pay you any more than they can possibly get away with. So gradually I learned to take credit when ratings improve, when I do a good story, and when I get good press. I definitely call my achievements to the attention of my superiors now.

Jo, too, has changed both attitudes and behaviors over the years.

> I was in court one day in an adversarial position. My opposing counsel was talking and talking and talking. I remember thinking, "I should be interrupting, but nice girls don't interrupt." And then I thought, "Wait a minute!

My role at this time is not to be a nice girl—it's to get my point across, and if that means interrupting, that's what I should be doing." It was a real conflict for me at that moment. Even thinking about it later, it remained a conflict. It's taken me some time to overcome this. Even now I go into court, and I get nervous, and my heart pounds. But I'm not as intimidated by it as I used to be. I've gotten much better at interrupting and speaking up.

Equipped with skills, responsibility, and some seniority, women are developing their own forms of management and are demonstrating power in ways they can respect. The most commonly cited avenue for doing so was increased employee involvement at every level of decision-making. Whether their field is law, insurance, or manufacturing, women are consciously promoting leadership skills among people they supervise. Brenda, as ever, offers philosophy succinctly. Natalie and Louise fill in with details.

In terms of motivation and employee involvement, I'm convinced that people who get to participate in setting objectives and designing how those objectives are to be accomplished are more committed to satisfying those objectives. I know what it feels like when it's dictated to me what I'm going to do, versus where my commitment is. On the other hand, I know what it feels like when I get to participate in those decisions, and what my spirit is like in terms of striving toward satisfying those objectives I helped set. It feels damned good. Simple as that. You feel good. You feel proud. You feel more committed. You feel accountable.

Natalie has worked her way up. She now draws a six-figure salary at a construction company in the Northwest. "My life wasn't always like this," she assures me with a twinkle. Yet from the beginning, Natalie's goal was a consistent one—to increase production through making work humane.

When I was a secretary, the shop people were very nice to me, very cordial. That's probably because I was particularly employee conscious. I set up a Christmas party where I had food brought in, and we gave out turkeys. I started a company newsletter where I could tell whose birthday it was and whose wife had a baby—in-house sorts of things. I set up wage and salary guidelines so that people could all be treated more equitably.

When we moved into the shop and one women's restroom was finished better than the other, they came to me, probably because I took enough initiative to show that I cared. I remember starting an "Employee of the Month" award. At lunch, we would have a presentation ceremony. I'd stand on a chair and say, "OK, the Employee of the Month is going to be so-and-so." It was terrific. It was fun. It was a neat feeling.

I found that we always got more people motivated by having the Employee of the Month award than we did by increasing salaries. That's particularly interesting for shop people, who work on an hourly basis. But what I found was that all of a sudden, they too were interested in what their peers thought of them. And then it became more than that. It became a situation where, within their own areas, they wanted to put out the most of whatever that product was. Or they wanted to inspect the most that day.

Then it became a competition between divisions—which division was going to do the best that month, which one was going to have the most items finished. I'd been continuously told by management, "You can't do that. You won't have anybody interested. Shop people don't care about doing anything other than coming to work, getting their paychecks, and going home." But it wasn't true—they took pride in their achievements as a group.

I remember when we moved to a new area and a bowling alley opened. The staff there came in and wanted to have a party for all of our people. Management said to me, "There's no way you're ever going to get anybody to

153

come." And I said, "Well, I'd like to try, and if people do show up, I'd like to have a bowling league." Management said, "Fine, but it won't happen." Well, we had to cancel the first game because so many people wanted to go bowling that the bowling alley couldn't accommodate all of them. Then we set up a bowling league, and those people did like seeing each other outside of work—not just sitting there next to each other on the line, seeing how fast they could get something out.

Louise is realistic about the challenges women face as they try to institute participatory management. She warns that since most organizations are hierarchical, people challenging that structure will become targets of suspicion. Even though she has fiscal responsibility for her company, Louise's decisions are still scrutinized by a skeptical all-male group. She adopts what she calls "my masculine stance" when answering to executives, but returns to a more personal style when managing day-to-day.

I think men look at women using participatory management techniques and feel that women are being indecisive. What we're really doing is looking for the group's buy-in to the objectives, and ensuring that everybody gets a chance to speak their minds. Even if a decision has been made, I find that if I walk into a meeting and encourage the pros and cons to come out on the table, the input from ten people is probably going to be better than what I may have decided myself. I try to keep an open mind so that I can use my management team's input to make the right decision. A lot of authoritarian, ego-driven men (I suppose women, too, but I've only dealt with men) look at my management style as being indecisive.

From some people I hear I have a reputation for being tough, but from other people I hear the question, "Is she tough enough?" I suppose it depends on who's dealing with me. I'm known to be very direct. I insist on having a management style that I call "No Hidden Agendas." That

154

means that we get everything out on the table, and we talk about it. I look around the room in a meeting, and if I see that someone's uncomfortable with the decision we've made, I'll stop and say, "Frank, you're obviously having trouble with this. What are your concerns? What are you feeling?" My management team knows I'm going to do this, and I encourage them to do it with each other. We've been through some professional training in this, and we know how to do it in a way that is not psychologically harmful. When there's discomfort or disagreement, we stop and talk about it, get it out there. I feel it's the only way to get the really good decisions.

Some of my bosses ask, "Is she tough enough?" because I don't do it their way. They're used to forcing people into doing something before they've had a real discussion about it. That's what they consider "tough." I believe in teamwork. What I've been able to do is to learn to work as a chameleon. I've found a culture where my style is acceptable, and I've created my own niche. I've put up enough buffers so that I can use a participatory management style when I manage down, and I've developed another style for managing up. In corporate America, you have to adapt your style to fit what you're trying to do.

Staunch on Ethics

Part of the women's concern about gaining more power has to do with their dismay at the violation of ethical principles condoned in the name of business. Indeed, almost every woman I met voiced serious doubts about her employer's ethical standards and practices. Though in all other areas they had learned how to compromise, when it came to questions of ethics, these women drew the line. Here's how one woman tried to cope.

Women often have this sense of ethics, or a value structure, that gets hurt or crippled in business, because business doesn't fit into that. War doesn't fit into that. A lot of things don't fit into that. But it may be reality, too, you know. I've been doing a lot more work in the community, and that feels really good. I'm giving my time over there to take care of my values and ethics, and trying to do things here that I can at least swallow—but I don't know how far I can go and still make it palatable to work in this industry.

Unaccustomed to stating aloud what they'd been holding inside for years, women appeared nervous when discussing ethics and law. When I asked Gina about the thoughts she harbors after ten o'clock at night, she shook her head slowly and murmured, "The secret thoughts I have about what really goes on here? Honey, I can tell you right now—you don't want to know." Yet, without much further coaxing, Gina told me everything. She talked about corruption until very late that night.

Getting somewhere in this company isn't about being terrific at what I do. I can be the absolute best at whatever it is I do, and I will never go anywhere. Beyond your first assignment, moving up depends on your performance rating, your whole personnel file, and who in the company knows you.

The advantage to the special assignment I'm on now is that I interface with a lot of people on a lot of different levels. I am visible to people at higher levels, and I make sure I keep my face in front of theirs. I write memos I don't have to write. I make sure my name gets mentioned more than the next guy's. My skills are good, and my talents are right, but I also have to be sure that I come across well socially and that I make many phone calls for no reason at all.

It used to really puzzle me, why these managers were on the phone so much. I didn't understand at the time that they were doing the most important kind of business: They were playing political games. They were networking. They were the ones who knew what was going on in other companies. They knew what was going on in other stores and in other territories. If you don't make those phone calls, all you're left with is what public relations sends down. And they are the biggest liars.

After I had been in many areas and had become knowledgeable about many different systems, I would read some of the official news blurbs from our company and say, "It just isn't true." At first, I thought someone had made an error. I assumed somebody got their facts mixed up. I would mention to people, "This isn't right," or "We haven't finished this test yet," or "But look, it says this, but the date is wrong." I was simply brushed aside with, "Gina, you don't understand." And I didn't. I honestly didn't.

I was totally naive. I thought everything you read should be true. I thought everything you do should be done properly. I thought everything that occurred should be reported as it happened. I had no idea that the news had to come out a certain way so that it fit into the big picture. But it's strategically necessary to report a gain before fourth-quarter earnings. It's strategically necessary to report a positive test result before the next board meeting. When I figured that out, I felt let down. Here I was, working for this big retail chain, and it too was dirty. I had a hard time admitting to myself that I was now in the dirty world of business.

When I started out, I looked for all the clean and good things in my field to justify my being here. I decided that whatever work I did would be upright and honest. I would not make sleazy decisions. I would not uphold sloth and laziness. I would not condone cheating and lying. And then, whenever I would see the company paper, I'd see it was full of lies. For a long time I wouldn't admit to myself that the lies were there. I kept saying, "There has to be another side," or "They just didn't print the other statistics," or "Somebody didn't get all the information before it had to go to print." I would hear stories about other companies, and I'd say, "Oh, here we would never do things like that."

Everybody else was getting slapped with fines for things like price fixing or switching bait, but we weren't. The first time I saw my company get hit with an FCC fine, I was totally wiped out. I kept waiting for the "Oops, we made a mistake" to come out. But it never did. Eventually, I was disillusioned. In the beginning, to me, my company was unique in the industry. And somehow, in order to be where they were, I figured they rode in there on a big white horse. It didn't occur to me that they just sidestepped better than the others.

Unlike Gina, Emily has grown accustomed to dirty dealings in mortgage banking. While certain that she would never inflate loan estimates or "discover" a low interest rate for her home, Emily is more worried about subtle ethical compromises. To her, every play of the game is decisive; moral overtones are present each step of the way.

I would say that playing the game means giving up something. Either giving up a frown and putting a smile on your face when you don't want to, or moving out of the city that you want to live in, or traveling somewhere you don't want to go. Doing what it takes to be in favor with your boss is playing the game. If you know when you're doing it, it's one thing. I'm very clear about when I'm doing it and when I'm not doing it, so I can elect to play the game when I want to. The sad part is when you find yourself playing the game unconsciously, or you watch other people playing the game to the degree that they're out of control.

When I'm playing the game, I feel like a whore. It's compromising. As much as possible, I try not to play it. I've also positioned myself so that I'm not a direct report to the president, or in a position where I have to play the game more than I want to. I like running my own shop, not having to contend with a lot of political influence. I don't like being phony or dishonest. If I'm encouraged to do something that I don't want to do, I feel cheap and uncomfortable about it. Having to play politics is very costly, as far as I'm concerned. It goes against my beliefs as a person. So I do try to avoid doing things I don't want to do, or don't believe in, as much as possible.

Over and over, women returned to the subject of psychological abuse. They told me they were shocked to find that in their organizations yelling was tolerated, criticism was expected, and painful humiliations were part of the game. They shuddered as they watched adults take abuse silently, accepting the unreasonable behavior of people higher up. The women were incredulous when they witnessed verbal tirades, but worried about what would happen if they dared to interfere. Many confessed that afterward they agonized. Remaining passive in the presence of torture was a violation of ethics that most could not endure.

Not surprisingly, the women ranked more humane treatment of coworkers as their primary ethical goal. The following incidents represent hundreds. Each describes individuals enduring injustices, yet feeling economically powerless to resist by speaking up. As Janet, Mandy, and Maureen relay their stories, I notice the same look of anguish on every face.

Usually buoyant and enthusiastic, tonight Janet is subdued. She grimaces as she recounts recent history, remembering how her company treated its employees when they were most in need.

I didn't like the way the layoffs were handled here. I felt it was almost immoral. At the time I reported to a vice president whom I liked. I thought he was a good leader and a good man. But he was a politician.

Two fellows who were my peers also reported to him. They'd been stroking him for months. They would go out and have a drink together and play golf together. When push came to shove, their two departments remained intact but mine did not, even though mine was the only one of the three functions that was producing bottom-line impact for the company. But those departments were like old-boy fraternities. They included some senior people who had been asked to leave other functions—to some degree, they were big elephant graveyards. But when the layoffs happened, those two departments were left completely untouched. It was totally obvious to me why that happened.

And that's when it hit me that politics are powerful—very, very powerful. At that point, I knew I was going to have to decide whether I was going to play the game. If I wasn't going to play it, how was I going to survive? That was the number-one question in my mind at the time.

The immoral part was the way the layoffs were handled. I saw fifteen-year veterans of the company, hard-working veterans, being told at 8:30 in the morning that this was their last day. Security guards stood there while long-term employees packed up their things. Within a half-hour, they were quietly escorted to the door.

What I'm arguing is that you just don't treat people that way. The jockeying that must have gone on two weeks prior to the layoffs—the jockeying for keeping people and positions—is not based on a value structure that I can relate to. You know it's all about who knows what about whom, who's sleeping with whom, and who's a favorite son. I felt so sorry for those people who were laid off with no notice, no discussion, no nothing. I watched as they packed up their belongings, and my heart went out to them.

Mandy gets up from her couch and paces about the living room. Her voice and gestures show agitation and despair. As she finishes her story, Mandy sits down slowly and thinks for a time in silence. She then adds a final image. It captures the moment well.

One time I was asked to hire a secretary. We had some-body working for us then on a temporary basis, and she was very good—efficient and accurate. I also felt she had developed a lot of loyalty to me. So I said to my boss, "I want to hire this woman." But the word I got was that she was unacceptable because she was an ethnic minority, and her ethnic identity was obvious on the telephone. It was incredible—my boss, who is of that same ethnic minority, said we shouldn't hire her because he didn't like the way she sounded on the phone.

My first impulse, considering my experience in public relations, was to call the *New York Times* and tell them what was going on here. But then I thought, "I might as well jump out the window. I might as well commit profes-sional suicide." Because not only would I be killing my-self in my own company, but who in the world would ever hire me again? It would be all over the *Times*, and my company would accuse me of slander.

Being put in this position really upset me. If I'd been with a small company I would have marched right in to my boss and said, "What in the heck are you doing? And who do you think you are? And if I want to hire this person, you give me a good reason why I shouldn't."

I was really upset because I'm used to standing up for my own principles, but I feel powerless to do that in a big corporation. Here I feel totally expendable. I feel like a penny that you drop into a river, and then watch how fast all the ripples disappear.

Many women expressed empathy for men who also report to abusive individuals. They know that men too put up with the tirades of leaders who have never matured. When Maureen was promoted into senior management, she expected a forum that was civilized and sedate. The interactions she observes now have changed her views entirely. She understands much more about egos and the game.

A certain vice president at my company was just made chief operating officer, and he's supposed to be made president next year. I'm worried about this because I feel the values that are held at the top are the values that trickle down throughout an organization. Our current president has a healthy outlook, but this guy who is coming up doesn't.

With management changes, people go in and out of favor. For women, I don't think that has to do with general values as much as with attitudes toward the male-female issue. For a woman, it depends very much on how that person at the top feels about women being in positions of power. For the men, there are other factors involved. Of course, somebody who's a golden boy under one management structure isn't necessarily going to be a golden boy under the next.

Some of the men feel they're between a rock and a hard place. I see some of them in high-level positions acting completely subservient to the man on top in order to maintain their positions. And the people who work for these high-level guys get the brunt of that. You know, the rest of us have the idea that people at high levels are some kind of superhuman beings. I tell you, when I see them cower and watch the subservient kinds of things they have to do, I can see why they all get ulcers and have heart attacks.

When I first started noticing what was going on with these men, I thought, "Gee, the glow is off of this whole business thing." Then, as I saw more and more of it, I said, "This is why men act this way." No one seems to know what they go through day in and day out. No one knows that they have these degrading things going on all the time. And these guys don't have any choice, especially after they get up in years. I suspect, as a result, some of them have totally lost confidence in themselves. I also know that I don't see it at its worst, because when I'm there observing it, they're very aware of my being there.

162

But I've seen enough to imagine how much more of it goes on behind closed doors.

The personalities of the people in power take the mystique out of business for me. I've learned that it isn't some sophisticated system, it isn't run by the books—it's based on somebody's personality or values or leadership style. So many petty things go on. And I see so many men directing their energy toward saving their positions—covering ass or just saving face. I've realized that business is not only frustrating for women—it's frustrating for men too.

In addition to questioning abuse, women are also looking at other kinds of dishonesty in the professions. Whether deceit takes the form of cheating on expense accounts, forging government documents, or lying to customers, sometimes it too is rationalized as a political need. The women I met had assumed that high business standards would be the norm. When they met all the exceptions, some went into shock. Lynn told how one manager's blatant use of lying hurt her psychologically and curtailed her career.

Recently I made the decision to start a family and stay put for a while. Right after I made that decision, I signed a long-term contract. And right after that, I was, in effect, demoted. I feel trapped. There is nothing I can do. Three months pregnant, I can't pick up and move to a new job. So right now, I'm trying to weather that storm.

There is an important lesson in this for me. I've learned that in business, I will never again believe what I'm told. From now on I want everything in writing, because on this contract my manager had given me his word. He had looked me right in the eye and said, "I give you my word I will do this." But as soon as he could, he changed the terms of the contract completely. When I asked him about it, he threw up his hands and basically said, "So? I lied."

I had expected fairness, honesty, and integrity. When I was growing up, I knew that everything wasn't going to be completely fair and that some people would be difficult to deal with. But I never expected that someone would look me in the eye and lie.

I still have to live by my own code of ethics, and I refuse to compromise myself. I will not be dishonest. I will not get down in the mud with them. I have allowed myself to be dragged down in the mud on several occasions, and I've never liked it. I don't like fighting dirty. I don't feel good about those kinds of victories.

Andrea discovered powerful group dynamics that tolerate cheating but punish the deviant who dares protest the norm. Out on the road, among fellow sales reps, Andrea found that pressures to conform were especially strong.

I don't talk about this incident a lot because I used to think people hearing it would assume I was a bit of a prude, a Miss Goody Two-Shoes. Now I don't care. I simply don't believe in being dishonest. I think it's wrong, and I think in the long run you're the one who cuts your throat. There's a core deep inside me that says, "No matter what, don't do anything dishonest."

Once a bunch of us went out to lunch, and all the other reps said, "Andrea, you've got an expense account. Let's put lunch on your expense account." I said, "No," and they said, "Why? They'll never know." And I said, "Maybe, but I'll know."

So I stood by my guns, and I got razzed. I felt like a little girl standing up for a friend that everybody's picking on. It was hard. For the first time you're really testing your moral fiber.

But of all the deception they encountered, none was more upsetting to the women than the question of adultery. Many said that the most painful realization about working in corporate

America was that certain company cultures implicitly condone cheating on wives. Ann explains that from her strategically located cubicle she hears men planning visits to their mistresses, all on company business trips, all cleverly disguised.

> The issue of ethics in business is a very sensitive area for me. Some of the things I've seen executives do go very much against my personal standards. What I've learned to do is to operate independent of them, to not let the dishonesty I see pull too much at my heart strings.
>
> There's a double standard in my company. In special services, I'd say 75 percent of the vice presidents "played" —they stepped out on their wives. They had regular gals in regular cities, and they traveled to those cities on company money. They used their corporate expense accounts to make sure their social lives with these women were taken care of. They all knew this was going on, but they covered for each other. That's just what they do.

Tips From the Trenches

Live Your Values

When I asked the women to share political advice, they spoke fervently. Most agreed that gaining power requires direction, planning, and a sophisticated knowledge of people. In spelling out their strategies, women stressed the need for reassessing goals and keeping one's values foremost in mind. The answer, they emphasized, does not lie in denying the game's existence. The challenge is to play while preserving self-respect.

The women recommend that newcomers begin by carefully studying the power status quo. Here the goal is not to mimic decision makers but rather to identify subtle corporate norms. In time a woman can discover how and when behaviors get rewarded. The idea is for her to use this data strategically, to compare cultural expectations with her own professional goals and standards.

Susan explains how she surveyed the power parameters of aerospace. She decoded a set of quasi-military customs, grasped the corporate culture, and formulated her plan.

> You get ahead in the job world by understanding the system and making it work for you. I really believe that. Just watching people has been very important to me. I watch who's in charge, who makes the decisions, and who gets people to listen to them. I internalize what I see working. I take pieces of successful people, and then establish my own reputation.
>
> Women must develop the techniques men have used so effectively—how to play the game, how to understand office politics, how to cultivate the right people. These are things men have learned how to do, but women haven't. We women have learned in our upbringing how to manipulate, how to be seductive, how to be cute, how to be helpless. As adults, we have to unlearn these things. As for me, I'm constantly feeling in conflict with the way I was raised, because I'm trying to be something that I wasn't ever taught to be. But gradually, as I observe, I'm learning.

Susan's ideas sounded good in the abstract, but I found myself wondering, "How did you get there? What did you do?" When I pressed Susan further, she revealed the specifics—and was delighted to find she had systematic techniques.

> I started out by asking naive questions or saying things like, "Gee, I worked on this project, and I'd really like to see what happens with it," or "I'd love to see how so-and-so runs a meeting. I'd just like to sit in the back and see how decisions are made," or "I'd like to hear the discussion that goes on about this paper I wrote," or "I'm really curious—when the budget was reviewed, how come this number was chosen, and that one wasn't?" or "Tell me, how did you evaluate this?"

People love to tell you how they make decisions and what their thought processes are. So I asked, and eventually I was invited to meetings. They'd say, "This one might be about something you're interested in. Why don't you come?" So I went a few times, and I sat in the back and observed, and slowly I learned who the players are and who's making the decisions, who listens to whom, who's prepared and who isn't. Then I found out which ones seemed to be in control, and I got to know them. That's how I created a need for myself.

Another reason to study the dominant culture is to recognize subtle invitations. Several women noted that they had missed key opportunities simply because they hadn't understood how the offers were conveyed. Mary Ann recommends being able to move on suggestions quickly. She counsels women to be alert for added responsibility at any given time.

I'm persuaded now that you can't stay in any position for a long period. Positions don't stand still. Jobs don't stand still. They change. Women need to understand that.

For one thing, reporting relationships change. Also, interest in a particular operation or in a particular way of doing things can change, and the people in particular operations can change. We women need to be realistic about the fact that ongoing changes are sure to be there. We need to think constantly about what we're going to do next.

I was walking down the hallway recently with a senior vice president who is now an executive vice president, and I barely knew who he was. I should have known a heck of a lot more about him. At the time, I didn't realize that he was a very bright guy and is probably going to be the next CEO. Anyway, we were walking down the hall and he said to me, "If you ever feel unhappy with what you're doing, give me a call." Now that's when the door opened. I should have walked through it that very afternoon. At the time, I was in the midst of some things I was committed to finishing up, so I didn't call. A person who had a clearer sense of how upward mobility works would have called him immediately and said, "What did you have in mind? Yes, I'm interested."

A number of women warned against relying too heavily on a male mentor when trying to learn the political ropes. Mentors, they noted, can be invaluable for fostering skills and mastering content, but often they don't understand the special political challenges that professional women face. Courtney solved the problem by emulating just a few of her mentor's talents. Jane, in contrast, feels that none of men's strategies can really work for her. What Jane has found more helpful is sharing political know-how with women. With typical midwest pragmatism, Courtney leads off.

If you ask, "How do you get from here to there?" my answer is that there's competence and there's hard work, but most of it is pure street fighting skills. And I can tell you one thing for sure: I didn't learn street fighting skills in my MBA course work. Street fighting skills are things you learn from mentors, from being savvy, from watching people who are successful and modeling your behavior after theirs, from trial and error. That really can't be taught, but what can be taught are specific lessons: "Watch out for this," "Here's how to get ahead here," "There are the land mines; look out over there."

Business isn't academic. I spend a lot of time and energy teaching other women about the "streets" of business. I tell them, "If you find a winner, latch onto him and learn everything you can from him. But figure out what it is about him that makes him a winner, because he's still going to have bad points. So copy only the good ones, and let the bad ones go." Early on, I made the mistake of copying everything I saw, until I found out that some things are good, some are bad, and some I could already do better myself. So then I learned to dump the bad and go on.

168

You have to ask a lot of questions in business. You've got to be tuned in to nonverbal signals. People will tell you exactly what they think if you just watch them closely and evaluate how they in turn respond to you. Above all, you've got to empathize and listen.

As partner in a management consulting firm, Jane is often the only woman meeting with top-level clients. The triple-layer dynamics of gender, power, and consulting combine to make Jane's task tricky at best.

Certainly, if a woman can find a mentor, that's a help. But one of the difficulties with mentors is that they don't always understand the rules of business for women. I was on a seminar panel for women in business last February, and the audience was mostly female. The only two people from my company who attended were my chairman and a male staff member I had recruited. It was funny because these two men were the only two people in the room that I was nervous about. In fact, I was terrified. I wasn't used to dealing with them on women's issues; I was used to dealing with them as a manager. And while most of the women on the panel gave their personal stories, I tried to present lessons that would be useful to other women.

My comments were addressed to women who are climbing the ladder, and also to male managers of women. When we got back to the office, the chairman said he was so impressed with my speech that he wanted to send a copy of it to all of the employees in the company. I said to him, "I'm not really comfortable doing that." Partly, I was reluctant to send out some of the personal comments I had made, and partly I didn't want to be put in the spotlight as the spokesperson for women at my company. His response was, "There aren't any politics here."

He then proceeded to send my speech out, with a memo emphasizing the company's commitment to equal employment opportunity. It made me sick to my stomach to realize I'd been betrayed—that I'd been used by the person who said we don't have any politics here.

The conclusion I reached from this was that neither of these men is aware of the kind of politics women deal with in this firm. Men simply aren't aware of the subtle little rules. That's because they live and breathe them every day. Women have to do more networking with women who have experienced those rules, so that together we can figure out what the hell is going on. I'm trying to provide coaching for the women coming in here—help that I didn't receive because I was the first one.

I'm suggesting that we women figure out for ourselves how the politics work. From a networking point of view, I think we have to be independent of men, because the coaching we get from them may be inaccurate for us.

The women I met with agreed that to be politically effective, every professional must strive to develop both formal and informal ties. At first, Nancy despaired when she couldn't join in on discussions of boats, hunting, and cars. But when she finally admitted that she didn't like the topics, she set about devising other ways to get herself known. Now visible and active on task forces and committees, Nancy is convinced that informal contacts have made her career.

What do I recommend? I recommend not ever missing an all-management meeting. Even if you're out of town, try to arrange your schedule so that you can get back for it. You never know who will see you at that meeting, and it may make a difference. People sit in those meetings and say, "Hmm, who's here? Who has power? Who doesn't?"

Another thing I recommend is, no matter how boring or how trite they are, don't miss the cocktail parties. They are old and tiring, but if you can, at least make an appearance at them. Let the host and hostess, or whatever department is sponsoring the party, know that you appreciate the invitation.

Also, when promotions go through in my company, and new executives are announced or career moves are made, we get an executive memorandum on that person. Then I usually write a note congratulating him or her. Maybe I only did a seminar with them once or twice, but if I know them at all, I congratulate them. I got notes from a couple of officers after my first promotion, and you can believe I remember who they are. So I do a lot of little things like that.

I'm also not afraid to speak up or make suggestions for business strategies or directions. I may suggest a new program or seminar, or recommend a twist to something we're already doing that might make it a little bit different or a little bit better. I'm careful about the way I propose things, but I plant my seeds at cocktail parties or before and after meetings. I might say, "We did this last week, and you might be interested in having one of your people check it out and see what you think." A lot of it is so informal.

What's funny is that people in this department think I just love doing that kind of stuff. It looks as though it comes naturally to me, but it really doesn't. I get just as many butterflies in my stomach, and my insides tie up in knots, when I know I have to get up the nerve to go over to someone and say something. But I just focus on what I want to talk about, and go say it.

Every individual I met urged other women to take concrete steps against losing their identity and getting overwhelmed in a power-hungry environment. Moving up is one thing, they contend, but sacrificing deep-rooted values can never be worth it. Over and over women spoke of the need to maintain perspective. Doing so may take the form of drawing clear lines on which games one won't play, or leaving an organization when work goes unnoticed. Janet said she learned her lesson the hard way, but looking back now, she's glad she did.

One lesson is to separate formal from informal politics. There is a formal reporting mechanism, a formal organizational structure, a formal organization chart. But there's also the informal structure, and believe me, the informal structure runs everything. That was a valuable lesson for me.

Also, after many years, I learned not to put my whole heart and soul into a company, because it's simply not reciprocated. Companies really don't give a damn about the individual. That was the hardest lesson for me to learn, because I'm a total commitment person. When I commit to something, I expect that whatever I'm committed to will have the same level of commitment coming back to me. But I found out that in corporate America, the commitment is not bidirectional—it's only unidirectional. Therefore you must guard yourself, and especially your heart, against getting on any bandwagon. I tell myself that they can have my brain—they purchased my brain—but never, ever can they have my soul.

Jane used to go to bat for all she believed in. Undiscerning but energetic, she'd argue hard on a variety of fronts. When most of her arguments weren't taken seriously, she backed off to study the scene. She analyzed the politics and mapped out a strategy. After two long years of frustration and embarrassment, Jane found that choosing her battles was the way to succeed.

I've become harder and tougher and I've learned to hold my ground. I've also learned that I can get away with holding my ground, because in the end they need me more than I need them. That's been a critical lesson for me. I finally know my value.

As a result, I've gotten to decide when to be hard and when to be soft. And that it's my right to decide. Nobody can tell me that the principles I decide to fight for are inappropriate, so I have to be very careful to pick and choose my issues. That's why, when I look at what people do here, I may say, "OK, that's not part of my agenda.

That's not one of my fighting points." But when something worth fighting for does come along and I say, "Over my dead body. . . ." I really mean it, and they know it. I have learned to pick my issues and to articulate my bottom line, and management has learned to believe me.

These are the things I consider when I pick my battles: (1) Will it have financial impact? (2) Will it impact my ability to attract or retain staff? and (3) Will it affect my credibility to run an organization? I am always concerned about things that may undermine a position I've taken with my staff, and certainly with things that I don't agree with philosophically.

Some women believe that the real way to win is to sidestep the politicking and refuse to get involved. Sarah, in publishing, and Heidi, in a savings and loan, agree that in their industries the real superstars are those who avoid petty politics. Keeping their perspective while others clamor for turf, those with talent and real leadership focus on the work. From her publishing office, Sarah speaks first.

The people who have real power are the people who haven't played the game. I think the people who have succeeded are the ones who haven't done what we're all supposed to do: They have not accepted the status quo, they have not waited their turn, they have not paid attention to the current wisdom, whatever that is. They have not played the game. They have said, "I know this is the way we've always done it, but now let's do it this way." They're not the "why" people. I think it's really quite the opposite from the ways it's usually discussed. I think people who say you have to play the game are just giving you part of the standard line that involves self-justification for not doing what they want to do.

While Sarah is worldly, Heidi is more down-home. With nearly the same message, she abandons formal logic and tells a fable all her own.

Once upon a time, the CEO of a company became tired of all the people who kept coming to see him. So he fired off a memo to the head of personnel and said, "Hire me an aggressive young male to screen these appointments so that I'll have more time to do my own work." The personnel guy came up and said to the CEO: "I appreciate your employment need, but you have 'young' and 'male' written down here, and it's illegal to use those words in a requisition. Besides, this is a perfect opportunity for us to get a female in at this level. Do you have a problem with that?" The CEO said, "I don't care who you get, just get me some people to interview. I've got to stop having all these interruptions."

So the personnel guy set up interviews with three women. The first woman came in, and the CEO chatted with her for a long time. Finally he said, "Imagine this situation. You are on a jet airplane. The plane crashes in the middle of the ocean. You wind up on a deserted island, just seventeen men and yourself. How are you going to handle this situation?" She said, "Well, I would have to hope there would be a high cliff, because I don't know how I would handle it. I'd have to jump." The CEO ushered her out.

The next woman came in, and he set the same scenario. She said, "Well, I would align myself with the dominant male, and I'd be supportive of him, and I'd know I would be well taken care of." The CEO liked that response. He thought, "This is my team member."

But since the third woman was still sitting out there, he figured he had to interview her. She came in, and he went through the motions. They chatted for a while, then he set up the scenario. "You end up on an island with seventeen men and yourself. How are you going to handle this situation?" The third woman sat there and looked a bit puzzled. So he said, "Do you understand?" She replied, "I think I understand what you said, but what's the problem?"

Now, I tell that story because women need to realize, and feel, that they're equal; they need to learn to play the game, yet never take it too seriously. It's only a vocabulary game, after all. It's really only a dress-up game. Until you realize that, you're going to fight an uphill battle, and you're probably going to have a heart attack by the time you're forty. Playing a game is never worth that.

I asked the women how it feels to sense their own power. Faces lit up suddenly. Cigarettes were snuffed out. The women welcomed the chance to bask in their accomplishments, to recount achievements that once had been dreams. They talked with gratitude about how their careers had increased their confidence, creativity, and self-esteem.

When I arrive at Flo's house in Beverly Hills, she's on the phone, arguing with a *Wall Street Journal* reporter. She hangs up, shrugs, and explains that the press is upset about a controversial piece on the television series she produces. Throughout our discussion, Flo monitors press calls, directs her staff, oversees her daughter's homework, and somehow manages to keep my teacup full. I am amazed at her energy, and ask how she does it.

Flo stops moving. She looks at me—for the first time, really—and remarks that no interviewer ever inquires about her; they mostly are concerned with the ratings of her show. Startled but curious, she begins to reveal herself. Instead of Flo, the glamorous Hollywood producer, I meet a complex artist, an inspiring individual the media rarely see.

I have the need to live on the edge. I don't like it when it's all orderly—I like the unpredictability of things, I like the game. I like fencing with men. I like finding ways to negotiate with them, and I do, in order to get where I need to go. I think at some point men do know I'm a strong negotiator. I'm not a screamer, but I'm very forceful and direct. And I'm very outspoken—now. Much more than I was before. I think it took years until I could negotiate the way I do now. Back then I was much more adaptive, always trying to please, trying to figure out what the other person wanted. I still need to figure out what the other person wants. But now I figure out what I want too, and I do everything I can to get it.

Like Flo, most women spoke about power by comparing the present to the past. Tracing their histories, they noted gradual yet cumulative growth. Because many had been raised to be passive and dependent, when they assumed more control at work, they were awed at their own latent strength. Janet saw that as she began to develop internally, her relationships with colleagues shifted in response.

> I discovered, as I went along in my management career here, that I was beginning to make people do what I wanted them to do. That's not something I had ever thought I should be doing—to manipulate other people or make them do anything. I could comment, very critically, on what they were doing. That was OK. I could analyze what they were doing; I could point out ways that would be better—these were OK, too. But I could never go out there and push them around, in essence, whether it was verbally, in a nice way, or in a business memo, or whatever.
>
> But I suppose for me that was an important moment, when I realized I had shifted from passive-analytical-critical to active-managerial-powerful. You can take either set of those things and make it negative or positive. My business experience has given me the opportunity to learn about the positive side of being an active person.

At a New York deli, Carolyn remembers a recent lunch at which she and three friends proclaimed their collective joy. Before that time, Carolyn had been caught amid divisional power plays that kept her from getting the position she wanted. As a neophyte to office politics, she had been confused and hurt throughout the episode. A full year passed before she could view it objectively, understand the dynamics, and appreciate how she had grown.

When I was trying to land the job I have now, it was very difficult—incredibly hard. But the fact that my friend Mary was having as much trouble as I was helped. It was the realization that we could sit down together and say, "OK, they're not just doing this to me. They're also doing it to you. And we know they're doing it to Nancy and Jill and so many others." It's very helpful to be able to say, "It's not just me, it's everyone."

When things finally got squared away and we all had wonderful jobs, four of us were sitting around at lunch one day. I said I'd just closed the such-and-such deal, and I did this, and I did that, and wasn't that great? And then Mary said, "You know, we have a situation like that in my company, and I was talking to so-and-so and here's what we did about it." All of a sudden we sat back and looked at each other and said, "My God! We like our jobs!" That was finally the up-side we deserved. That day we told everybody back at the office, "You know what we decided at lunch? We decided we like our jobs!" That was a wonderful day. We were really happy.

Of all the women interviewed, Louise best described the highs and lows of executive life. Having focused on the struggles for most of our talk, Louise looks surprised when I ask about her own power. Unaccustomed to answering personal questions, at first she seems thrown, reluctant to respond. Gradually, as she recounts how she built up a company, her eyes start to sparkle and her face is alight with pride.

I'm proud of what's happening in this company now. I'm proud of the people, and I'm proud that they feel the way they do about coming to work. People love it here, and that's my job—to make sure they continue to love it here. When I see the product in the stores, it looks great and it's selling well. I have a tremendous sense of pride that I've been the guiding light of that.

No longer naive, professional women throughout America are coming to grips with power in their own unique ways. They have survived culture shock and disillusionment. They have gone through a painful, eye-opening process of confronting insecurity and greed. Repeatedly they have been forced to clarify their values and ethical precepts. They have had to spell out what they stand for and just how hard they'll fight.

Jane, like most, believes that despite the struggles of transition, the workplace will improve as a result of the values and talents that women continue to bring. Her words of advice echo those of countless others whose stamina and enthusiasm have triumphed.

> Ultimately, a male-dominated environment is a great place for a woman to be. It's definitely worth it. The real message from me is to know yourself. Every woman needs a very hard, realistic assessment of what she brings to the party. She needs to know honestly and truly how good she is and where her weaknesses are, so that she isn't blindsided, surprised, or put in a position to do something she's not yet ready for. She needs to learn the networks, the rules of the game, and how to play the game without giving up her values.
>
> If the game contradicts her values, she's got to ask herself whether it's worth playing. So far, I've never had to compromise my personal values. I think once you do that, you don't have much of anything left. I may sound naive or like a prima donna, but I don't want to be part of an organization that forces me to give up my values. It's my hope that women can get ahead without fundamentally compromising. Maybe the world could use some female influence where value structures are concerned.

6
Hitting the Cement Ceiling

No Room at the Top

The difficult lesson for women professionals is that the work world ensures no happy endings, no final guarantees. If the story of this book were filmed as a fairy tale, it would be at this point that the cameras would move in, the music would swell, and all across America women in blue suits and with briefcases would move triumphantly into boardrooms. The story would be complete. The scene would fade, and the audience would smile.

But fairy tales are fantasy, after all. In the real world, something radically different is happening. There, women find that they are not living happily ever after in their companies. Most do not move steadily forward beyond a certain point. They do not have access to executive offices or to boardroom retreats.

These women feel they have hit a cement ceiling. They've topped out. Whether in midmanagement, in staff jobs at professional firms, or in nonmanagement positions, they find themselves stuck on plateaus with nowhere to go. Nowhere, that is, but out.

In record numbers, some of America's most talented women are now leaving mainstream institutions to create institutions of their own. As seen in the previous chapter, one reason for this trend is their collective disdain for a world dominated by power, ego, and competition. An equally compelling reason is their sense that access to the top is virtually cut off. Armed with skill, talent, and ambition, this group of women is saying goodbye to organizations that have denied them opportunities for leadership. The women have concluded that making it into senior management depends more on whom you know and how you'll fit in than on actual ability and what you can do.

For the majority of working women, there are few options. Not all can financially afford to leave their companies when they feel they've reached a dead end. Nor do all want to strike out on their own. To them, hitting the cement ceiling has become a looming psychological threat.

In this chapter, women tell the story of the culmination of their careers. They describe what it feels like to look ahead and see doors closing—doors that appeared to be open just a short while ago. They talk about the pain of having their accomplishments overlooked, of feeling underutilized as others move on by. Their images and anecdotes document a waste of brain power, a precious national resource that is still relatively untapped.

Despite this reality, the women tell a parallel story, one of determination, guts, and energy. It is a tale of perseverance, of a willingness to fight. Surprising even themselves, women today remain doggedly hopeful. With that hope, and with a sense of realism gained from experience, many see themselves as entering a totally new phase. These women predict that during the nineties, other women like them will continue to raise hard questions about leadership and power. If there's even one crack in the famed cement ceiling, this is a group that will somehow inch through.

Topping Out

American women appear to have made it into all realms of business. The casual visitor walking through major corporations sees them everywhere. They hold jobs in all functional areas, from manufacturing to finance, from R&D to sales. Women seem to have made it firmly into the professions, too. They hold good jobs and earn decent salaries. Judging from the surface, the visitor might conclude that equality has been achieved, that women in the United States have become fully integrated into the system.

But for most, things don't work that way—at least not yet. In interviews across America, women with responsible jobs and top credentials reported that they still do not hold a place in the informal circles where real decisions are made. They still cannot bank on promotions without anticipating long, bitter delays. Most have little access to policy and strategy, and many assume they will never have more. Their sentiments are summed up by Dorothy, an expert in finance and a remarkable survivor.

> My advancement has taken a very great effort on my part, much more effort than I should have had to expend. It's painful to think back and realize that I had to stage brinkmanship-type one-woman wars. I was always taking extra courses, and I've always had excellent reviews. There was no reason for me to have gone through the kinds of emotional challenges I did, and I don't like remembering those things. It's hard to think that simply because you're female, a corporation won't accept you, or develop you, or recognize your talents. It was very painful for me to realize that, though I think it was always true. It's as if I wanted to pretend that the world was never like that.
>
> And now I have a desire to rest for a while. It was a difficult struggle, and I'm not willing to deny that it existed. I'd go out there in a minute and start fighting all over again, if that's what it took. But it's so exhausting.

When I asked the women why there are so few females at the top, I got two very different responses. One group said simply, "It's just a matter of time." Noting that most men don't advance into senior positions for twenty years or more, they argued that it's unrealistic to expect women to be there by now. The under-

181

lying assumption here is that with time, energy, and demonstrated skill, men and women will eventually have access to the same leadership positions. Meritocracy will triumph.

Others are not quite so sure. The second group, the majority, believes that the dynamics involved in women's moving ahead have turned out to be far more subtle and complex than anyone first imagined. To them, the solution is not simply time. It involves slowly changing entrenched traditional views of women that still permeate male-run organizations, however subtly they may be manifest. The highest-ranking women I interviewed believed this most emphatically.

Maureen is definitely one who feels this way. Having served on two senior management teams, she's convinced that women are up against a seemingly intractable all-male culture. "It's not that senior men are adamant about keeping us out," she explains matter-of-factly. "It's just that most would never consider bringing any of us in."

> I'll tell you, some of those men at the top deserve the money they make—not because they're running a company so wonderfully, but because as individuals they are surviving. The closer to the top you get, the more pressure there is and the more vulnerable you are.
>
> I don't think they're threatened economically by me. I mean, who am I? I'm making $50K a year, and that's nothing to them. I don't think it's the economic side. I think it's the tradition. It's the values that say women can't be equal to men or smart enough to do the things that men are doing. Men at the top say, "Women can't do the things we do. We all know that."

What makes the issue so problematic is that there is no clearcut sense of right and wrong; there are no heroes to cheer or villains to blame. Instead, what's at stake here are deeply held convictions about reality, about people, and about the way life should be. Women recognize this complexity, and as a result, feel an uneasy mixture of frustration and restraint. They understand that older executives were raised with traditional values, that they have wives who have never worked outside the home, and that many still feel awkward doing business with a "lady." Unfortunately, the women's insights help only temporarily. They do little to diminish the anger and impatience that have been building for years. Most important, insight unaccompanied by action does not take away the obstacles talented women face.

Hitting the cement ceiling may be hardest on those who have been encouraged to be leaders. For a large number of women I met in my travels, this was clearly the case. Recruited from graduate school to become "the" female MBA or "the" female architect, they entered organizations and at first moved quickly. They were the superstars, the ones destined to get ahead. For a time, being female was a definite advantage.

Diane's career fits this pattern. A superior student, she joined her company right out of school. She excelled in an in-house training program, landed opportune assignments, and soon caught the attention of a fast-track rising star. For ten years her mentor made sure that all doors were open. Diane was excited and grateful; for years, she loved her job. But recently, as the payoffs for loyalty have subsided, Diane has adopted a different point of view.

> There are only short-term advantages to being a female in business. A woman can sometimes get away with certain things that a man can't. A woman can use appeals that men can't, but it's a real catch-22. The appeal will get you what you want in the short term. You can be less hardheaded, and you can advocate the interest of the people who work for you in a very personal way. I think that for a while women can get away with being a lot less formal with senior men than the other men can. In the short term, that all pays off. In the long term, however, it doesn't, because those are the very same things that keep you from getting appointed to a senior position.
>
> When someone is being considered for top management at this company, they look at a lot of things other than competence and performance. They look at style

issues, and deportment, and whom that individual knows in the community. Having a female style doesn't get you into senior management. If you happen to know a lot of professional women in the community, that doesn't get you very far either, because women are still not the movers and shakers. In the short term, being a woman pays off; in the long term, it certainly doesn't.

Men in power communicate their ambivalence in a variety of ways. Women are sensitive to the hints and are on the lookout for subtle clues. When they realize that the same messages aren't being conveyed to male peers, they grow suspicious. They start to put the pieces together and to make connections between messages conveyed over time. When a woman finally recognizes that her options are limited, sometimes she feels relieved just to be rid of the ambiguity. More often, when reality hits, she feels discouraged and lost.

Sandy, Tina, Heidi, and Marilyn all received a similar message, but heard it in different ways. In Sandy's case, the word was communicated through a puzzling set of interviews. Having moved up steadily through the management ranks, she found that Big Oil had a new set of standards awaiting her at the top.

I've often been astonished at how much more deeply women are critiqued than men. I'm a perfect example. To be permitted into the controllership position of an operation that generated less than a million dollars of revenue, I had to be interviewed by a regional vice president who oversees $75 million of revenue. That's absurd. That's a waste of management time. But it's done all the time, and it goes further than that. What will happen is that the interviewing process will be much more in-depth for women, because the senior men are afraid of making a decision that will give them so much exposure. They're afraid of taking a woman that they really like, who has a good track record, and putting her in a high-risk situation

> where the odds are that she will fail. It gets really scary for everyone. The higher up you go, the more subjective the interviewing process gets. It's no longer who worked X-hours on X-projects and has X-qualifications. It's become totally subjective.

A sense of personal comfort often dictates those subjective evaluations. Tina notices that the senior men in her company have become good friends. When they invite someone new to join in a golf game, within weeks he's promoted onto the team. To Tina, that putting green has become a powerful symbol of all-male solidarity holding firm at the top.

> I think the higher up you are, the more important it is to be in tune with that informal network, because that's where most of the real decisions are made. I don't think decisions at the very highest levels are made in meetings. I've attended enough of them to know that decisions were made beforehand, informally—the meeting is just a formality. At my level, this isn't important yet. But as you go higher, it gets increasingly critical. I think women are going to have to find a way of getting into that informal network, because now it acts as one big barrier.

A second way women notice they have plateaued is when they find themselves isolated in either a literal or figurative sense. Many claimed that as they rose in status, they were quietly frozen out of meetings, physically separated from peers, or given tedious assignments that required virtual hibernation. It seemed to them that they'd been cut off from real power as soon as it was within their grasp. Heidi believes that rank per se is not the issue. As a senior vice president, she's still kept far away.

> My relationships with senior management are generally pretty good. But there are problems with my salary and my office location. My salary is well below the salaries of

the men at my level—that's a known fact. In addition, each of the other senior vice presidents in the company has an office in corporate headquarters. But not I. That is really a disadvantage, because the men have impromptu meetings all the time, and here I am, stuck at a different location. I asked my boss, "Is there any chance I could have an office here? I'm having trouble functioning the way things are, with me at another location." His response was, "Heidi, you're a woman." He didn't mean it negatively—he and I are good friends—but the message is that the boys want to keep me out of the club. That completely undermines my role in the company.

Often I find out that the guys were sitting around over coffee, and made this or that decision—decisions that will have a direct impact on my department. But no one from my department was there to represent us or to have an effect on the decision.

It's hard to play the game when you aren't on the same field. I feel cut off at the knees. I'll go to a meeting and find out that someone is planning something that is under my jurisdiction, but they forgot to include me because my office isn't over there. Being left out has had more negative impact on my work than anything else.

When I talk with my fellow senior vice presidents, my peers, I can feel the male club arching its back. There was one guy who really wanted to learn my job. He wanted more say on my turf, he thought he could do my job better than I, and I didn't have the support at my peer level to maintain my ground. By my not being located in the same building, he actually got to do a lot more.

In the end, it's just a matter of egos. If any of the others had come to my defense, they would have been booted out of the club for violating club rules. The basic feeling of the group is, "We're not going to let her have an office here." So if someone says, "I think she should have an office here," he's suddenly put himself outside the circle.

I'm convinced that women can't make the last leap into senior management because of the club.

When women inquire directly about hitting this impasse, few feel they get a straight answer. Aware that the reason may in fact be discrimination, yet also acutely aware of federal laws, managers devise an array of alternate explanations. Marilyn has watched this back-and-forth interaction go on for twenty years. Women like her find themselves in an increasingly distressing psychological bind. On the one hand, they know that the answers they receive are only half-truths. On the other hand, if they allow themselves to accept the fact that their futures are limited, they'll think as Marilyn did: "With twenty years' service, I'd feel like a fool for hanging in so long."

I don't think anybody's ever honest with you about why you don't get promoted here. In my case, it's easier for me to believe the reason they've given me than to accept the fact that somebody in senior management thinks I don't have what it takes, or that there aren't two full vice presidents who support my promotion. Frankly, I'm sure the reason they've refused my promotion is the fact that I just won't relocate again. I have chosen not to move, and that is seen as a problem. But I know there are other women who aren't getting honest feedback either. They're being told that they aren't "ready," and that they need to do "X," "X," and "X" before they'll be promoted. The women in my firm are sure there's discrimination here. They continue to get feedback that says, "You've done everything, you're great, you're on the promotable list, you're going to be promoted soon." But then more and more men get promoted, and more and more women don't.

The cement ceiling reflects fundamental laws of group behavior. For example, social scientists have observed for decades that people will gravitate toward those who share their personal characteristics. As a sense of mutual understanding evolves among the members, a group becomes a safe refuge from the plurality and confusion of the world at large. To the degree that it remains homogeneous, its members feel comfortable and protected. But as soon as someone "different" joins, the safety factor disappears.

Given this dynamic, it's not surprising that all-male management teams subtly or overtly resist the presence of women. Men at the top are responsible for decisions that involve vast amounts of money and affect thousands of lives. Decision-making at that level requires an ability to take major risks and to live with the consequences of those risks. In a climate filled with such tension and pressure, executives wish to be surrounded by people they can trust. Unconsciously, many pick associates who resemble themselves.

The problem comes when maximum performance is sacrificed in the name of personal familiarity. In the short run, choosing a group of like colleagues builds consensus and support for the leader's goals. Over time, however, intellectual inbreeding can seriously limit the group's capacity to grow. With few divergent opinions represented, leaders can inadvertently overlook the full range of talent available for making the most important policy decisions.

When competent women are excluded from the senior ranks, organizations and individuals suffer. As the pattern continues throughout American industry, the trade-offs may have profound economic effects. In their efforts to preserve group solidarity, corporate leaders may be shutting off the contributions of some of the sharpest individuals available. Heidi found to her dismay that even a Harvard MBA didn't help. It took her ten years of working at a Fortune 500 company to appreciate the resilience of long-standing traditions.

What's really going on with all this chain of command stuff is that it perpetuates itself. We have one female vice president in this division, and that's a very new thing. She was hired from the outside last fall, and she's great. She has done some really good things for the division. But it's interesting that she wasn't promoted from within. I think I'm the third-highest-ranking woman in the division, but by having the chain of command, they keep it an all-boys club. It used to be all male, and it still is very predominantly male. They promote people who look the way they do, who act the way they do, who play the same sports they do. It's not that they exclude women or any other group—it's more of a consolidation of the one given group.

Today, when professional women should seemingly be pleased with their progress, many are worried about their futures and those of other women. They constantly look around their companies, studying who's made it how far and how fast. They keep careful watch, and they take careful notes. When they realize that few women move beyond a given level, they see a bigger picture and start to view the challenge in a radically different light. Even in a conservative public utilities company, Marilyn sees trouble brewing among the female ranks. She predicts that soon the quiet revolution will be over, and widespread litigation will take the place of fear.

What worries me is knowing that no one has jumped above the women who came up ten to fifteen years ago. After a group of us trailblazed and made it to this level, we haven't seen any women capitalize on that. There are tokens, one or two or three here and there, but that's a very small number. Soon we'll have a female vice president, but that's still only one person. It's not as if women as a group were moving up—not at all. Instead, we're seeing management select a token here and there so that they can silence the outcry, or at least keep it stilled. I'm worried about that. I'm forty-three years old, but there are many women five to ten years younger than I who don't have any of the constraints I do. There are women in this company who are single, who don't have children yet, who still haven't made it above my level. I really wonder why. Time seems to have stood still.

I think it's still a matter of time before women will start to demand recognition and promotions. But one thing's for sure—women aren't going to continue to take this kind of tokenism here. There are going to be internal rebellions soon. Things today aren't the same way things were twenty years ago, when women wouldn't open their mouths for fear they'd be fired. Not so today. No so at all.

Those women who have hit a barrier talked candidly about their emotional reactions. Some have become listless and unmotivated at work. Others try to battle feelings of depression, but over time, they find themselves losing ground. In the most severe cases, disillusionment can affect physical health. For Anne, a dramatic incident that could have cost her her life made her reassess quickly her scramble to the top.

It was during the morning of the first day of an important three-day strategic planning session, with only senior managers, that I started having some very noticeable cardiac arrhythmias. About every other beat was going haywire. I could tell I was having big problems.

But I waited until noon to go down to the company's medical facility. They immediately put me on a heart monitor and said, "This is serious." Then they sent me over to the local hospital, where again they put me on the monitor. They wanted to keep me there, but I said, "No, I have a meeting that I absolutely have to get back to." So they released me after I promised I'd see my doctor right after the meeting and would definitely get on medication that very night.

In the meantime, when I was at the hospital emergency room, the I.V. had come out of my hand and blood had spilled all over my skirt. Before I left the hospital, I went to the washroom and tried to wash it off, but I was covered with blood and water stains when I returned to the meeting. I had bandages on both hands from the I.V.'s. I was pale. Frankly, I looked as if I'd been run over.

I went back to the meeting a little bit after three in the afternoon, but nobody had even missed me. Nobody said a word to me when I came in. Nobody said, "What in the hell are all those bandages for?" or "What happened to you? You look like death warmed over." Nothing. Absolutely nothing.

So I waited until the meeting was over. At about six-thirty that evening, I called my boss aside and told him I had a problem and wanted him to be aware of it, because I'd be going to the doctor the next day. From the expression on his face, I saw that nobody really cared if I was there or not.

It hit me then that my company is a very impersonal arena in which everyone is totally expendable. It's like burning long matches when you're lighting a fire. When one burns down, you light another one from it, and you burn it until it's almost gone, and then you light another. I realized that this is the way people are treated there, and I made a decision that very moment that the next year, when my daughter graduated from high school and was off to college, I'd be saying "ta ta" to that company for good. And that's just what I did.

Rethinking Everything

For many women, hitting the cement ceiling marked the first time they'd lost control of their lives. Having played by the rules, they had expected to be offered opportunities they could adopt or reject. It never occurred to most that one day the series of choices would end abruptly. When it did, each woman had to view her career in a much broader personal and political context. "Only if you keep in mind the bigger picture," Anne explained slowly, "do you regain the idea that you have life choices. You regain the feeling that you're in control."

In most major companies, there is a level past which women simply do not go. As you move from company to company, that level floats—in some it's very low, and in others it gets to be fairly high. What a woman has to do is recognize where that level is, because it essentially acts as a wall. You do have a choice when you find you're hitting your head against it. One route is to keep hitting and hitting and hitting, trying to move the wall up another level. The other is to say, "Hell, there are better places to put my energy," and go some other place where the wall either doesn't exist or is positioned higher up in the company.

Two years ago I was having a conversation with a senior manager about this, and he said to me, "Anne, there is a point at which a woman's voice doesn't get heard anymore, and you've reached it." I told him how frustrated I was about not being able to contribute more at my level. He helped me understand that it boiled down to my having so much more to give than the company could possibly absorb. That's basically what it was. I knew I wasn't being heard, but I also knew that they needed to hear what I had to say. I felt that I was whistling in the wind. He was right. He told me the truth.

In some organizations, women hit the cement ceiling long before they approach senior management. As Anne so aptly put it, "the wall" is not consistent; it surfaces in different subtle ways in different organizations. Julie observes that despite Silicon Valley's reputation for innovation, when it comes to promoting women, even high tech is slow. After working for twelve years at defense contract firms, Julie has concluded that the stronger the male tradition, the lower the ceiling for women.

In technical fields, it's still a man's world. I don't know how much longer that will be true, but right now it's impossible to break through a certain level if you're a woman. I know the opportunities will come someday. It may be five years down the road, but it may be more like another twenty. In my opinion, it will be a lot longer. Right now, it's a distinct disadvantage to be a woman if you're really career-oriented. If you're just there because you want to do a job and learn a little, make social contacts, and have a good time, then it's OK to be a woman.

For women to break through the cement ceiling in the technical industries, we're going to have to wait for female graduates of engineering schools to get business experience. It's going to take time, and it's going to take technical women coming up through the ranks and slowly moving into managerial slots. Personally, I feel there will always be some tension between men and women in business. I don't believe it will ever be fifty-fifty.

A bigger issue is that when women examine the lifestyle that accompanies top positions, many question whether they want it after all. Jennifer, for example, watches thirty-five-year-old CEOs darting about Silicon Valley in red-hot Ferraris. When she sees the frenetic pace and their workaholic existence, she's no longer sure she wants to join the club. Nonetheless, she feels angry for not having the option; she still wants the right to choose or refuse.

If you asked women to be honest, I think they'd say they have mixed feelings about whether they really want to go any higher. I know I always look at that. You know, jobs can give you satisfaction, but they can never make you happy. It's true. I'm at a point in life where I'd like to make some more money, and I'd like to achieve a few more things. But I also want to be happy. I get a lot of satisfaction out of this job, but I'm much more likely to find happiness at home. At some point, the desire to have kids and a nurturing relationship becomes a very powerful instinct. I think a lot of times women get to a certain point in their careers, and then choose to walk away from it all. I may do that. But I sure as hell want it to be my own choice. And right now it isn't.

Both Nancy and Natalie are grappling with reality. Each believes that no matter how limited her ultimate horizons may really be, for now she must maintain high performance and try to infiltrate the all-male network inch by inch. Remarkably, both women appear calm—neither frustrated nor resigned. They're willing to pace themselves and wait for change that may occur only over a very long haul. Nancy speaks first.

I think the cement ceiling is a reality for women, and breaking through it is going to involve getting into that fraternity, or that network, and being totally available. The big problem is that when you get to an executive level, the company does own you. I don't think one of our senior officers takes a family vacation without its being interrupted with a call from the president or an emergency at the office. Very often they have to fly back here for one day of business. It's an incredible drain. I look at what these men have sacrificed: They have women at home that they barely know, they have children who have grown up without their fathers really being there, and many of them have moved every eighteen months.

I think women are saying, "I do want to get there, but I might be just as happy being at the director level rather than becoming a vice president." When you're a vice president you have to be on call twenty-four hours a day, 365 days a year. I haven't sorted this all out yet for myself. Fortunately, I'm married to a man who's supportive and who knew me professionally before we got involved personally. His point of view is that even if I did stay at home, I'd probably be running the Red Cross, or the Y, or the neighborhood association. No matter what I do, I go whole hog. My husband says to me, "If you're going to go whole hog, be sure you get paid for it."

Natalie sounds a similar refrain.

I'm as high as I'm probably going to go, and for right now that's OK. As long as I'm making a comfortable living and can afford what I want, why should I worry about not getting a promotion or moving up in the company? Men in my MBA class talk about this timetable everybody should have, and how you should constantly move up or change jobs. Well, I can't change jobs as easily as they can. I worked my way up from the bottom here, and if I go somewhere else, I may have to start all over again. Realistically, I have the best shot at advancement if I stay here and keep showing them that a woman can handle the responsibilities I have. The important thing to me is, "Do I like my job and the people I'm working with, and does the company treat me right?"

It's not easy for men or women to know how high they want to aim or what sacrifices they're ultimately willing to make. The women described a noticeable dichotomy between what they say in public and what they think about in private. Most are convinced that their options would vanish if they appeared anything but thrilled about every possible job. At the office, they present themselves as totally committed, sometimes just for the sake of appearing always open to options.

In the privacy of their homes, however, many are less certain. Julie points out that the very idea of "goal-setting" is something foreign to women like her, raised for marriage and family life. To determine how high she wants to go in aerospace, she must adopt entirely new ways of thinking about her life. As I spoke with others struggling with this question, I realized that Julie is not the exception; she's just more candid than most.

I'm forty years old, and I still don't know what it's like to have long-range goals or aspirations. I ask myself, "Could I be the president of some company?" And I answer, "Hardly." I simply don't want to put out the hours. So then I ask myself, "To what level do I really want to go?" And I answer, "I don't know." That puts me in a really awkward position, because by this time I should know. In my case, I think not having any goals set for myself is directly related to being female. Women in my age bracket and older were raised differently than women who are younger. What I hear from my friends who have children is that young women today know what it's like to have goals. But when I was a teenager, there was nothing more on the horizon than getting married and having children. That was the only goal I ever had. It's still the only goal I know. I think it's that way for a lot of women my age.

People experiencing confusion internally often have a hard time assessing the external world. Women who have hit a cement ceiling and are also ambivalent toward ambition reported difficulty reading the dynamics of their offices. Usually they interpreted their career plateau as a personal rejection, a final condemnation of their capabilities and work.

The process escalated. Women obsessed about whom they had offended and where they had gone wrong. Finding no clear-cut answers, they vacillated, blaming first themselves, then their employers. Cynthia remembers that when she found out she could go no higher at a radio station, her immediate reaction was to examine how she had failed. It took her time and a great deal of soul-searching to appreciate that the problem was institutional and she was not at fault.

For a while I thought, "Maybe I haven't gotten a promotion because I'm not good enough." Well, that's garbage. I know I'm good enough. Every time I call a headhunter there are seven or eight companies interested in me immediately. I do good work, and I know what the people I respect think of me. Still, when I look at myself stuck at this plateau, I ask, "What am I doing wrong?"

I blame myself. I think, "Maybe I wasn't aggressive enough when I was putting this or that show together. Maybe I made a mistake. Maybe I didn't contribute enough. Maybe I didn't have enough good ideas. Maybe I'm not playing the game right." Yet, at the same time, I know all those things I say to myself are ridiculous. I haven't missed a day of work in three and a half years. And I even had a baby during that time! My supervisor keeps saying, "Talk to the news director," but I've talked to the news director, and I could keep on talking to him until I turn green. I've decided I'm not going to talk to him about this anymore. I don't have anything else to say. He knows what my goals are, but he's busy grooming other people—who aren't women.

Tips From the Trenches

Broaden Your Options

For many, the cement ceiling is a crossroad. Already fed up with hostile corporate cultures, some women decide they finally must leave when they continually confront discrimination in promotions. Many opt to start their own businesses. Five women considering the entrepreneurial option spell out their thinking and offer their advice. For them, leaving has little to do with status. It has more to do with compromises they refuse to make.

Brenda speaks softly in her office at the plant.

I've been taking a serious look at leaving this organization, because I've made up my mind that even though compromise is part of every life, the day I have to compromise my personal ethics is the day I decide this is not the job for me. This doesn't mean I always get to do what I want in order to solve a problem or deal with a situation or complete a project. But it does mean that if I have to compromise a basic belief that I value, I'm just not going to do it. I've found in industry—and I don't think it's just this company—that sometimes to succeed you have to become a liar. I have refused to do that. If I screw up, I'll tell you I screwed up. If I made a mistake, I'll tell you I made a mistake. I always hope I'm going to learn from my mistakes, but if I don't, I'm prepared to accept the consequences that go with it. But I'll be damned if I'm going to lie about my mistakes, because I've found that one lie leads to another, and I have to be able to sleep with myself at night. I detest lying.

I've been thinking about this a lot lately, because I've been watching carefully how the system operates here. To me, there are two ways to be a liar. You can out-and-out tell a bald-faced lie, or you can not tell the whole truth. Corporate America tends to promote CYA types of managers—cover-your-ass types of managers—and CYA people lie and cover up.

If ethics is the primary reason why women leave organizations, the desire for control is a very close second. Like their male counterparts, women in their twenties, thirties, and forties were surprised to discover how much control they surrendered when they started corporate life. Unlike men, however, women are weighing the loss of that control against the idea of limited options. Even Linda, who genuinely loves the corporate environment, finds her need for autonomy can no longer be met in the world of Big Oil.

One of the things I've been dealing with recently is whether I want to stay here. I've reached a level where I think it is very unlikely that they'll promote me any further. There's no place to promote me to; there's no other place for me to go in this company. There are many things I could do here, and I know there are ways I can continue to have an impact.

I like the corporate environment. I enjoy it. I enjoy corporate politics. But I always have this question in my mind: Should I be doing something else? I've worked here for nine years. I feel I need some different experiences. My friend and I have even put together a prospectus for opening our own business. We're beginning to feel that having our own business will probably be the best way to change our work environment and to have more control over our lives.

Several women I interviewed give frequent lectures to professional organizations. They travel, conduct workshops, and develop a feel for the cultural landscape. Courtney's achievements have won her national recognition and genuine credibility among legions of women. When she analyzes why they're leaving corporations, I know she's speaking not only for herself but also for the hundreds of women she has met.

A large number of the people in senior management positions in America are egomaniacs. Every story you read in the paper about unfriendly takeovers is true. Those self-centered, egocentric, and obnoxious people really do exist. The women I know don't want to work for people like that. They don't want to work for people who expect their lives to be their jobs. Most women have a diversity of interests and responsibilities. They can't relate to somebody who thinks "job, job, job." Egomaniacs are petty and very rank-conscious. They believe people at lower levels really aren't the same quality of human being that they are. Most women I know just don't think that way. Many who are leaving to start their own companies disagree with how power is used or abused. They're comfortable with themselves, and they feel it's not worth the price they have to pay just to be around immature men. You know, people at that age should not be immature. But what you often find is that these men have basically stopped growing.

Courtney also sees the cement ceiling as a problem in demographics. With a chuckle, she apologizes for "sounding like a numbers freak," then explains that in large part the problem is statistical. Now that too many baby boomers are competing for too few desirable jobs, people with seniority win and newcomers must wait. If waiting meant working in a supportive environment, women would do it with pleasure, Courtney maintains. But since waiting may mean accepting hostility and no hope of advancement, women are choosing alternative routes.

> I'm seeing a lot of women topping out right now. Some of it has to do with age and the fact that we've moved so fast: What do you do if you're treasurer of a $7 billion company at age thirty? Most men in those kinds of jobs are fifty-five years old. Many women feel they've topped out too early. These older gentlemen still have some life in them—they can't be expected to leave just because women are ready for top positions. Until people in the forty-year-and-under range are ready to lead, and that whole over-forty-five crowd is gone, there really isn't much that can be done. We also need to wait until younger men get used to working with women. They have to have the experience of respecting women in the workplace and of actually working for women. To most men at work, women are still sort of an odd animal. If I had to predict what's going to happen, I'd say a lot of the women are going to drop out. They won't stop working, but they'll start their own companies or do something different in the business world, basically to get away from discrimination and egomaniacs.

Many women fantasize about the companies they wish to start. Central to their vision is a new style of management based on perceived feminine qualities of nurturance and support. In designing their ideal organizations, these women emphasize that in no way do they wish to mimic those they know now. Ginger, who is leaving Madison Avenue to start her own ad agency, outlines for me the essentials of her dream.

> I don't have a platform of steps that I'm going to lay down in my new company, but I do know that I want to create a healthy and flourishing environment for all personnel. If you look at Japanese corporate structures, they

really are very familial. People in Japan go to a company and stay there for a lifetime. They know they're going to be protected and taken care of, and if they have an emotional crisis, there are people in the company they can go to. It is very important to Japanese companies that employees be in good shape, both physically and emotionally. It is definitely a patriarchal family core, very interdependent, and you always know you are working for The One.

Now, I know that's a bit of a socialistic notion and it can't really work here in the purest sense, because in America men and women are in business for themselves. When it comes right down to it, we are a very self-centered culture, and it's hard for individuals to play for the team's sake. But as I start my business, I'd like to personally examine every old habit I've seen in this industry.

What I want to develop is an entrepreneurial spirit, a pioneer spirit, where everyone is free to challenge every old notion that exists out there. Here in advertising I want to challenge the sixty-second increment in ads and the problem-solution-reward formula for writing. Why not collaborate with another agency, for example? Let's say one agency has Xerox, and I've got McDonald's. Why couldn't we get together and do something creative like sponsor a Special Olympics or a youth group activity? Why can't we even do a commercial together?

I want to challenge everything, to question everything. I want to turn problems into opportunities. I know it sounds too good, and I don't really know how far I can take it. I just know I want people who work for me to be confident that their jobs will never be threatened, that they can bring the most outlandish, ridiculous ideas to me, and I will listen. I don't want people working for me to feel that they are in constant competition with one another. I want them to compete with themselves and try to outdo themselves over the years. A hostile environment, in the end, doesn't breed a profitable operation. It can't.

Surviving on the Inside

Though women like Ginger have chosen to leave, the majority of working women will not be exiting the corporate world in the immediate future. Whether lacking capital for new ventures or enjoying the security of a regular paycheck, most women remain with employers and continue to do so for most of their careers.

These women have designed ways to deal with the reality of the cement ceiling. They know that economic survival depends on keeping their jobs, and that their emotional health depends on how they deal with the fact of discrimination. No longer naive and no longer in shock, women who choose to remain in corporations respond to the cement ceiling threat in a variety of fashions.

Cynthia and Mary Anne stress the importance of maintaining contact with others. Though each recalls times of being tempted to give up, "Those are the moments when we must view this collectively; those are the key times not to fight alone," Cynthia asserts. Her hope is contagious.

> I encourage women to believe that the top is accessible, because unless you believe it, it won't ever be. I think women have to understand that the top will be accessible sometime, and that nothing's ever permanent. As long as you're doing what you believe is right, and doing it as best you can, a lot of circumstances can change. When you feel you're the only one hitting a barricade, remember, you're really not. Look for somebody else who's going through the same frustrations you are, and I'm sure she'll want to talk. Never be afraid to ask other women for help.

Mary Anne's insurance company is a massive bureaucracy. Inching her way up for twelve years, she's learned that nothing moves quickly in a complex organization. Mary Anne advises women to keep that in mind when working for change. "The only way to tolerate how slowly they accept us is to cultivate a sense of patience and to keep on moving through."

It's true that not many women are going to climb up to the next rungs in the very near future. This impasse has to do with the amount of experience women have in the business world and the degree to which professional women are accepted in various corporations and in the world at large. I feel strongly that for women to advance in business, a wide foundation of support is going to have to exist.

One of the things I've learned about power is that leaders are perceived to be omnipotent, but in reality the decisions they make are constrained by the ways their organizations work and the internal acceptance of what they say. Leaders can't be there all the time to monitor the implementation of their decisions. This means groundwork must be built that creates an acceptance of women in senior management positions. There are growing numbers of women who are executive vice presidents now, and that's the foundation we need to strengthen the possibility of women becoming CEOs. I'm confident that as the foundation is strengthened, we'll get there.

The women have devised ingenious plans for maximizing success despite the cement ceiling. Most fully believe that traditional attitudes will gradually be forced to bend, and when they do, women best prepared for advancement will benefit most. Though aware of current obstacles, these women are practicing tactics now to use in the future. Kay is certain that in any large organization, only those who know the system inside out will be called upon to lead.

I want to know the rules. I don't think that the females in our company know the rules. We don't know how to have what you call a mentor, somebody who's actively helping us get where we want to go. I had a discussion with an executive vice president recently, telling him what was going on here. I said, "You know, I really would like to have a mentor." And he said, "Well, you have one, your senior vice president." I said, "That's not the same thing. You should know if you have a mentor."

My senior vice president may be telling other people that I do a good job, but he doesn't come to me and say, "OK, now how are we going to get you to this next step?" Or "To get to this next step, you need to do this, this, and this." There's none of that going on with the females, but you see it all the time with the males. Like this one fellow who is being groomed for vice president. They've taught him, and he's learned. He's one of the best among the people in our age bracket—thirty-two, thirty-three, thirty-four. He's the best one in the company for the vice president slot, but what exactly did he learn? I don't know. What is it?

Others agree that having a mentor is not the easy answer that some would like to believe. Though a mentor can be helpful in learning the system and in initially opening doors, implicit sexual energy can eventually get in the way. Sandy knows what can happen if a woman entrusts her professional future to just one senior male.

Having a mentor is a very fragile relationship. I think it's even more fragile between a man and a woman, because there's always a hint of male-female sexual dynamics at play. I don't think you can avoid it. What happens is that because you have two professionals who respect their own and each other's professionalism, you never let the sexuality develop, yet it's always there. The mentor is giving, and if the person receiving is not appreciative, the mentor has strong grounds for resentment. I think, in my case, that is precisely what happened. It was a case of my mentor saying, "I've given all this to you, but what have you done for me?"

It's a question of independence. I noticed it in him from the beginning. I've always had a hard time with it, but it was never major enough to take issue with. My mentor made it perfectly clear that people were not to mess with me because of him. He made it perfectly clear that what I said was endorsed by him—almost to the point where it became uncomfortable for me, because basically I don't see myself resembling his clone.

I'm sure he saw putting his authority behind me as positive, but to me it ultimately went too far. Having him as a mentor, I became more of an alter ego, which is not particularly flattering when you want to succeed on your own merit.

Rather than depending on one senior executive for access to opportunities, an alternative strategy is to develop very systematically a broad professional network, both inside and outside the organization. Over and over, women stress the importance of reliable contacts, for advancement, learning, and reality checks. They are excited to discover that in contrast to the Old Boy Network that still keeps them apart, the New Girl–New Boy Network is fast emerging in all cities. Mary Anne believes that soon this national alliance will have substantial influence and will make the ultimate difference in her getting to the top.

The higher you get in an organization, the more important relationships are. Knowing people is a crucial element of getting the job done, which is what it's all really about in business. Even if you're shy, you have to make those important contacts. Since most of the people I deal with are interesting, I push myself to explore common interests and be myself around them. It's true, you have to make an effort to be open and friendly, but it's all part of doing your job the best you can.

Just as Mary Anne has had to push herself to develop contacts, many women described a similar need to become more bold and forthright in all aspects of their careers. Having struggled to prove themselves professionally, to fit into a male culture and to be liked in the social realms, they have begun to seriously question that accommodating role. Their goal now is not to worry so much about appearing impolite, but rather to speak up forcefully and to articulate precisely what they want.

Ingrid knows that this change is often trying. Like most, she was raised to consider others first. But as she has become an accomplished businesswoman, Ingrid has found out that pursuing her own goals doesn't necessarily deprive others of theirs.

> I'm learning a lot about myself in this business. Basically, I'm learning you can tiptoe too much. In the past, literature and workshops for women in business emphasized that we must always be careful, because if we make a mistake, then we have to mend it. But I think I've been too careful about not hurting other people's feelings and not getting people bent out of shape. I'm trying now to live with the fact that if I get someone bent out of shape, that's tough. I get bent out of shape all the time, and the world's never once fallen in just because I've been upset.
>
> I think this fear of hurting people's feelings is very strongly related to being female and wanting approval all the time. Not only do you want to do a good job, but you also want people to like you and think you're nice. Personally, I've found it difficult to get satisfaction just from the fact that I've done a good job. So I'm trying to develop emotional independence. If I'm always concerned with everyone's feelings, I end up allowing myself to be held hostage.
>
> I do think women feel a great responsibility for people's feelings. It's how we've been socialized. Men don't bear that. My husband will have a fight at the office, and he'll be pissed about the position a person took or what they said, but he'll never be particularly concerned whether he made them angry or sad.

No one gets anything in business without aggressively pursuing clear objectives, the women emphasized. As young professionals join the workforce, too frequently they wait for assignments and rewards to come automatically. For anyone in the transition from campus to cubicle, learning to take the initiative is a critical change in style. For women, this shift from passive to active may be difficult. Yet, given discrimination, it has become an immediate need. Melissa tells how she learned this lesson years ago. Then Marjorie describes the dynamic in the oil industry; in the rough-and-tumble atmosphere that oil men thrive on, demanding one's due is how things are done.

> When I started on the advertising sales staff of a major magazine, one of the best things that could happen was to get a cigarette account or a big-volume advertiser. Well, one time after I was about three years into my job, one of the people on the staff died suddenly, and his cigarette account was given to a young man who had far less business experience than I, and who wasn't nearly as good. About a week passed and I finally said to my boss, "How come I didn't get that account? How could this have happened?" My boss said, "It never occurred to me you'd be interested in a cigarette account." At that moment I realized, "There it is; the writing on the wall. They simply do not take women seriously here."
>
> I learned something else from that experience. To this day, I constantly tell people who work for me, "How am I going to know what you want to do in this company, or in your job, if you don't speak up and tell me? You have to tell me what you want. It's not up to me to figure it out."

Marjorie recounts her Texas career.

> I've always demanded my promotions. They've never been given to me automatically. I've always had to wage all-out war until I was promoted. I had one boss who told me, "You have to be a little bit aggressive, Marjorie; you have to ask for these things if you don't get them." In a way that's nonsense, because men are always perceived as

ambitious, and they're always promoted if they can be. And I don't think I ever was. My work has been above average, but I've always had to pound on the door to get the promotion. I don't think a man would have to do that, especially if he were performing at my level.

The way Sarah speaks, I'm reminded of a sage. There is gentleness in her wisdom and kindness underneath her tough, pragmatic exterior. In her publishing career, Sarah has supervised numerous women over the years. Those who've made it farthest, she argues, are those who at some point very nearly failed. Leadership comes not only from asking for what you want, but also from taking major risks for what you believe.

I've heard many young women say, "But they never give me the real stuff to do." And I say, "That's right. They never do. You have to ask for it."

I find that a lot of women wait to be given permission to succeed. But people who succeed in the business world by definition don't wait to get permission. You have to look around, identify the people who are not doing entry-level work, and find out how they got there. You must always do your work, but you also have to set realistic goals. I don't care if you're a man or woman, if there's something you want to do, you simply have to say, "I would like to try this." The truth is that most people are so overworked that they're delighted when you want to take on additional responsibility. Show them that what you want to do is something you can do reasonably well. It's easy to ask. Just say, "Maybe I could do this," or "I see you're in a bind. Could I try doing that for you?" The worst that can happen is that you won't do it well, in which case you pick your moment to get the person you're assisting to explain what went wrong. That way you can correct it the next time.

Above all, don't be afraid; failing is not the worst thing that can happen. You learn more from mistakes than from successes. Failing in itself is not a disaster. Everybody fails from time to time. It's better to try something and have it not work out, and then be able to draw a pencil through the things you're not going to do again, than to not try and just stay where you are. Women don't need to be so scared. Everybody's scared. I'll tell you something—the guys are scared too.

Finally, the individuals I met urge other women to learn from men's mistakes. They seek to devise new models for managing people and for managing careers. They're convinced that such innovations are vital for surviving the system and making it work more on their terms. The key, they concluded, is maintaining a sense of values and focus, then developing specific strategies to enhance chosen goals. Three senior women executives, Emily, Tina, and Heidi, reflect a consensus opinion that the American economy needs maximum creativity to compete in worldwide markets, and that it cannot afford much longer to overlook the intellectual resources talented women bring.

Emily leads off. She believes that the global starts with the personal.

I watch the men in my division become so dedicated to the corporation that they would do anything, including move three times up and down the state, to please senior management. I see this and I think, "Do these men even realize what they're giving up?" They're giving up everything. And the company makes no promises. I watch these men and I think, "There's no way I would do that." I'm happy where I am, because in a sales commissioned job, I have the capability to make all the money I want, and at the same time, I get to run my own shop.

Women need to notice the pitfalls of what men high up in the corporation have gone through. Women have to see what men go through to attain their high-level positions and then decide very carefully whether it's what they want or not. Too many men are losing their families, their children, and their friends as a result of all this moving around and all this corporate change.

What I want to do is establish a balance and be very clear about how much I'm giving to my career and how much I want to maintain for my personal life. I want to be in control of this career, instead of letting it control me. If women can do this, I think maybe men will strive to create a balance too. Men will look at how women are running their families and homes, maintaining relationships there while succeeding as executives. I think men are going to look to women to see how it can be done, because they can't do it. Someone did a study recently, asking senior executives, "If you had to do it over again, what would you do differently?" And all of them said, "I'd spend more time with my family, my kids, and my wife." To implement true change in any corporation, you don't start with the exterior—first you change the interior.

Tina, once an English major, uses images and metaphors to understand her present world. Hers is a unique perspective on business. She brings to the environment a decidedly different analysis and a fresh point of view.

The business world is made up of a whole group of values and systems, and they all intersect. It's a series of little trade-offs, and if you get what you want out of a situation, great. If the other person can get something at the same time, then you've got a good business deal. I think a lot of us women feel we're being short-changed on the exchange side of things, and therefore we need to learn how to use the system better for our own needs.

In some ways, business is the equivalent of reading a long Dickens novel. Maybe a single character isn't all that interesting, but he has a certain personality quirk, and the timing of the arrival of the quirk and the intersection with other quirks suddenly makes an interesting thing happen. And that's exactly what I've discovered goes on in this bank.

Heidi has a vision. She's not given up on the corporate world, nor is she convinced that she's reached a plateau. Thinking of the future, she can envision the day when men and women work together toward more common goals. But, she argues, this will happen during our lifetime only if the feminine and masculine sides of everyone are successfully integrated and finally used.

Each of us has our own approach as to how we're going to effect change. What I hope is that we'll end up with companies where a balance is met. I don't think women have to become men. I've learned to hunt on male terms, but I've found that what works for me is to get into the club and effect change from within.

I've been on the inside, and I've stayed there for a while, so I know my success hasn't been a fluke. I've been successful with more than one boss, and I've even survived a merger.

I know other people whose style is to stand on the outside and point fingers to draw attention to possible solutions. But that's not for me. I'd like to see structures that allow a softer side of men to come out, so that they can finally relax from the pressures of this macho stereotype that our culture has pushed them into. I also hope women can get out of the dependency stereotype. We'd all be so much better off if we combined these capabilities. We'd be better off, and so would business.

7

Striking a Balance

Back to Basics

Work can't keep you warm when you're eighty years old. You know, that's what I worry about—that work can't keep you warm. And then I say to myself, "Wait a minute. This is a double-edged sword. I may say, 'Work can't keep you warm at eighty,' but who says I'm going to live to eighty?" And then the second voice says, "There's always somebody out there, whether it's male, female, or dog, someone who can give you companionship. And there can always be some form of work, even if it doesn't provide money."

I guess I've concluded that I have to be busy. Even when I'm looking for a strong relationship with someone, I've got to have something to do, some kind of job to do, or else I'd go bonkers. I've never really not worked. Even though I may say I don't want to work, the truth is I always want something to do.

Patricia is at a crossroad. She has made it big in television news and is now a local celebrity. People stop her in the grocery store, asking for her autograph. Churches and schools invite her to speak. Viewers name their babies after her, and network executives offer enviable contracts. Yet even with all the attention and glory, Patricia wonders whether sacrificing her personal life has really been worth it. She thinks about a pending divorce and looks back on several relocations, and asks herself when the sense of balance began slipping away.

Like Patricia, women across the country are feeling a need for more balance in their lives. They're well aware that their careers have provided them with advantages—working has increased their self-esteem, given them financial independence, and in most cases, allowed them the chance to go places and do things their mothers and grandmothers never dreamed possible. Professional life has expanded women's horizons.

But with these opportunities have come trade-offs. Women who have concentrated exclusively on their careers reported problems in their relationships with men, in beginning and building a family, in maintaining their emotional and physical health, and in developing friendships and enjoying the community.

As problems build, women wonder how they can direct more time toward their personal lives and still put out the energy needed to make it in the world. Their consensus is emphatic: You can't do it all. The first step toward balance is selecting priorities.

Emily has struggled with balance since she started work. Back then her husband, also on the fast track, had little time for their marriage. The subsequent divorce taught Emily a lesson about the dangers of a one-dimensional life. In her eyes I recognize a certain brand of wisdom, the wisdom that can come only from working through pain.

> I think about what I'm supposed to be learning as I observe corporate life, and I've come to the conclusion that in almost every case, balance is the answer. If we could learn to balance our work lives with our personal lives, we'd all live much more happily.
>
> If work is the most important thing to us, then what happens is that we lose our sense of balance. If in our

personal life we're too madly in love with the new boy on the block, then soon our work suffers. Each time, one or the other suffers. Everything is fine as long as it all stays in balance. It's almost as if balance should be my life goal. If I could only keep balance in every aspect of my life, I would live a harmonious existence.

To me, making it is being an independent woman and earning as much money as I elect while maintaining a satisfying personal life. A person is not making it when he or she has to give up something valuable in order to have money. And the same is true the other way around: I could never be content in a relationship if I didn't have a strong feeling of self-worth through my contribution to the world.

Unfortunately, "making it" in corporations is defined only as going for the top. But the narrow definition doesn't talk about personal life. Making it as a human being would be making it on both sides, and balancing them somehow so you could be happy. I think we all will find that if we have one without the other, we're going to be miserable. I hope that women and men realize this before it's too late.

It is hard to describe the change that came over the women as we talked more about personal life and less about work. For one thing, their bodies visibly relaxed. Faces that had been held taut softened, and eyes that had been boring into me suspiciously welcomed me at last. Women put down their cigarettes and took off their jackets. When we began to discuss babies, men, and friendships, the corporate armor all but disappeared.

Diane is an executive whose armor seems impenetrable. For most of our interview she answers questions politely yet indirectly, as if careful never to show her hand. Watching her, I get the clear impression there's a discrepancy between how she acts at the office and how she really feels. It isn't until our last fifteen minutes together that Diane the person finally emerges. In a soft embarrassed voice, she tells me that six months ago she became so depressed she lay in bed crying for more than a month. Ending a marriage, moving to a new city, and finding herself utterly alone, she'd hit bottom and was forced to confront issues she had previously avoided. From that experience came Diane's new priorities and standards for success.

> During that period of reevaluation that I went through shortly after I got to Chicago, one of the things I took a long look at was how good I was at being a person instead of how good I was at being a professional banker. When you look at it in that context, what you come to see is that although the success of this bank is very important—it's very important to me, it's very important to other people who are here—in the total context of the world it doesn't mean a hill of beans. In the context of this country, in the context of this city, it really doesn't make any difference. What's important for me is how good I'm becoming at being a person. This is very much judged by my personal feelings about how good I am, the friends I have, and whether they see me as a valuable person to know.

In this chapter, the women describe the choices they confront as they try to build rich, full lives. They talk about what it takes to become multifaceted when there are no role models to emulate. They talk about the consequences that trying to "have it all" inevitably brings to a woman and her family. They talk most poignantly about the problems they face as concerned working mothers, and with joy about the perspective on career life that motherhood provides.

In the following comments, three women describe what "balance" means to them in everyday terms. For one, the juggling act boils down to not having time. For another, the challenge is building self-esteem through work after five grown children have left the home. And for a third, balance means developing different parts of one's personality in different arenas of life.

> What's problematic for me is that I can't fit in all the stuff I want to do. I've got three full-time jobs: I'm Mom—

that's a half-time job; then I'm a community volunteer—that's probably a two-thirds-time job; and I'm a manager—probably a time-and-a-half job. And here I am, trying to do it all at once.

Even though nobody's accused me of being unfair to any of these priorities, I feel the need to get more done, and I feel it all the time. I especially feel inept, inadequate, and unworthy of all the good things people say about me, because I'm not measuring up to my own standards in anything I do.

They're saying I'm a superwoman and a supermom, but really I'm not. I'm just regular. I work hard. I'm certainly not intimidating because, after all, I'm just me. Yeah, I guess I'm talented because I was born with certain qualities. But that doesn't make me more special than anyone else.

I've proven to myself that I—just me—can work and achieve things and it can be OK. I myself can make my life OK. My greatest accomplishment, obviously, is raising five kids. They're great, they're contributors to the world, they're good friends of mine, and I like them. I have a whole lot to do with their being who they are. They're strong and independent, they care about people—all that good stuff.

But if raising those kids had been the only thing I ever did, that wouldn't be enough. I'd never know whether I could be in any situation and really deal with it. By working, I've learned that I can do just that.

One of the basic things for anybody who's been working in the home for a long time is to know that in fact you can go out there and make the kind of living you want—that you can, in fact, support yourself. You find out that you could be independent if you had to, that you could definitely take care of yourself, and that you could earn a good living to boot.

I think there's a tremendous amount of new self-confidence in knowing that you can do that. It made me feel so good that after many, many years, I entered the workforce and after not too long a time got a position of real responsibility, a job that was challenging and interesting, where people respected my work and my judgment. You just can't depend on a family situation to give you all that. I mean, what poor husband could do that? Really, truly, what poor anybody could do that—to give that measure of gratification to any other person?

Superwoman Is Dead

I'm finding that I'm fighting with myself. I'm fighting my own perceptions of me: There's the way I've always been and there's the way I am now, and I find I want them both. I feel they're conflicting with each other, and I don't believe that needs to be. I don't believe I have to give up one to have the other. But I haven't figured out how to marry them yet.

Sometimes at work I think I'm grooming myself to be somebody I won't like. I'm worried that I'm working toward becoming something I'm really not going to like at all. The stress I feel from juggling two identities often results in my pulling away from the feminine part of me just to be able to achieve on the job. And then a voice inside says, "Wait a minute, Susan, you need to do this other thing. You really do. Believe that. Being good at work doesn't mean you can't be sensitive. It doesn't mean you can't be pretty and sexy and even make love."

Sometimes I'm afraid life's going to pass me by, and I'm going to look back and say, "What the hell were you doing all that time, Susan? What did you give up? Where did you really think you were headed?" Sometimes, yeah, I'm afraid of that. Deep down, I am really afraid.

As their careers progress, women like Susan grow aware that major decisions confront them. They recognize that no longer can they pretend their lives will be simple. Women realize that if they're to become multifaceted people—to have challenging careers and to maintain rich personal lives as well—certain tough choices have to be made.

Most women never expected these conflicts. They entered the professions at the height of the women's movement, at a time when the media proclaimed that being superwoman was an option for all. But faced with the stark realities of long hours away from home, high-pressure jobs, and little support, women learned quickly that the mythical superwoman does not exist. Their stories tell vividly what they discovered instead.

The women's most common fear is that pursuing success will take over their lives. Though for a few years a workaholic life seemed tolerable, they look around after a decade and worry when they see no end in sight. They scrutinize the lives of executives and often conclude that the personal trade-offs just aren't worth it. Torn between concentrating on work and making a conscious choice to broaden their lives, women with strong leadership potential agonize the most. Gerry, a newspaper publisher, told me it took a series of personal crises to show her just how immersed in work she had actually become.

Recently, when I was given another offer, I felt totally compelled to move. It didn't even occur to me not to move because of personal commitments. It's funny. Once that job came up, it was just, "Oh, my God, I have to move. They want me."

Once you get on these corporate ladders, it never occurs to you to say no until it's too late, until you realize all you've given up. And finally that happened to me. The other day I thought, "They've been so good to me. They've done this, they've done that, they've given me a car, they've given me all this stock and all these benefits." And then suddenly out of nowhere I thought, "Yeah, but I gave them my whole life. Wait a minute. It hasn't been for nothing that they've done all this."

Once you get on that corporate ladder, you become obsessed. You think, "The job, the job, the job. Whatever they want me to do, by God I'll go do it." A friend called me up once and said, "Gerry, is there nothing you'll not do for your career?" At the time I thought he was rude, and I told him so. But later I thought about it and said to myself, "I'm not so sure there *is* anything I wouldn't do."

At that time, I was driven to be publisher of a paper. That was my goal, and it seemed that anything that was necessary to accomplish that goal was OK by me. Recently, I've started to question that too, and to see how much I've really given up by even thinking that way.

A second unexpected conflict revolves around femininity. Although some women reported allowing themselves the freedom to bring feminine characteristics into their lives at work, others still felt uncomfortable about appearing "too soft" on the job. The problem came as these women discovered that their capacity to be vulnerable and gentle had in many instances all but disappeared. When they tried to be more feminine away from the office, many were terrified that they no longer knew how.

Mandy feels like two people. There's the competent businesswoman who's adept at PR, high-powered negotiations, and overseas travel; in her public persona, Mandy seems cool and at ease. But back at her apartment, another self emerges. As she struggles to acknowledge a hidden sensitivity, Mandy seeks to carve out an identity that will incorporate both sides.

When I have problems socially, I think maybe I've forgotten how to be a woman. Maybe with all this great assertiveness training, something important backfired. Recently I've found myself thinking, "Have I learned something here that is adaptive in a work environment but maladaptive in a social environment?" I wonder.

220

I feel that I have to be two people—I have to be one way at work and then turn it all off. The strange thing is that I've always been told how feminine I am. But now that I've worked so long, maybe I'm just not as feminine as I used to be. Maybe something fundamental isn't there anymore.

When I try to talk about all this with my closest friends, suddenly we stop cold because it's so scary and demoralizing. It's as if we don't want to look at it. Sometimes I feel like giving up all of this career stuff tomorrow, because now that my personal life is shot, all I have left to look forward to is even more work.

I find myself wanting to say all this every day out loud in my company. I want to shout to them, "You're asking me to blunt my individuality, just to work here. How would the whole world be if everybody did that?" Yes, all of this is scary—I started to say it's like 1984, but then I remembered it's beyond 1984.

Nowhere are the women's dilemmas more intense than in their personal relationships with men. Single, married, divorced, or separated, many working women find that their careers have raised significant problems in their love lives. Some of the problems have to do with logistics, with the mechanics of having time together as a couple, of dividing household responsibilities, and of coordinating complicated schedules.

More painful issues go deeper. The main concern of the women I met was that in growing more independent, they are seeking from partners a psychological equality that they claim few men can give. The women end up torn, on one hand knowing that they value their careers and the growth their jobs have provided, yet on the other hand determined to preserve their marriages and other personal ties.

What are now secret arguments in homes across America may be the beginnings of a profound social change. As women attempt to broaden and enrich their lives, men who love and care for them must reevaluate their own lives as well. When

221

men feel entitled to demand more balance, changes in the workplace will undoubtedly evolve. The issue for the future will not be the grooming of multifaceted women; it will be the support and development of multifaceted adults.

Jennifer and Emily are single, and each makes over $75,000 a year. Both feel up against the biological clock and want to be married. Yet each of these successful women often feels discouraged. Having made it professionally and now being ready for commitment, they are certain their salaries scare men off. Just when they've decided to cut back on career life, they're discovering that their personal goals may be hard to reach. The first comment is Jennifer's.

> I don't think success at work will ever make your social life better—if anything, it makes it worse. That's one thing I've really been struggling with, because I have tremendous self-confidence when it comes to business. If I want to run a company, I'll do it, and I'll be successful at it. If I want to get some big executive job in a large corporation, I'm pretty convinced that given time and effort and a little bit of luck, I can do that too. But if you ask me if I can find and keep a really good relationship or raise a child or have a rich home life, the answer is—I really don't know. I certainly don't think anything in business has equipped me to do that.
>
> How many people want to date someone who travels 140,000 miles a year and lives three nights a week in an airplane? Just the practical side makes it very, very hard. The other thing is that most men would like to be with a woman who is stimulating and interesting, but who basically complements and supports them. And most women want to do exactly that.
>
> I have mixed feelings. What's hard is that the very moment I want to be soft and supportive, the telephone rings and it's the sales manager in Denver, and I've got to tell him eighty-five reasons why he needs to get off his butt and charge ahead with the account. That may sound strange, but it happens a lot. So I feel isolated by realizing

that most men my age are simply not aspiring to the level of my current job. It makes me feel misunderstood. I tell them I'm not really two people. I mean, I am that person on the phone with the sales manager, and I'm also the one who is soft and just wants to go cook dinner and talk. It's hard for most men to handle both sides of me.

For the most part, men who like me tend to be powerful, strong, tough-minded, career-addicted, workaholic professionals. I'm not as attracted to that kind of person as I am to someone who's softer, more supportive, and more interested in building a relationship than in getting ahead. I need somebody who is not threatened by my career identity, and at the same time is sensitive to the fragile parts of me. It's terribly difficult to find that mix.

I'm finally realizing that there are very few men out there who will treat me as an equal. Many of them are frightened and insecure, and scared of a woman with power, a woman who knows what she wants. I want somebody who's going to say on an issue, "Well, look, let's talk about this." I don't want a man who's going to say on an issue, "No way, this is how it's going to be." On the other hand, I don't want one who'll say, "Yes, dear, whatever you say, dear."

I want a partner. I want that in business and in my personal life. And I'm finding it's very difficult, because a lot of the men are turning out to be less strong than they've always appeared. A lot of them have had power by virtue of default, just because they're men. And now these same men are starting to come across women who have personal power, who know what they want, and who are assertive.

A lot of these guys just don't know how to deal with us—in business or in life. They don't know if they should open the door, and they don't know if they should open their mouths. It's amazing. There's a lot of change going on, and people are looking at their old roles and trying to see what adjustments to make. They have to, because it's very clear now to everyone—the old stuff doesn't work anymore.

The women were adamant that a wife's career has tremendous impact on her marriage. The stress that comes from male-female interactions in an office affects after-work relationships in a variety of complex ways. For one thing, many women no longer talk to their husbands about what goes on all day. Having recounted horror stories, and still facing problems, women worry that their husbands will grow tired of complaints. As a result, they deprive themselves of advice and coaching in order to preserve what they consider "the peace." Then, cut off from the potential understanding of the very men they love, these women sometimes feel isolated and resentful. Their marriages suffer, and divorce results.

Women who chose to involve their husbands in their careers reported a range of responses. Some said their husbands "just feel proud" of their wives' achievements. Others described men's humiliation when their wives bring home more money than they do. Many talked with gratitude about the perspective their husbands had provided on their work. The great majority of the women feel proud of how their husbands have come to grips with their careers.

Still, they acknowledged, the process wasn't easy. The fact that a woman is attached to her career will invariably evoke emotions in both partners. In strong marriages, the women felt that struggling with their husbands over these issues had, in the end, been worth it. In cases such as Ellen's, the marriage had to end.

It was impossible to develop a career when I was married. My husband didn't like my working at all. He even resented my substitute teaching when the kids were in school. Even though he wasn't there, he didn't want me away from the house. It was extremely difficult.

When I did go to work, and especially when I started getting promotions, that nearly killed him. He couldn't cope with the fact that I was earning more money than he was and that I loved my job. I couldn't understand that. I always thought he should be proud of me. I think it would be great to have a marriage in which you both have careers and you give each other space. That must be wonderful, because when you do come together, you're both so happy in what you're doing.

But with him, it was a battle from day one. And looking back now, it's a good thing that I kept up my career. It really is. When we finally divorced, if I hadn't had some sort of career commitment, I'd have been in the pits.

To Emily, housework is something highly symbolic. With a twinkle, she describes a system that she and her boyfriend just devised. On Saturdays, she does the vacuuming and he does the laundry. On Sundays, she buys the groceries, he changes the bed. Every Thursday night she washes the dog while he does the dishes. Reciting all this with a deadpan expression, Emily bursts out laughing and then shakes her head. She knows very well that what's at stake here is not just the dishes. What's really at stake is what all of this says.

We working women don't have the background to know how we're supposed to interact with men at home, because in most cases our parents didn't both work full-time. We don't know who's supposed to do the laundry and who's supposed to do the dishes—how much you're supposed to do and how much I am. We're struggling ourselves, in our own breakthrough for achieving equality in our homes. As far as the chores, is it still "half yours and half mine" if I make more and you make less? And if I make more, does that mean you do more chores than I do? It's absolutely crazy, but that's where we're at. We women are trying to establish equality with men at home and in the business world. And men are still trying to learn how to deal with it and with us.

For all their struggles, most women I met have concluded that they are indeed multifaceted, that they do enjoy both work and home life, and that they want to apply their talents in a variety of places. But since doing everything at once is impossible, the challenge lies in developing clear individual priorities. The question women ask today is not "Can I have it all?" but rather "In what fashion can I get the career and personal satisfactions I need?" Nancy is convinced that as women become comfortable with multiple roles, the men who know them will grow comfortable too.

Most men find it surprising that a woman can be multifaceted. Until recently, most of the men I've worked with have had wives who stay at home, and I don't think these men had ever seen the multifaceted female they're encountering now in today's professional woman.

Personally, I love being a mother. I love being affectionate. I love being sexy. I love buying groceries and being the housewife. On the other hand, I like coming to work. I like doing business. I like high pressure. I like being taken seriously in meetings.

There's one senior executive vice president in this company that I keep bumping into at the Big Star—that's a grocery store—and it's always on Saturday nights, though I don't know why. He shops there with his two little boys, and I shop there with my son. You know, we carry on the best conversations at that grocery store. Of course, I never see him here at work because there are so many levels of bureaucracy between us. But when you bump into somebody at the grocery store, all of a sudden he's a human being and a parent—just like me.

I think that what goes on with the men who aren't married to career women is a kind of shock, a kind of surprise. When you're competent they say, "Gee, you know, she really has something to say. She isn't as dumb as she looks." Or "I guess she can be professional and pregnant at the same time." They're learning. It's slow, to be sure, but they are learning. We have to give them time.

Trade-Offs

One reason women become preoccupied with balance is that many suffer physical or emotional reactions to stress. When reactions occur, a woman begins to rethink commitments. Part of the reevaluation involves recognizing realities and letting go of romanticized expectations. The next part involves dealing with the inevitable disappointments. As each woman goes through this personal assessment, she weighs the joys of her job against the costs it has levied.

The internal search takes many forms. Some women talked about fantasies of giving up work altogether, of staying home, baking cookies, and becoming full-time mothers. Others imagined rediscovering friendships and curling up with good books. But for most, no fantasy is realistic. The women believe that despite the ups and downs, despite the frustration and isolation, despite the physical and emotional consequences, for important psychological reasons they have come to depend heavily on their careers.

Yet, listening to these women describe how their jobs have affected their lives, I was surprised how many sounded clinically depressed. Over and over they matter-of-factly recounted the symptoms of depression: sleep loss, anxiety, fluctuations in weight, a constant lack of energy, and decreased sexual desire. When I asked how long they had been experiencing these symptoms, most shrugged and said they were used to them and really didn't know. It is apparent from these interviews that in many parts of America, bright professional women may be suffering chronic, low-grade depression—a circumstance that could become a serious mental health problem for one of society's most promising populations.

Edie is twenty-six years old, and already she's exhausted. After working all day in "the ring" of Wall Street's commodities exchange, every night she drags herself home, listless yet agitated. Though her depression is mild, it has gone on for months.

I get depressed very easily. I almost get immobilized. Instead of going home wanting to do something, I just think, "Oh, thank God, I'm away from work." I feel that I have to keep busy at night, but I can never concentrate. I might do something to look busy, like flip through a magazine. I think I'm doing something worthwhile when in reality my mind is a million miles away, and I'm just sitting there spaced out. After standing all day without taking lunch, I'm physically exhausted. I'm lucky if my legs can make it up the train station steps.

Ruth's bout with depression was far more dramatic. A young brilliant attorney, she recounts the events of four years earlier, and her face looks fearful. She clenches her teeth and her fists. The memory of an acute depressive episode is clearly terrifying for her. Ruth confides in a whisper that she worries constantly that if she's not careful, suicidal depression may creep up again.

My first year of practice I began to suffer from very, very serious bouts of depression. I was unable to do anything. I would find myself sitting at my desk in my office with the door closed for hours, just staring at the papers. I was unable to read. I had a feeling of real terror and a sense of being overwhelmed.

One night I went home and for no reason started taking my blouse off. Instead of unbuttoning it, I pulled it off, and then I put on every blouse in my closet, nice silk blouses. I'd put each one of them on, button it up, then rip it off. I kept doing this until I was standing in the middle of a pile of blouses, crying, with no idea why I had done that.

When I started having this kind of really whacked-out thing happen, I went to see a doctor. She said, "You are seriously depressed. But it's not your fault. You're not a failure. You need to take medication, and you'll feel better." So I did. I took the medication for six months, and I was fine.

I've come across a lot of professional women who have had early experiences just like mine. You come into a job and you think you're really competent—you did very well in school, and everything looks fine. And then suddenly, for no apparent reason, you can't perform. You're frozen. The terror and the depth of my intimidation at success or failure was so overwhelming that it was just enough to trigger a final leap into a serious depression. It was scary. I was terrified. And I still am.

Depression can be manifest through a variety of physical symptoms. Many of the women I met complained of painful ailments they developed on the job. They talked of headaches, chest pains, bad backs, and stomach disorders. All of these symptoms may express anxiety and pressure, though a surprising number of women seem to take them for granted.

Laurie's story moved me more than most. The contrast between what she told me and the cool, detached way in which she said it demonstrated clearly that a woman working on Wall Street makes certain her feelings always stay contained.

I find the isolation of this job very difficult. I'm sure that's one of the reasons that I got so sick last summer. I remember all the pressure was building back then. It's the pressure inside, of wanting to be right, wanting to be perfect, not ever wanting to make a mistake in my decisions and in my opinions of a company.

I felt the pressure mounting. I wanted not to work for a while, but you don't give up a position on Wall Street just like that. I'd worked far too hard to let it all go just because of some stress. But suddenly my back started bothering me—it was really bad. Within a week I had gotten very, very sick.

I was totally laid up, lying flat on my back. I couldn't move. I had terrible pains down my legs and all over my lower back. I went to a chiropractor, but it didn't help. Nothing seemed to help. A similar pain had gone away in the past, and I figured that soon it would go away again.

But this time it didn't go away. While I was waiting, I got terribly scared.

Finally, I heard about a doctor who believes that most back pain is caused by anxiety, and I started seeing a therapist that he recommended. Within about five weeks, the pain went away.

That whole experience was difficult for me. First of all, I never thought I had an "anxiety problem." I didn't think I needed to see a psychologist. At first it was difficult to accept that I did. But then after a while, I started enjoying it—I started getting into it, in fact.

One of the things I worked on is having to keep up this air of aloofness on my job. I really don't know how to make that toughness go away when my day is finally over at seven o'clock at night. It's almost like putting a mask on when I come to work, because that cold, formal style is what the organization requires. It's very difficult to work in an environment where you have to wear a mask, especially if the mask they give you doesn't fit your face.

Three months later, Laurie chose to remove the mask. She quit her job on Wall Street.

Many working women ward off depression through fantasy. Particularly when they feel powerless to change their work conditions, some start imagining other ways to live. They retreat into the past and daydream of motherhood, child-rearing, and a life led at home. In a posh Madison Avenue office, Fran captures the trends of the past several years. "When the career bubble bursts," she asks me straightforwardly, "what can you do but become just like your mom?"

I remember feeling very strongly that when women first started coming into the work world, being there was like a reward of its own. It was like "Hey, I'm a woman, and look at me. Man, I'm working! I'm a real career woman." I certainly felt all that. I'd say to myself, "God,

I've gotten out there just like everyone else. I've got a good job—I've got a career."

But later I went through a phase of realization: "So what's so rewarding about working? It's a grind. It's a rat race. It's horrible, it's competitive, and you never have free time. My stomach hurts in the morning. I don't sleep at night. I feel like drinking nearly all the time."

You go through this incredible soul-searching. You ask yourself, "Why did I want this? What's so good about working? Why would any woman in her right mind want a job like this?"

At a certain point after all the rah-rah magazine articles had gone away, after all that networking business had slowed down, all of a sudden there was the reality of "God, I fought so hard to get where I am, but why? Why do I want to be here? This place is awful. It's cold. It's unemotional."

And then, after all of this questioning, suddenly we see this big return to more traditional feminine characteristics—like sensitivity and love. And that's when this whole maternity thing began. I think the new baby boom evolved out of women's disappointment with what the work world is really all about.

I remember fifteen years ago if you said that you were going to have a baby, people said, "Oh? Why? What, are you crazy?" It was as if mothers got no respect back in those days. But now all of a sudden, if you don't have a baby, it's like "What's wrong with you? What's the matter? Don't you want to have it all . . . just like me?"

Wendy and Don decided not to have children. Both are executives who have jobs that keep them constantly on the road. For the past twelve years, their decision was fine with Wendy. Lately, however, when she can't sleep, Wendy is wondering if she's made a mistake. A senior vice president at age forty-two, she looks back on her sacrifice and feels deep regret.

I want to quit my job. Wouldn't it be wonderful just to play tennis all day? I wonder if I should have been a mother after all. Maybe that's what I really should have done.

Who needs this job? Just last night I was thinking that I now face an awful lot of pressure that I wish I didn't have to face. I ask myself, "Is this normal for people? Do men feel this way too?" I'm certain that my husband feels this kind of thing a lot, but he evidently handles it much better, because I never even know about it. Yet here I am with my eyes wide open, anxious and awake at three o'clock in the morning.

I don't want all this confusion in my life. I want order. I want happiness. I don't want all this. The wish to escape is my strongest reaction. I ask myself, "Am I doing the right thing by being in this job? I really don't like banking. I don't like it at all. Do I want to continue doing all this? Or do I want to take ballet lessons and go back to school and go shopping and maybe make a special dinner for my husband? Don't I truly want to do all those things instead?"

In the same way that some married career women dream of creating a family when work seems impossible, single women also dream of creating a home. Ironically, many women despair more about the future as they start to get promoted, for they recognize that to many men, their achievements come as a threat.

Andrea lives in a lovely apartment. As a sales rep constantly out on the road, she considers a comfortable home especially important. Looking over her place proudly, Andrea tells me she started with just twenty dollars. Her expression changes abruptly, though, when we start to talk about men. With her head down, Andrea admits that no elegant furniture is worth the pain of loneliness she feels every night.

When a guy tells me I'm really "established," I feel hurt. It says two things to me. First it says that men aren't thinking of meeting needs of mine that are other than financial. The other thing it does is make me angry. Why shouldn't I be established? Who says I have to be living in some dinky little apartment and not have nice things and not go traveling? Why? Why should I be sitting around waiting for the prince to come rescue me from some squalid life? It doesn't make sense.

I refuse to settle for anyone who is not as successful as I am. And given that, I really don't know if it will ever work out. I've dated lots of men, and maybe my expectations are too high. But usually what I'm finding is that we'll go out a few times, and then I just won't hear from them. I went through a stage where I wondered what was going on, so finally I called one of them. I just wanted some feedback. And he said very clearly, "I don't see a place for a man and a family in your present life."

Attitudes like that are a problem, a real problem, for women like me. I guess my idea about marriage has boiled down to "Well, if it happens, it happens." If it doesn't, I'll be darned if I'm going to turn around and go backward. Forget that business.

Another career trade-off the women cited is the loss of friendships. Swamped with responsibilities both at work and at home, they find that friends are often the first thing to go. Looking back, many regret this sacrifice most of all. They miss the long talks, the frivolity, and the ease of support that comes only from deep personal friendships. On stage all day long at the office and generally swamped and busy at home, women find themselves longing for the impromptu visits, telephone chats, and outings they remember from the past. Their lives have become so regimented by schedules that many have forgotten how it feels to have free time. Even more striking, some admit they no longer know what it means to have a friend.

When Marsha had her second child, the public relations firm where she works said she could keep her job if she came in three days a week. At first, she thought she had lucked out. She was working part time, which for most mothers is considered a coup. Gradually, though, Marsha realized that now she was expected to do in three days the same amount of work that used to take her five. When I met Marsha, she felt overwhelmed by work and by two children under two. More than anything, she felt desperate for the support that only friends can provide.

> My biggest sacrifice has been friends. I never see my good female friends anymore. Maybe I talk to them on the phone once a week for ten minutes while kids are screaming in the background on both ends of the line. We don't have time to be friends. I don't feel that I have one good female friend left—I mean a friend I can talk to about anything, be listened to, and be understood.
>
> That makes me sad. That's the one thing that makes me consider not returning to work full time and trying to be a mother too. I find myself thinking, "If I didn't work, would I have time for my friends?" I find that every time I'm with women who don't work, I'll say, "Do you get to go out to lunch with your friends? What do you do during the day? Do you see so-and-so?" I so much want to know. I so much want them to say, "No, I don't do that." I want their lives to validate mine. Sometimes they'll say, "Oh, yeah, we get together with such-and-such every day." But usually they say, "No, I'm just as strung out as you are. I don't see friends either."
>
> I think somehow men manage to see their friends a lot. I know my husband sees his friends and is with them a whole lot more than I'm with mine. This is probably because he doesn't feel the multiple responsibilities. It's easier for him to add friends to his life, when in fact I've chosen to sacrifice mine. It's sad, but it seems as though friends just have to rank below children, husband, and job.

When I asked the women how they minimize stress, all voiced different opinions. Some, like Jennifer, are convinced that everything has to be done in sequence—first you're a career woman, then you're a full-time mother, and later, when the kids get older, you're a professional once again. Others, like Bonnie, insist it's possible to do everything at once, provided a woman accepts the fact that nothing will be done well. Bernice's view is that as long as the individual knows her real priorities, commitments can always be juggled. Caroline represents the opposite point on the spectrum: She feels that since no woman can really hope to have it all, ultimately she must choose between children and career.

Jennifer can't imagine how she could physically keep her job and have a baby at the same time. Having just recited the details of her eighty-hour work week, Jennifer already looks tired and worn out. When I ask her to define her formula for balance, she looks at me weakly and mutters, "One step at a time."

> Women of my generation are making a fatal mistake. It is not humanly possible to have a family and have a really big career, and do both well. You cannot be superwoman. You cannot raise your children with the same level of stimulation, creativity, and love that your mother did without making basic sacrifices in your career. Right now the bottom line is that I will always outsucceed a woman who has a family, simply because right now I don't have one. But the same is true the other way around: You can't succeed in your career and always stay on top of the pile and continue to outperform if you need to devote your energy to your child and husband. My attitude is that I have made a conscious choice. For now.

Bonnie should know about having it all. She's a mother, a wife, and the only woman partner in a prestigious law firm. She even manages to serve on five citywide commissions. After struggling to maintain high standards everywhere, one day Bonnie realized that it couldn't be done. Laughing at herself and at how seriously she used to take things, she tells me the story of how she changed her mind.

I've finally come to grips with the fact that I simply cannot do everything well. I really can't "have it all," as they say. That's been a hard thing to internalize. But the truth is I can't have a career and be a wife and mother who makes little pumpkin sandwiches and goes to PTA meetings and does all kinds of community things. What I have to accept is that I'm going to do some things with a lot of mediocrity and just do other things much better. Shifting from being a perfectionist to this kind of understanding has been wonderful.

It's interesting the way I figured this out. A friend of mine, a writer, came to interview me for an article on women attorneys. But when the article came out it wasn't on women attorneys after all. It played up the theme of "The Superwoman Myth." I remember seeing it and thinking, "Oh, great. What on earth did I say?"

For the last part of the article, my friend had asked me, "How is it that you can have a marriage and a child and a career and be involved in all of these community things and do it all so well?" Totally off guard, I'd said, "I can't. I don't do it all well, not at all." Well, I saw that quote in print and nearly died.

But it turned out that many people called me and said, "Congratulations. That's the neatest thing I've ever heard anybody say." What had happened was that I had finally given myself permission to say I was really screwing up in parts of my life. And the best thing I could do was just not to try to be perfect at them all. I had to hold back on that, and, in the process, try not to screw up absolutely everything.

Bernice sits behind a big walnut desk. She wears a navy blue suit and a red bow tie. She appears every inch the corporate tax attorney. But she feels that because she is black as well as a female, no one at the firm can understand what sitting in that office really means to her. On the issue of family and career, Bernice, too, feels torn.

Sometimes I wish that all I wanted was to marry someone successful. That's so easy in comparison to this. I look at other women—and I know they aren't faking it—and I see that being married to a successful man really makes them happy. So I find myself wondering, "Is there something wrong with me? What am I missing?"

Repeatedly, it seems, I have to make a decision about which I want. When I look at the pattern, I find I always choose me. *I* say I'm choosing me—outsiders say I'm choosing my career, but I know I'm really choosing what I want for myself. I think almost intentionally they characterize it as my choosing a career, because somehow that's less noble.

I ask myself, "Why is practicing law more satisfying to me than I imagine another lifestyle might be?" And then I admit to myself that it's never really been an ambition of mine to get married. In the end, I believe each of us has to evolve to the point where we trust our own decisions, where we never really feel we've chosen the lesser thing.

Caroline got married at thirty-nine. Like many professional women, she married a divorced man older than herself. He didn't want more children, but she felt up against the clock. At that point Caroline evaluated her television career and concluded that if she poured herself into it, she could really make it big. Now, ten years later, she talks about her decision not to have children. In a large sunny office overlooking Hollywood, she speaks with the perspective that only time can bring.

I'm vital and alive and achieving, and every day, even with all the frustrations of this job, there are moments when I'm proud that I'm fighting this war. I'm not just sitting on the sidelines saying, "Gee whiz, I wonder what life is really all about?"

On the other hand, I haven't had a decent vacation in years. I can't remember the last time I had a two-week vacation. I miss that. I also wish I had time to smell the roses. I wish I had time to read a book just because it's a good book, and not because it might make a good movie for television.

But I don't wish anymore that I had children. At one time I did. Do I consider that a loss? Let's talk about that when I'm seventy years old and wondering where my son or daughter is. I did get two wonderful stepchildren along with my husband, and they're grown up and they love me a lot. I think all this comes down to the fine art of compromise. If I am willing to compromise in my business, I've got to be equally willing to compromise in my personal life. You just can't have everything, even though everybody says they want everything.

The past fifteen years represent the story of a profound loss of innocence. Coming into the work world with exaggerated expectations, women were shocked as they witnessed the realities of business. Unlike men, who were brought up aware of these realities, women had to come to terms with the shattering of glamorized notions. They had to confront the consequences of a life strictly dominated by getting ahead. In the end, they had to see for themselves what fathers, husbands, boyfriends, and sons had felt for decades, but rarely shared directly with them.

Along with this loss of innocence came new understanding. The professional women I met now appreciate the complexities of problems in the real world. They recognize that the pressures they take home at night are not unlike the pressures men have felt for years. Above all, they realize that mixed in with the disappointments and disillusionments, there is joy to be found in stretching one's mind and achieving one's goals. In a stockbroker's office high above Wall Street, Michelle captures well the women's hopeful tone.

I feel very good about myself right now, simply because I have become stronger. I have become my own person. And it's been a long, hard pull. It's been two broken marriages. It's been having to live life on a day-to-day basis. When I was a military wife, my husband took care of it all—just the way most women used to have it. It wasn't until the past five years—not until I was thirty-eight years of age—that I finally became a woman. That's a real late bloomer as far as I'm concerned.

Why do I feel good about myself? Because now I'm able to stand on my own two feet. Now I feel able to face the world without having to depend on a man to take care of problems for me. And fundamentally, I no longer feel afraid.

I think the biggest thing women struggle with is fear. A man doesn't have the same kind of fear that a woman does. She's afraid constantly. She's afraid she's going to lose her husband. She's afraid to face life. But what I feel about myself right now is a powerful lack of fear. I feel what a man might feel. I know that I can come in here and earn $80,000 a year and take care of myself. I don't have to depend on a man to pay my bills. If he leaves, I know I'm not going to starve.

I realize I have no children, and that having children would probably change things immensely for me. Right now I have only myself to worry about. I know plenty of women who do have children, and they have to worry constantly about their kids, as well as themselves. It's much tougher for them, and I can't give you any answers there. But I still believe that as soon as women stop being afraid and reach out and grab what they can grab, that's the only time we're going to be any different from what we've all been for generations — generations and generations and generations and generations.

The Mommy Question

Nowhere in the interviews were emotions as raw as when we discussed children. Single women spoke of their longing to have families, and the yearning was evident in their faces and words. Married women trying to get pregnant looked tense and preoccupied. Women who had decided not to have children still found themselves wondering if they'd made the right choice. And working mothers, often drawn and tired, said that no matter what the career sacrifices, when it comes to satisfaction, being a mother is well worth the cost.

Each of the 125 professional women I met had gone through a period of anguish over this issue. Those without children agonized whether having them would jeopardize further advancement in their organizations. Those with children explained in detail the compromises, trade-offs, and psychological justifications they had negotiated all along the way. In both cases—whether a woman was considering motherhood or whether she had made the commitment—the issue itself stirred up profoundly ambivalent feelings. Each woman identified the decision to have or not to have children as one of the significant turning points in her life.

Single women in their thirties feel in a bind. Large numbers of them entered the workforce a decade ago, oblivious to all but getting ahead. For five years or more, they worked hard and stayed late, pouring themselves into their jobs. They rationalized the personal sacrifice by pointing to promotions and salaries. High achievement made them feel competent and powerful, and those feelings, in turn, raised their self-esteem.

Now that they find themselves up against the biological clock, these same women are suddenly confused. While they long to become mothers, they fear that withdrawing from their jobs will mean the loss of power and responsibilities that took years to create. Most important, these women fear that without work they may lose a strong sense of self that their careers have provided. Natalie, an expert in videotape productions, sums up the conflict well.

> I'm at an age where I'm feeling torn. I'm thirty-six and I know that if I'm going to have children, I need to do it quickly. But I'm still very career-driven. It's difficult for

me right now because I feel the old biological clock ticking away.

A lot of women have children when they're young, so that by the time they get further along in their careers their children aren't quite so demanding. Maybe that's the answer if you want to try to do both. But I'm sure it's very difficult for those women too.

I definitely believe that if I had had a family, I wouldn't have succeeded to the degree that I have now. Because I'm single, I've been willing to put in a lot of long hours and work exceedingly hard at my job. I truly believe that's had something to do with all the promotions I've gotten and the movement that has taken place in my career. If I had had a child, I'm sure it wouldn't have happened the way it did.

Claudia said she couldn't "get out" to have a child even if she wanted to. As chief litigator for a state regulatory agency, she supervises the work of fifteen attorneys. Though the demands are extensive, Claudia loves the pace and drama of going to court. Yet somehow she doesn't feel in charge of what's happening. Her desire for children is almost forgotten in the frenzied intensity of a litigator's life.

Work is very demanding. There are a lot of expectations of me here, particularly at my current level. I find myself routinely putting in sixty-five and seventy hours a week. This drains you, from a physical and a mental perspective, both. It also has a very negative impact on your social life. Finally, there's a point at which you say, "Enough is enough."

All of this is very difficult to balance. That's one of the reasons I've shied away from having a family—it's even harder to balance all that. I'm the type of person who feels very committed to doing my job the best way I know how. I'm certain that if I were raising children, I'd have the same attitude about that. I could devote only a certain amount of energy to my career, because I'd have this other huge responsibility that would require my dedication as well. I admire women who raise families while they have careers. I think that must be incredibly difficult.

Ruth, another lawyer, has skyrocketed to leadership within her community. She publishes regularly, sits on blue-ribbon commissions, and has a clientele that seems to keep growing. When she thinks about a family, she feels paralyzed. She finds herself envious of her husband and the fact that his own legal career would not be affected by the birth of their child. Angry at herself for feeling competitive, Ruth nonetheless cannot imagine giving up all that she's built.

I'm thirty-five this year, and I'm dealing with the issue of whether I'm ever going to have children. I am really agonizing about that, because I don't think it's fair to have a child just to have one, and then spend sixteen hours a day, seven days a week at a job.

Frankly, I think about work all the time. I never leave it behind. I ask myself, "What kind of mother is that?" Unless I'm willing to change that dramatically, I don't have any business having a baby. Is this something I'm going to be sorry about in five years? I honestly don't know.

If I did become a mother, I'd have to change my style of working completely. I would have to become more efficient. I would have to commit myself less. I'd have to do fewer things, turn down speaking engagements, probably get off the board of governors of my professional association, and not write so much. I'd have to leave the office by six. I'd have to learn to leave all of it behind.

While single women intellectualize, mothers learn by doing. Their comments are pragmatic, clear, and to the point. They talk about becoming realistic, learning what is possible and where compromises must be made. They agree that cutting back on career ambitions is an absolute necessity—if not in a permanent sense, at least for a time. Throughout the mothers' statements, a new kind of perspective stands out distinctly. When I asked the women about that perspective, one replied, "Just when I thought the corporation was my world, I had a baby, and that other world looked so small." This added dimension of knowledge and insight helped working mothers balance their lives.

Ginger, her husband, and their five children live on a farm fifty miles outside the city. Each day at dawn, Ginger, in white Bloomingdale's slacks, feeds the cows, then feeds five kids, then jumps on a train for an hour's ride to work. When I go to meet Ginger, I find her office in a mess. Papers are scattered everywhere, pictures of kids cover the desk, and marking pens, photographs, and layouts fill every chair. Ginger laughs, apologizing for the chaos. She tells me that raising five children is excellent preparation for maintaining sanity in the advertising world. Later, her tone turns serious when I ask about her family. Even she, who seems to fit the superwoman profile, has serious doubts that she ponders late at night.

> I just don't buy the idea that it's not the quantity of time, it's the quality. I really don't. Having a family and having a career requires a very, very, very difficult balance. I ought to know—I have five kids.
>
> Anytime I'm away too long, or if I go on a production, I feel the problem more. Last year I was in the middle of a major production for a long time, in and out and in and out every day and every night. One night I actually got home on time, and my little one looked at me and said, "Oh good, Mommy, you're babysitting tonight!" Well, that just broke my heart. I felt so terrible—really, really terrible.
>
> Looking back, there have been times when the kids have had stitches, and I haven't been there. Or it was the first time one of them got on a school bus, and I haven't

been there. Or, as in the commercial, "Today my daughter took her first step . . ." and I was away at a meeting. That all comes right out of real life experience.

The other part—which I very much agree with—is that you can't be a great mother unless you go home at five, and you can't be a great businesswoman unless you stay after five. The way I handle that is that I am not great at either. That's my answer. You know, I kick up a lot of dust, and I come on as though I can do it all. But, to be honest, it's a real stretch. It's a strain on my relationship with my husband. And it shows up in all those squeaky-wheel neuroses in the kids.

I've had some problems in recent years because I am a nine-to-fiver. I've always made that very, very clear. At five o'clock, apron strings sprout out of my sides. I go home. I don't take business with me. And I never bring my kids to the office.

I like what I do. I really like working. In fact, I can't imagine not working. But I also want to go home. I like to go home. And a lot of men in this agency simply don't understand that.

This may be a generalization, but I'm afraid I'm going to have to make it: A lot of men I work with either can't share my feeling because they don't have that desire or that drive to go home, or they don't have a need for that fifty-fifty balance. Instead, they choose to devote more time to the professional side because they think of themselves as less needed at home.

I think that's tragic. Men in this country just don't realize how much fathers are needed at home. But I'm certainly not blaming them for it. That's a sin that comes from the moms as well.

Most women agreed that you can't do it all and plan to do it all perfectly. To deal with this reality, working mothers devise a host of ingenious schemes. Some admit to lowering their standards and giving up perfectionism in hopes of keeping both family and job intact. Others choose to prioritize commitments, deferring certain job goals until the kids are grown. Those who try to raise a family while staying on the fast track find that the only way they can do it is by structuring their lives in almost rigid ways.

As I listened, I couldn't help but wonder how many women would soon burn out. With no historical precedents and little support from employers, mothers in professional jobs are charting new courses entirely on their own. The psychological challenge is enormous, and the task of sustaining it takes energy as well.

Sarah recognizes this fact. She is proud of having raised her son alone, and she likes how he turned out. Sarah remembers when she decided to put motherhood first, though all along she was working full time. Her advice is to choose what you value and focus on it, while believing, as she did, that "the rest falls into place."

> I've been very serious about being a decent parent to my son. I was conscious that there were many things I could have done that would have moved me forward in my career, but all of them would have involved my not being at home. I very consciously decided that I was going to defer certain things.
>
> I do not believe you can be a good parent and remain on the fast track. It's not humanly possible. You can pretend to be a good parent and be on the fast track, but you are usually a rotten parent, because being on the fast track involves just not being available to your kids.
>
> One of the things I've had in my mind during the last three years is the realization that in another two and a half years my son will be going off to college and I'll be forty-five. I have felt very much that that will be the moment at which I can make another set of career moves.
>
> Considering all the things I haven't been willing to do for work, when I look at my career thus far, I think I've done extremely well.

I worry about Nancy. She is trying to do everything with skill, talent, and flair. Just hearing her describe a typical week, I feel drained and exhausted, though Nancy herself beams with energy and pride. To make sure that all her responsibilities are covered, Nancy has adopted one simple rule: Do everything as best you can, but keep all your roles distinct. Listening to Nancy describe how she moves from job to mothering, I wonder if at any time she'll yearn for an integrated life.

> When I'm at work I'm giving 100 percent, and when I'm at home I'm giving 100 percent too. I rarely do work on the weekends. Now, that doesn't mean that I don't entertain people from work. I do. But usually from Friday night to Sunday night it's exclusively home. We have home renovation projects going on, and there are always shopping and cooking and all those household things. All those are things that I want, things that are important to me. My friends outside of work are very important to me too. So I use discretion, but I try to make sure that those people aren't getting cheated in my life.
>
> When I'm at work, on the other hand, I'm a devout loyalist to the job. I would go to the ends of the earth if my son's babysitter didn't come to work one day. I'd take him to child care or do anything I could to keep from having to stay home. I don't consider that kind of thing an excuse for missing work. To me, it's just part of what we have to learn to struggle with, to be received and perceived as being very professional employees. When I say I give 100 percent, I really do mean that. Monday through Friday at work I give 100 percent.

Working mothers worry about preserving their marriages. Running from job to kids to job again, they discover that time with their husbands is too often lost. To avoid that predicament, Cynthia and John consciously decided that having a child would be a two-parent enterprise. John quit his job to work out of the home and take care of the baby. Even though she appears to have the perfect set-up, Cynthia still feels panicked, with no time of her own.

> I had a baby because I looked in the mirror and saw how old I was. It was suddenly like, "Well, if we're going to do it, we'd better get on with it." For the past nine months, my husband's worked for himself because he's wanted to spend time with our son. He's a great daddy.
>
> But my frustration has been that there's just not enough time. I haven't read a magazine since I was in the delivery room. I'm really bummed out by this. I do have some time, of course, but certainly not a lot—especially with the amount I work. By the time I come home every night, we can only play with the baby awhile. We don't eat dinner until the baby goes to bed because it's just ridiculous. So suddenly it's ten o'clock and that's it. There's just never enough time.
>
> I have a friend who always says, "Life is not a Hallmark card." It's really not. My child and I do not walk barefoot on the beach every day. When I thought about child-rearing, all I thought about was walking on the beach. I didn't think, "I'm never going to read a magazine. I'm never going to go anywhere. I'm never going to do anything." I guess if I didn't work fourteen hours a day, I'd have a lot more time.

The working mothers I met feel unsupported by their employers. Time and again, they told me stories of how they had been subtly teased throughout pregnancy, as if childbirth were an embarrassment to the organization. Maternity leave was also a major bone of contention. Women described the intricate plans they devised for stretching out their leaves without jeopardizing their jobs. Rarely did a woman note that the company applauded her decision to start a family. Rather, most felt that their bosses and colleagues secretly believed they would not return to work.

Dual-career families now dominate the workforce, yet few

personnel policies have caught up with social change. Almost none of the women I interviewed work in organizations that offer flex time, job sharing, paternity leave, part-time employment, or the option to work at home. But seeing the women's determination to preserve family and career, I'm convinced that organizations that present creative solutions for dual-career couples will be those that will attract and retain top talent in the coming years.

Gina and Fran talk about their companies in hushed tones. Gina is a single mother. Fran is married and thinking of having a child. Gina has had to compartmentalize her life to a frightening extreme. Ever since she adopted her son thirteen years ago, she has avoided mentioning him while at work. To make sure no one there views her as a "mommy," Gina pretends her son doesn't exist.

> I rarely mention anything about duties concerning my son while I'm at work. When I first adopted him, he needed a lot of special attention. Back then, I had to do triple duty to try to maintain my work presence and still be a mother, because when any of the other women managers called in saying that their child was sick, the guys' retorts were totally unfair. So to protect myself I wouldn't say anything.
>
> It was OK for the men to tell stories about their kids. But I couldn't talk about my son for years, and that hurt. The men could be proud or angry or whatever at their kids, but I would have to sit there at that lunch table and not say a word, because if I did it would be, "Oh, just like a woman," or "Oh, listen to Mommy," or "Well, why did you get that kid anyway?" or "Well, if you weren't a single parent. . . ."
>
> Even though a woman's biological role is to produce and care for her family and home and hearth, you get the clear message that you can't do that in business. And you really better not bring those issues in. If somebody asks you, then it's OK to answer. But I can never go into a

room and burst out with, "Oh, you should see what my son's doing this week." No way, I tell you. No way.

Fran thinks that women are conflicted about having children not just because they fear the loss of intellectual stimulation, but also because their organizations subtly punish them for taking time off. Wearing fashionable jeans and bright argyle socks, Fran looks every bit the part of a Madison Avenue designer. Yet behind her colorful exterior is a young woman who is longing to have a child. As she wavers in making her decision, Fran is carefully scrutinizing the fate of other women.

Maternity benefits stink. They let you take six weeks off with pay, but I don't think six weeks is enough after you've just had a baby. In general, I think the men here see having a baby as a handicap. One of my supervisors said to me, "We're all for women having babies, but there's a certain place in this agency for women with babies."

My case is actually a good example, because right now I'm working on one of the best accounts in the business, and I've worked very hard to get there. But the implication is that if I have a baby, I'm no longer going to get to work on that account. Instead, I'm going to be assigned to an account that's less challenging, less exciting, much more tedious, and not as much fun. Their argument is always, "Well, you'll have a baby and you won't have as much time to put in."

I recently heard of one place where a woman has two new babies, and the company values her skills so much that they don't care how she uses her time. She's still the editor of that magazine. She doesn't work all day, but she gets all the work done, so she's still the editor.

But around here, and probably in most corporate environments, the assumption is that as soon as you have a baby, somehow your intelligence drops and you're less capable of functioning. Personally, I think that's real disrespect for a woman who's trying to juggle everything.

But business is so competitive that I understand their reasoning. And sure, if I were a supervisor I'd want somebody who was going to be able to put in the hours at the drop of a hat. But I've seen too many women in this agency who have had babies, and they all get overlooked, put out to pasture. It's very unfair. It's a terrible waste.

Emily thinks a lot about these issues. Having described her concerns, she walks me through the list of divorces in her office. She then moves on to count the divorces in the division. When she gets to the point of naming divorces among executives, Emily stops and sadly shakes her head. She gets up then and goes to the window. Late afternoon sun makes the office golden and still. For a full five minutes I wait in silence as Emily ponders her final statement.

If getting in with the guys means that you have no family and no friends and no time for the things that are really important to you, and after all is said and done it's just a matter of whether somebody likes your face, who really wants to be in?

One day, I realized that I don't want to be a part of that if it means another divorce—or worse, if being in means that at any time I could lose it all because I have put all of my energy into letting the company have me. They could fire me anytime, just like that. You have to save a piece of yourself, the important piece that keeps you in control and centered. I look around and I see all these people who are giving away every piece of themselves. It's scary.

This is all crucial now because there's so much change going on. Women's roles are changing tremendously. We're all putting a lot of energy into getting ahead. But we're going to have to be fully conscious about what "getting ahead" really is and what that "pie in the sky" might mean to our relationships, our marriages, and our children.

I'm fearful for women who are now moving into the corporate world, because the pendulum is going to swing very far for them, and if they don't catch it, suddenly it'll be too late. They will lose the things that are most valuable. They will never accomplish personal things like a loving relationship or a family if they don't watch out for the pitfalls of executive life.

There's also a big issue about maternity leave coming up now. A lot of women are not getting their original jobs back once they return to work. I think that fear of not being able to go back to one's position might keep women from making the decision to have children. And if that happens, it's a national tragedy.

Tips From the Trenches

Know Thyself

The women's recommendations about balance range from attitude change to new strategies designed both for home and for office. Recommendations cover the span of career life, from the time a woman starts working to the time her children are grown. Achieving a balance will never come easily; it is a concentrated process that takes energy, soul-searching, and time.

Women emphasized that the hardest part of thinking about these issues is self-understanding and deciding what you want. Many told me shyly that they had been swept away by careerism in the 1970s and 1980s, and thought then that they no longer wanted a child. It wasn't until much later that they acknowledged the desire for a family, realizing that this was still a priority in their lives. From that experience, women learned a critical lesson—that self-understanding must come before goal-setting and that goal-setting comes before making a choice.

Patricia presents a framework for thinking through the issue. What she advocates is a version of strategic thinking that she learned through the civil rights movement. There, Patricia learned that once you're in touch with values, beliefs, and a strong sense of purpose, taking the steps to achieve them is least difficult of all.

> You have to plan to live, and then you have to live your plan. You've got to know what steps you need to take to get there, and then you have to follow those steps. You have to constantly reevaluate your work and your personal life and how they tie in together. You have to be honest with yourself about who you are and what you really want to be. That honesty is hard to come by.
>
> I want all of us to be sensible, and I want all of us to be honest. That's mainly it. Know who you are and be honest about what you want. Then follow those steps.
>
> And never say, "I didn't get something because I am female." First look at yourself and ask, "Did I do the best I could?" And then, if it does back up to being female, say to yourself, "OK, now how can I get around this?" You can get around it because everybody you run into has a weak spot you can use. You have to learn personality styles, and you have to learn how to work with them. You can't expect to like and respect everyone you work with.
>
> And to deal with this constantly, you must have outside outlets to get rid of all the anxiety. You're never going to make it if you don't have an outside life.

Setting priorities requires an accurate sense of one's strengths and limitations. Nonetheless, many women I interviewed still wrestle with the wish to be perfect in all areas of life. Having been excellent students, they strove to become superb professionals. Having made it in their careers, now they seek to be superior mothers. Unwilling to relent, many try to do it all and end up feeling drained. Disappointed, they feel that nowhere in their lives are they living quite up to standard.

Many women understand that they remain their own harshest critics and that to the extent they come to grips with limitations, they can prioritize career and family life in more realistic ways. Though the fundamental problem is internal, overcoming perfectionism is a long, difficult task. Women who recognized this tendency and challenged its validity found themselves much better able to cope.

When I arrive at Marty's house for an evening appointment, she looks flustered and apologizes for not having put the baby to bed. Her husband looks haggard as he lamely picks up toys scattered about the room. Marty and Bob are exhausted. They are high-level managers who work ten-hour days and raise three children besides. When Marty returns from the nursery clutching her wine, she can talk of nothing but the challenge of being both a mother and a senior executive. In her mind, the key is mapping out ahead of time the realistic consequences of every single choice. That way, when the time comes for living with the consequences—be they financial, social, or health-related—both members of the couple are better prepared to cope.

In recent years there has been a lot of change, but I think there are also some things that will never change. One thing that doesn't change is the need to recognize who you are. Getting a chemical engineering degree has nothing to do with knowing what you really want for yourself. A degree certainly prepares you to do something in the world, if you decide to utilize it. But the thing I've noted with the eight women working in my department is that they haven't wrestled with what they really want for themselves. They haven't wrestled with what they're willing to compromise.

Everybody has to make some choices. Nobody can have it all. My sister once said to me, "Marty, you've got it all." I stared at her and said, "No, I don't have it all. I've had to make some pretty tough choices in my life."

But I don't think most women are conscious about having control of themselves enough to know that they can choose who they're going to be. Somehow, too many of us think somebody's going to bestow it upon us, or somebody else will make our decisions. The thing I would advise is to really do some soul-searching on what you want for yourself.

If a woman wants a family, that's fine. But she can't expect that she can have three children, take six months off at each of those births, and convince a company that she is a committed professional. That just isn't realistic. That woman has to understand that each path is a choice. If she's committed to it and thinks that that path is best for raising her children, then she should do it, by all means believe in it, and expect to live with the consequences.

But if she decides to take only six weeks' maternity leave because she thinks that's best for her career, then she can't take herself on a guilt trip around her child. She made a choice because she believed it was important either for her family or for herself or for her child. And that's the choice she's made.

Emily believes that a life plan is meaningless unless a woman is willing to present that plan to her employer directly. Recalling the months leading to her divorce, Emily said that it never occurred to her not to work every night. If she had thought through her priorities, she could have stated them clearly and then negotiated them one by one with her boss. To reduce her chances of another divorce, she now states exactly what she won't sacrifice.

Women have to be very clear about where they want to go and what they're willing to give up. If they don't take charge, the corporation will take everything, and they'll be allowing that corporation to take everything from them unless they draw the line. Women must learn to say clearly, "I will not work on weekends," or "I want to have a family," or "By the time I'm thirty, I'm going to take a leave of absence to have a child." Unless they're perfectly clear going in, they will lose sight of their goals and ultimately lose it all.

We all need to be very clear inside ourselves about where we ultimately want to go and how much we're willing to give up to get there. Then if the company doesn't allow us to do that, we'll have to reevaluate. At that point, we'll have to assess whether we still want to go with our original goals or whether we want to alter them because we particularly like this company or these people or how much they pay.

Women have to constantly reevaluate goals. They have to make sure that in the end they can truthfully say they always did it their own way, that they were the ones in charge, that no one made them do it. Really, the company never "makes" us do anything. We either allow them to do it to us or we don't.

Many of the women offered tips on how best to balance career and family life. Some mothers advised against having children in the early days of one's career. Courtney noted that once she had become indispensable in the office, she had more leverage than she'd expected when the issue of maternity leave came up. Worried that she might lose ground professionally, she discovered, instead, that during her absence the senior managers she works with missed her expertise. She advises, "Prove yourself first."

Power and success and all that stuff are not the sum total of life. There's also being a mom. But wait awhile to get established in your career before getting pregnant, because then the company will need you desperately, and you can write your own ticket. That's basically what I did. By the time I wanted to have a child, the company had decided that they couldn't afford to lose me.

Also, don't take it all so seriously. Most important, don't take yourself so seriously. Get involved in the community, keep a happy marriage, have kids—do all that. But don't try to be Superperson. Above all, learn to compromise. If women really feel that they have to get to the top, I guess that's fine, but it's not necessarily the world's most noble ideal.

Women, like men, are going to be a whole lot happier if they don't let other people make them into something they don't want to be. I still get that old pressure all the time. People here say, "You haven't had a promotion in three years. Don't you feel there's something wrong with you? Better watch out. People are going to stop seeing you as a fast-track person and think you're actually going backward." After you hear that a few times it's easy to start getting upset. But then I say, "Well, I didn't want to be that big-time executive anyway. Big deal. Go away from me."

While you have to disregard pressure like that, it's important to listen to everybody who has solid advice to give. Don't put your armor up when people say something you don't want to hear—they're probably not going to say it again. Listen. Ask for feedback and accept it, because people really do want to help. You can always find coaches and sponsors—maybe not mentors, but you can find people all over the place who want to help if you've got something to offer. If you're a good person for the company, they've got a reason to want to invest some time in you. Be open to it. If somebody says, "I will help bring you through your career" and they're a good person, don't ignore that. Don't try to do everything on your own.

If you think you can do everything on your own, you've lost your mind.

Another tip in planning is to confront the possibility of burnout head-on. If month after month, year after year, working women have had no time to themselves, it's inevitable that they will spiral downward in both a physical and emotional sense. Swamped with deadlines, travel, children, and housework, women still tend to put themselves last. Over a protracted length of time, the pattern can lead to fatigue, poor health, and decreased motivation. Too often it leads to depression as well.

Becoming conscious of these physical and mental dangers means taking deliberate steps to escape responsibilities and to create a certain time for oneself. The working women I met agree that even though finding time may at first seem impossible, leisure and relaxation are the only ways to guarantee sustained mental health. In Nancy's case, the hardest part about taking time was overcoming her harsh internal judge.

To be successful you have to have a clear sense of self, and of what you want to do. Then you have to go about getting it in a real no-nonsense way. The way I was brought up, and the way a lot of women were brought up, was not like that at all—instead we were expected to make people happy, all the time. We were always worrying about offending people or worrying about saying no.

Working here, it was so difficult for me to learn to say no—like saying no to assignments or saying no to working overtime. But soon you find out that you really achieve a lot more and earn a lot more respect when you do learn to say no. You do so much better when you don't try to be coy about getting what you want, but when instead you go straight for it.

It's important to have goals. It's especially important for women starting out, because we tend to give up a lot personally to get ahead professionally. That's something we really have to watch out for. I'm talking here about striking that elusive balance. I still think it can be done.

I'm still hopeful all of this will work out for us. I know discrimination is there, but I'm still hopeful things will change. But in the meantime, be sure to take time for yourself. I think that's key. I once met with another television anchorwoman who has two children. I looked at her and said, "How do you balance all this?" She said simply, "I don't have time for myself. I haven't had a

257

manicure in ten years." If that's really going to be the case, I think twenty years down the road, we'll all look back proudly on our successes and we'll all look back proudly on our children, but we will constantly wonder why we weren't enjoying them all along.

For a long time I was afraid to make time for myself. I thought it was selfish to map out a couple of hours every week that would be my time to stay in bed and just read. Now, though, I think it's critical to make time for myself. All of that ends up benefiting you as well as everyone around you. You're more productive at work, you're a better companion for your husband, you're a better parent to your children.

I think as women we do get caught up in questioning ourselves every single day, asking, "Why am I doing all this?" We're constantly asking, "How am I ever going to get through the day?" To keep even the slightest bit of balance in our lives, we need to recognize it's not selfish to make time for ourselves.

The problem with goals and plans is that circumstances change unexpectedly, and suddenly the plan is obsolete. As a result, career plans must have built-in flexibility, and goals must be reevaluated on a regular basis. Lois learned that while events may change, a clear sense of values keeps her direction on track.

I think the hardest thing is to keep perspective on your own values. It's hard to keep in mind the importance of what really counts. It's hard not to sell yourself away too cheaply or too easily. So I'd say give your energies to what matters most in your heart.

Then make sure you reevaluate it constantly. What really matters to you won't always be the same. There are certain values that you'll hold all of your life, but you need to reassess them and reassess your direction every X-number of months—every six months at the max. Look at where you are and see if you're really pleased with the direction you're going. I always figure it's not where I am, but the direction I'm going that makes all the difference.

Re-evaluating goals comes instantaneously when a woman gives birth to her first child. New mothers told me that very quickly they came to view their careers in an entirely new light. Most were surprised at how profoundly they were moved by motherhood, and how daily work frustrations suddenly seemed petty. Every mother I met expressed the wish that she had given herself more options in returning to work. Hannah, a water rights lawyer, advises women to consider that their ambitions may change totally as soon as they have children. Fingering a silver-framed photograph of her daughter, Hannah speaks in a soft voice, as if to herself.

What I would like to be now is a good model for my daughter, in many senses. That includes being a professional as well as trying to be a calm, sensible, consistent parent. And let me tell you, being a part-time lawyer doesn't lend itself to calmness.

I really have to work extra hard at not being grumpy. That's why I sometimes think I ought to chuck it in and go home for a while, for several years. So what if my skills deteriorate and my mind vegetates? At least I could cook a dinner that's not a Lean Cuisine.

You know, it wasn't so much that my idea of success changed after I had my daughter. It was that the focus of *whom I wanted to be successful for* suddenly changed. I had always wanted to be a calm, considerate, consistent, whatever-I-was to whomever I was relating to—whether I was a wife, colleague, or friend. But there was something about my daughter's arriving that really brought it into sharp focus. It was a profound experience.

The thing that having my daughter did for me was to remind me that life is short and that for me, human values are always more important than professional values. I still want to be a good lawyer, but if it came to choosing between practicing law and going home full time, I would go home. And I wouldn't look back.

Before I had a daughter, I didn't need to make that clear a choice. Then it was OK just to keep going along this fast track. Now that I have her, that choice, if it becomes necessary, may also become inevitable.

How well a woman achieves a sense of balance depends in large part on her husband's attitude toward her career. Trudy and Sandy agree that balance is something couples must strive for together. Sometimes it means simple things, like sharing the driving, or understanding that a crisis at the office means an empty place at dinner. Other times the question entails much larger commitments, like the decision to relocate or to take a drop in status so a mother can stay at home. Considering the pivotal role of husbands, the women advised others to select only those partners who can appreciate the need for balance and who will act conscientiously to ensure that it's achieved.

Trudy got recruited out of business school to work for a top management consulting firm. Her husband, also an MBA, started his own company about the same time. When they decided to start a family, they wrote down a list of what each would give up. Trudy is convinced that the reason her child, job, and marriage are all surviving well is that she and her husband knew what sacrifices to expect.

I think a working couple has to accept the fact that there are going to be times when one or the other is totally preoccupied with what's happening at the office—when he or she must have the privilege of dropping out of the home and being totally into business. When both people are working, you have to accept that those things happen. If you've got a good relationship to start with, it's really much better. You understand each other and each other's worlds.

Sandy works in the oil industry, a place where fortunes are made and lost in a matter of hours. From living in that whirlwind atmosphere, she has come to appreciate the value of contingency planning and of keeping options open. Sandy believes that though a plan is important, knowing how to spot opportunities and when to move off the plan is, in the long run, a more valuable skill. Sitting in her living room on a warm Texas evening, Sandy sips a gin-and-tonic and offers her advice.

If women are aggressive and they really want to do well, they've got to be flexible. Being tied to one setting will take its toll. Either you have to find somebody who's willing to move around with you—which is highly unlikely—or you have to find somebody who's going to stay in one place with you. Then you have to find an industry and a company that are also going to stay in one place.

You have to keep your options open. You can't just work for one company and forget about all the rest. This is sometimes hard to do, but in retrospect, you have to. You owe it to yourself to look for a lot of options. You can be true and loyal, but you also need to keep your eyes open. And above all, don't restrict your activities to just your job. Get involved in other things, get exposure, and make sure you've got a cross section of good contacts. If some day you get laid off, or if you want to change jobs, or if somebody comes and knocks on your door and says, "Come work for us," the reason itself doesn't matter. The point is that none of it will happen unless you're out there and you know good people.

In the final analysis, achieving balance depends on discovering and maintaining a consistent sense of self. Women who had emulated men for many years said that the pretense hurt them psychologically and caused instability in their personal lives. By stepping back from the pressures and reassessing their larger goals, they are able to make choices more effectively and to feel their identities return. They've concluded that the only sustaining way to cope as a woman is to be who you are, refusing to pretend you are someone you're not.

Ruth is excited to be her own person. When she gave up trying to copy other lawyers, she knew intuitively that her life would improve. What she never expected, she tells me delightedly, is that being herself would raise her legal skills, too.

> Don't try to be a man. Don't allow men to intimidate you into wearing a bow tie. If you like frilly blouses, then for God's sake wear them. That's how you're going to be most comfortable. It's only when you're comfortable with yourself that you will truly be able to be relaxed about your work. And if you're relaxed about the work, then you're going to be much more effective. When you're relaxed, you'll have the best judgment to do what you want in the most efficient way. If we try to behave the way men think we should, or even the way other women tell us we should, and it's not really who we are, we'll all end up unhappy, professionally unhappy, and certainly not nearly as effective.

Shirley, a seventeen-year veteran, worries that few women are making it in the high-technology field. Watching young female engineers get lost in her company, she believes they have given up unique strengths in order to fit in. Shirley is convinced that this kind of adaptation robs women of the special skills the industry needs most. She feels that only if women retain their diversity can they really make a difference and see technology advance.

> A lot of women go into professions today and say, "I'm not a woman, I'm a lawyer," or "I'm not a woman, I'm a programmer." They pretend to forget they're women. But you can't. If you forget you're a woman, you forget that you have feelings, you forget that you care.
>
> One of these days that attitude is going to catch up with you. And when it does, you're going to be in for such a

shock you won't understand what happened. Invariably, it's going to happen right at that point in your career when you should be able to make the big leap, but you find for some strange reason that you can't.

I think a lot of that has to do with having forgotten you're a woman. You have to be a whole person to function. You can't just be part of a person. I really think that that's a big thing that a lot of women—especially young women, I'm afraid—forget about today.

In the old days, Suzanne, too, tried to be like a man. She copied men's behavior, dressed only in dark suits, and was careful never to reveal what she felt inside. For many years, her formula seemed to be paying off well. She became the only woman partner in an architectural design firm, commanded a salary of $200,000, and had full responsibility for a large professional staff. But six months ago, in her words, "something big came crashing down." Examining her life and the world she'd created, Suzanne described herself as "empty, a mere collection of roles." After agonizing self-scrutiny and some professional help, she decided she could no longer be two people—one woman at work and another at home.

Recently I started thinking, "I don't want to die and look back on my life and say, 'I lived up to all my responsibilities, but I wasn't happy.'" And you know, I think I can have both. I think I can have all these responsibilities and become happy in the process. Since I've always been successful at everything I've done, why can't I be successful at having a fine career, being a good mother, and having a relationship with a man where feelings go back and forth? I used to think, "Fine, but will that cost me my job?" I'm beginning to think that having a full life will not only *not* cost me my job, but that it makes my job easier and better.

A man told me the other day, "Suzanne, organizations don't really have goals. People do. What you're missing here is that you think you can sit down and write out business goals, and everyone will just go along with them. But that isn't the way it works. You've got to find out what people's personal goals and aspirations are, and weave that together. Only then will your organization get ahead." I remember thinking, "That makes a whole lot of sense."

But he went on, "The hard thing is getting people to lay their cards on the table." That's when I realized that the only way I'm going to get what I really want is to lay my own cards on the table. If I do that, then maybe others will start to do that too.

Well, after that meeting, I came back to the office and started doing that with my partners. I started saying, "Here's what I'm thinking of doing. What do you think about that? Here's how I feel about this. How do you see it? Let's go talk about this out of the office somewhere. Let's all get together for once and just talk."

And you know, the greatest things are happening around here now. We're getting all this cohesiveness and agreement on what we really want to accomplish. We're working together. I'm proud that my cards are finally on the table.

A search for personal balance is the ultimate challenge professional women now face as they continue in the world. Unlike men who were raised to be pragmatists, women entered the workforce with idealistic hopes. As they found themselves confronting barrier after barrier, hundreds of young women grew up overnight. Their realizations were painful, but always instructive. They grew savvy and wise, no longer naive. Looking back on their accomplishments, the women I talked with are glad that through it all they maintained a sense of values and personal beliefs. With the spirit and the determination that helped her survive Wall Street, Michelle sums up their sentiments in her own unique words.

If I could give one message to all the women out there, if they're coming into business, any business—doctor, lawyer, Indian chief, stockbroker, whatever—my message would be to maintain your own individuality as much as possible. Don't become enmeshed in what you think you should be.

Obviously corporations have rules and regulations that you have to maintain and keep. But still, within all of that, maintain your own individuality, set your own goals, work at your own pace as much as you can. Once you start falling into that old trap of being what everyone else is, you've lost.

You're a female. There's no doubt about it. You're different from a male. You cannot come in dressed like him and act totally like him. He's different. He's always going to be different, by God's nature. So do your own thing. Be equal to him in the workforce, do as well, study as hard. But don't try to become him.

I want to be a woman. I happen to enjoy being a woman. I don't want to be a man. I don't want to wear trousers or pin-striped suits tomorrow—I feel sorry for men in the summertime, quite frankly. I want to be a woman. And I am equal to or better than men in brains and in aggression and in assertiveness. I'm proud of who I am today. I have my own spark.

Epilogue

Men and Women Together:
The Only Alliance

For more than a year I traveled across the country, listening to the voices of professional women—a proud and stunningly competent group whose members have achieved an incredible amount in a very short time. But as their words so clearly attest, many remain essentially unfulfilled. Why, after all they've done, do professional women feel so discontented? What are the implications of the findings in this book?

To get at the deepest roots of this question, we need to adopt the broadest possible perspective. We need to view the phenomenon not only as psychological, but as historic and economic as well. Male-female tension, depicted graphically in these pages, is the result of fundamental shifts in culture that intellectually we acknowledge, but daily we deny. To date, resistance has surfaced indirectly, making it difficult to pinpoint and easy to overlook. Organizations today are riddled with anxiety, but few have addressed it in systematic ways. To the extent we pretend the problem is nonexistent, individuals suffer and collective energies are drained.

Our first task is to accept the trend as irreversible. Professional women are entering the workplace in escalating numbers, and once inside, they are unlikely to leave. Both economic necessity and pride in accomplishments keep women working even after they establish families. The question is no longer whether women will remain at work—today's coed workforce has become a way of life, unlike the era of Rosie the Riveter. A more relevant question has surfaced for the future: Can male-run organizations accept what women can give?

To consider this question, it helps to step back from daily pressures and ponder the uniqueness of this moment in time. Fundamentally we recognize that American men and women share many of the same global concerns. When we keep this bigger picture in mind, squandering energy on male-female tension seems adolescent and petty. But too often it is easy to lose track of mutual interests. When we are forced to compete, we abandon shared goals. As long as men and women struggle for limited resources, rarely will their overlapping concerns get the attention they deserve.

Imagine how much vitally needed talent is being wasted by the underutilization of American working women. Just as the introduction of computer technology has infinitely expanded our capacity for information, so too could unleashed female brainpower expand our problem-solving skills. Working in tandem, American men and women could be tackling issues with unprecedented vigor. We could be recognizing this potential as new intellectual energy, a valuable national resource unparalleled in the world.

Achieving this goal depends in part on how we redesign the workplace. Advanced technology, specialization, and a highly educated labor force require that we rethink how resources are used. Looking back, we recognize that women entered the professions at a time of mounting tension. Global competition and falling productivity meant that the system was already under considerable strain. Educated baby boomers scrambled up organizations even before females added to that squeeze. In most cases, nothing structural was done to accommodate this crowding. Business as usual meant that competition was extreme.

Given this demographic crunch, perhaps we need to take a second look at the male-female tension presented in this book. Perhaps some of the resentment women have encountered thus far has less to do with discrimination and more to do with men's realistic worries. Women themselves said repeatedly that, except in extreme cases, male colleagues rarely excluded them maliciously, seldom treated them unfairly in a systematic sense. To the extent scapegoating did go on, it was subtle and intermittent. Ambivalence was far more widespread than hostility.

The real lesson is that the American workplace has been inundated with more educated talent than yesterday's organizations can possibly take in. And rather than viewing the problem as structural, we have gotten sidetracked into a preoccupying fight. Male-female tension started at the bottom and has now moved quickly throughout the management ranks—and in the process, the focus has shifted from resources to gender. Since the mid-1970s we have wasted time and energy fighting the wrong fight.

What we need is a comprehensive effort, on the part of both men and women, to redesign organizations to better reflect the work styles of today's professional adults. Together we must reexamine the validity of the corporate pyramid, a structure that dictates top-down decision-making, individual competition, and centralized control. For a generation raised to value self-initiative, we need a new reward system, one that encourages group innovation as well as individual achievement.

A variety of incentive programs and employee ownership models have sprung up recently in disparate locations. We need to examine these experiments, evaluate their impact, and customize them for much wider use. Until we invent ways to reward the performance of all professionals, the scramble will continue, ultimately restricting our collective growth.

Many of the women I interviewed support this argument and have already begun restructuring the organizations in which they have control. Experience inside the system has helped them appreciate the pressures and sacrifices men have dealt with for years. In response, female managers are initiating experiments. They are involving the people they supervise in collective decision-making. They are promoting employees as a group, then sharing the rewards. In cooperation with key male colleagues, they are instituting flex time, job sharing, and rotating leadership. In all cases the programs are based on one assumption: that working men and women share the same human concerns.

A curious phenomenon occurred as I traveled to companies— a phenomenon that solidified my beliefs and strengthened my hope. As I walked down corporate hallways, male managers stopped me spontaneously and asked with sincerity, "Why not also interview me?" Noting that media attention has focused on women, these men wanted someone to document their views. When I asked them to summarize what they would say in an interview, their immediate responses caught me off-guard. I discovered that men and women today share similar workplace concerns.

The men I met argued that not all male managers condone today's corporate cultures, nor do all relish playing the game. Men, too, worry about careers restricted by competition and limited opportunities. They too wonder about how to be good parents and still get ahead. From more than fifty informal conversations, I learned that many men are challenging in private the costs of their careers. In city after city, men voiced concerns that echoed those of women. And their intensity convinced me that a powerful coed network will soon emerge.

We have moved from a time of clear expectations into an era that has provided no rules. For more than a decade, we have responded individually, each of us struggling to cope while wondering if others feel the same kinds of stress. Since it is evident now that changes are widespread, we're rethinking choices and decisions to be made. We recognize that redesigning the workplace has vast implications, not only for productivity and job satisfaction, but also for how we want to raise our children.

Resolving these issues will require clarifying and validating what we hold important. If we stop and assess basic assumptions, we will recognize that a deeper set of values outweighs our daily sex-role concerns. Already a "New Girl–New Boy Network" is emerging across America—a network based on interests, respect, and fundamental beliefs. The time has come to mobilize the energy of that massive network and to create changes in work life that will benefit us all. If we can design our collective future to reflect what we value, the battle of the sexes will become moot.

IMPORTANT BOOKS FOR TODAY'S WOMAN

___ **THE FEMALE STRESS SYNDROME by Georgia Witkin, Ph.D.**
___ **0-425-10295-5/$3.95**
Do you suffer from headaches, PMS, crippling panic attacks or anxiety
reactions? Dr. Witkin tells of the stresses unique to women, and why
biology and conditioning may cause the strains of daily life to strike women
twice as hard as men.

___ **THE SOAP OPERA SYNDROME by Joy Davidson, Ph.D.**
___ **0-425-12724-9/$4.95**
The learned behavior of drama-seeking is the need to fill out lives with
melodrama. Rid your life of unnecessary crises, end the heartache of
addictive relationships, discover your own specialness and self-worth,
strengthen intimacy with your partner...and much more.

___ **BEYOND QUICK FIXES by Georgia Witkin, Ph.D.**
___ **0-425-12608-0/$4.95**
Is a dish of ice cream your answer to a frustrating day at work? Does
buying new lipstick help you forget your overdrawn checkbook? Thousands
of women rely on a "quick fix" to feel comforted or in control—instead of
facing problems head-on. Find out how to change these temporary fixes
into real, long-term solutions.

___ **BEATING THE MARRIAGE ODDS by Barbara Lovenheim**
___ **0-425-13185-8/$4.99**
In this practical, clear-sighted book, the author offers a simple, down-to-
earth plan for women who want to take charge and achieve their personal
goals of marriage and family. The truth is, opportunities abound for
women who know the real facts—and know how to use them.

___ **SLAY YOUR OWN DRAGONS: HOW WOMEN CAN OVERCOME SELF-**
___ **SABOTAGE IN LOVE AND WORK by Nancy Good**
___ **0-425-12853-9/$4.99**
For many women, love and success seem like impossible dreams. Leading
psychotherapist Nancy Good shows that self-destructive behavior may be
the unconscious cause. Now you can achieve happiness by unveiling the
self-sabotage in love, career, health, emotions, money and compulsions.

For Visa, MasterCard and American Express orders ($15 minimum) call: 1-800-631-8571

FOR MAIL ORDERS: CHECK BOOK(S). FILL OUT COUPON. SEND TO: **BERKLEY PUBLISHING GROUP** 390 Murray Hill Pkwy., Dept. B East Rutherford, NJ 07073	**POSTAGE AND HANDLING:** $1.75 for one book, 75¢ for each additional. Do not exceed $5.50.
NAME_____	**BOOK TOTAL** $ _____
ADDRESS _____	**POSTAGE & HANDLING** $ _____
CITY_____	**APPLICABLE SALES TAX** $ _____ (CA, NJ, NY, PA)
STATE_____ZIP_____	**TOTAL AMOUNT DUE** $ _____
PLEASE ALLOW 6 WEEKS FOR DELIVERY. **PRICES ARE SUBJECT TO CHANGE WITHOUT NOTICE.**	**PAYABLE IN US FUNDS.** (No cash orders accepted.) 388